PAYBACK TIME

Following several years with the Special Forces during the Vietnam war, Phil Town returned to the United States and supported himself by working seven months a year as a river guide in the Grand Canyon. His annual income was in the low four figures. After some split-second heroics on his part saved a boatload of Outward Bound trustees from a white water disaster, a grateful financial expert who had been onboard took Town under his wing and taught him the first principles of Rule #1 investing. Town managed to put together a $1000 stake, and within five years had turned it into $1 million.

Also by Phil Town:

*Rule #1: The Simple Strategy for Successful Investing
in Only 15 Minutes a Week!*

PAYBACK TIME

EIGHT STEPS TO
OUTSMARTING
THE SYSTEM
THAT FAILED YOU
AND GETTING
YOUR INVESTMENTS
BACK ON TRACK

PHIL TOWN

BUSINESS
BOOKS

Published by Random House Business Books 2010

8 10 9

Copyright © Philip B. Town 2009

Philip B. Town has asserted his right under the Copyright, Designs
and Patents Act, 1988, to be identified as the author of this work

First published in the United States in 2009 by Crown Business,
an imprint of the Crown Publishing Group,
a division of Random House, Inc., New York

First published in Great Britain in 2010 by
Random House Business Books
Random House, 20 Vauxhall Bridge Road,
London SW1V 2SA

www.rbooks.co.uk

Addresses for companies within The Random House Group Limited can be found at:
www.randomhouse.co.uk/offices.htm

The Random House Group Limited Reg. No. 954009

A CIP catalogue record for this book
is available from the British Library

ISBN 9781847940643

Penguin Random House is committed to a sustainable future for
our business, our readers and our planet. This book is made from
Forest Stewardship Council® certified paper.

Printed and bound in Great Britain by Clays Ltd, St Ives plc

To Melissa, with love and thanks

This book is further dedicated to the brave men and women who serve our country and who have suffered harm in the line of duty. A portion of the proceeds of this book will be donated to the Wounded Warriors Project.

CONTENTS

I'll be using a lot of examples in this book that include numbers, such as stock prices, growth percentages, earnings per share, etc. These numbers were accurate when I wrote this book, but companies routinely update their financial information (including even historical data), so they probably won't reflect the actual current numbers as you read this. Don't let that affect your learning experience. My purpose in using these figures is simply to provide examples that'll teach you how to perform these analyses yourself. The specific numbers in the examples don't matter. The principles I'm teaching do.

I also mention and analyze several specific companies in these pages, but please don't take that to mean I'm telling you to buy or sell them. Again, these are used as examples only, and their purpose is not to tell you what to buy but to show you how you can figure out *for yourself* what you should be investing in.

In fact, please use this book as a tool to change your financial future from potential poverty to riches. You can start by reading carefully and taking notes in the margin; dog-ear the pages and review extra examples at PaybackTimeBook.com. Also, I want all of you to do this: Write me an email. Tell me what your situation is and where you'd like some help. I'll write you back with ideas and resources. Here's my email address: phil@PaybackTimeBook.com. Let's get a conversation going and help change some lives.

The ROAD from *RULE #1* to *PAYBACK TIME*

Stand up to your obstacles and do something about them. You will find that they haven't half the strength you think they have.

—NORMAN VINCENT PEALE

I'm about to teach you the very best strategy for investing — the one strategy worth pursuing regardless of how much time, money, and effort you *think* you have available. No, it's not as simple as handing your money over to some fund manager, who'll probably lose it. Yes, it does require that you actually *do* something. But what I'm going to get you to do is so easy that, yes, even you can handle it. Even if you've never invested in your life. Even if you can't stomach math or researching companies. Even if the thought of beating the market and realizing staggering returns of 15, 20, or 25 percent or more (yes, even in a volatile market) seems impossible and you don't want to try.

Let's start by getting something straight: The reason I've been able to make a whole pile of money starting with nothing is that my approach is the same one that's been making people rich in all kinds of markets for the last hundred years. Because I learned the *fundamentals* of solid investing, I've survived all the crazy market swings, including the recent one that began in 2008. In fact, on August 17, 2007, I appeared on CNBC and told you point-blank to get out of the stock market the next day . . . and I was right. On March 9, 2009, the Dow fell below 6,600 and I sent an email that evening to Maria Bartiromo at CNBC, Manny Schiffres at Kiplinger, and to my blog followers that said it was time to load up the truck. Right again.

We'll pull out of this economic crisis eventually no matter how badly we handle it, because eventually we always get back to the basics of a society that creates the most wealth for the most people. We're experiencing the down part of a cycle. Government got too loose with credit and too proactive toward people with bad credit, people got to thinking real estate can't go down, bankers got too clever with derivatives and leverage worldwide, and, in a nutshell, we were on a binge for twenty years. We overinflated. Now we're going to contract the economic balloon. We've been through it before and some of us always think there is no tomorrow. Warren Buffett described it as "an economic Pearl Harbor" and suggested we do what we did then—everything possible. And we will. But we're at war economically, and the impact of government meddling in the markets is going to be painful for a lot of people. What I want to do is make sure you're not one of them. Investors who take the correct action now will come out the other side in ten or twenty years really, really rich. Making that happen for yourself starts with knowing the rules.

Every successful investor I know—whether an active trader or a long-term investor—follows the same two rules of investing: Rule #1: Don't lose money. And Rule #2: Don't forget Rule #1. My first book, *Rule #1,* appeared in the #1 position on the *New York Times* bestseller list and has been translated into fourteen languages. Folks like investing guru Jim Cramer and SEC Chairman Arthur Levitt were nice enough to recommend it. In that book, I provided a straightforward explanation of how good investors use specific fundamentals to find the value of a business. I also presented a few technical tools investors can use to avoid losing money, and in doing so, make millions . . . and in some cases, billions.

There is, however, *work* involved. Being an active investor is a discipline that, like dieting or getting into good physical shape, has a huge payoff but does require effort and steadfast dedication. You wouldn't believe the number of people who read about dieting or working out or investing but don't actually do it. Okay, you would believe it.

I can't do anything about making you stick less food in your mouth or dropping to the floor for some push-ups and then dashing out the door for a run, but I *can* do quite a lot about motivating you to do your own investing. Getting you to do what you know you should but can't quite. And you probably have a sense that these days, it's more imperative than ever to learn how to take charge of your investments. Our entire financial system has nearly melted down and, in the process, created great problems for the average person's financial future. You know it's critical to do something today to secure your retirement later, because what you've been doing just hasn't, well, *worked*.

Most of the people I meet nowadays don't even want to talk about their retirement funds because they don't know if their money will be there when they need it. They are often stunned when I start sharing with them the facts about how those funds are managed, as well as the simple solutions to a great retirement completely within their reach—solutions that can make them rich in very little time. You could be starting with close to zero dollars today in a horrible stock market, apply what I teach you in this book, and have a bundle of money in ten years to do whatever. Maybe you won't be ready to retire just yet, but you'll want money for other things, like paying for your kids' higher education, starting a small business, or buying a dream vacation home and taking more time off from work. I'm not here to tell you what to *do* with your riches as long as you keep investing your money the way I'm going to teach you. The goal is to continue to grow your retirement money *and* have plenty extra to play with between now and the day you actually do decide to walk away from the workforce. And to do that with less risk than you are taking now.

How great would that be? All it takes is a willingness to embrace a style of investing that your fund managers—who probably just lost you a ton of money—cannot. And you have to accept that no one can do this for you. You must do it yourself.

Here are a few truths that might surprise you. I'll explain all these later in this book—for now, I just hope they'll prompt you to take what I'm teaching seriously:

FACT: Mutual fund managers get rich at your expense—stealing as much as 60 percent or more of your returns over your lifetime through *fees.*

FACT: The average individual will need more than $3 million to be financially independent in retirement in twenty years, and won't get there with mutual funds. Not even close.

FACT: Ninety-six percent of fund managers can't equal the historical market average return of 8 percent per annum. When the market goes down, they go down with it, no matter how "low-risk" their funds are supposed to be.

Another fact of the matter is that opportunities abound during volatile markets. This book will give you the intellectual foundation for getting rich during *any* type of market climate, but particularly during unstable sideways markets, which can last for years, even *decades.* As millions of people agonize over diminished or obliterated retirement funds, wondering what happened to their money and whether or not they will ever be able to get it all back, I offer you hope and a realistic solution for moving forward. Contrary to what you might think, the time has never been better for making millions in the stock market. If you know how.

The strategy detailed in my first book, *Rule #1,* starts with Rule #1 principles but success is anchored on active *trading.* The strategy explained in this book is about active *investing:* how to properly buy and hold a stock. I call this investing strategy *stockpiling,* because it's about how and when to accumulate a wonderful business while the price is going down.

The combination of Rule #1 principles with the tactic of "stockpiling" stocks is the winning ticket to a rich life—particularly *now.* In fact, this time-tested approach to investing is *exactly* how the best investors in the world turn a down market into an up portfolio. The richest people in America use this strategy as their basic way of making billions, even if they prefer to keep it a secret.

It's time you learned how they do it, and then go do it yourself. Follow what I teach and you will overthrow the financial industry that failed you . . . and seize the investing opportunity of a lifetime.

THE ONLY SCHOOL OF SUCCESSFUL INVESTING

I was taught by a man I admiringly call the Wolf, a successful investor I got to know really well after I nearly killed him along with my entire raft of whitewater adventurers in the Grand Canyon in 1980. I was a river guide then, making $4,000 a year, until he got ahold of me and dragged me into the world of investing. Understand that at the time, I'd been living more or less in a sleeping bag for thirteen years: three years in the Army and ten more in the Grand Canyon as a guide. But I'd just gotten married, and the prospect of raising a family on $4,000 a year was not all that thrilling to my wife. I was expected to make money. Enough for things like a house, for instance. The idea of living under a roof was novel enough to me at the time. Actually *buying* the roof . . . phew, baby, that was hard to get my head around.

And then along came the Wolf.

They say timing is everything, and in my case they are right. My mentor found me at the perfect moment and then he proceeded to drill into my thick head the basic secrets of successful investing — that high returns and high risk are not necessarily related, that I should want the highest return on my investment with the lowest risk, and that the way to achieve that was to copy the people who have already done it. I got that. I got that loud and clear. And in five years, after starting with just $1,000, I was a millionaire with a house looking over the ocean in Del Mar, California. Since then I've made a lot more money, lost some when I started getting clever and investing in things I didn't understand, and made it all back and then some by returning to good old Rule #1—Don't lose money. Which is why I told the world to get out of this market when it was hovering at 13,000. The great trick of investing isn't so much about making good money—it's *keeping* it.

It turns out that over the long term—any time period beyond about ten years—the investors who get the consistently high returns, the folks who actually *keep* their high returns and just keep getting richer all the time, almost all come from the same basic school of investing. Back in the 1930s, the original home base for this school was New York City, but in about 1960 it moved to Omaha, Nebraska, where it is currently located. Its original promoter was Ben Graham—a successful investor, an author, and a professor at Columbia University. The current head guru of this school is Mr. Graham's student, Warren Buffett, who used what Ben Graham taught him to become one of the richest people in the world.

Other students of the school include thousands of successful amateur investors and hundreds of professionals who regularly clobber the stock market for their (usually very rich) clients over the long haul. **This school of investing teaches you how to get the highest returns for the least risk of any strategy you can name.**

STOCKPILE YOUR WAY TO RICHES

In my first book, *Rule #1,* I taught you how to do a quick analysis on a business, find its value, and then trade it with the help of technical tools. Think of this book as the *prequel* to *Rule #1.* When I wrote that book, I thought I could teach investing without focusing on the *fundamentals of stockpiling.* I was wrong. You need this. In fact, I'm now of the opinion that, for most of you, it will be *all* you need to make millions and retire rich.

The readers of *Rule #1* have taught me that doing this on your own can be scary. Not because the techniques are hard, but because if you're going to do it, you've got to ignore the lies the financial services industry is telling you. As much as my readers and students want to be better investors, they are continually bombarded with advertisements and TV shows that tell them they can't do this on their own — that it's too hard, too complicated, that we should leave it to the "experts." There are bestsellers written every year that "prove" to you no one, not even Mr. Buffett, has beaten the market and, therefore, there is no reason for you to try.

These ads, books, and shows are wrong. And they are not just "mistaken." *They're lying to you.* They know that good investors beat the market all the time. It's an inescapable fact. But **what is at stake is so huge that reality is not going to be allowed to intervene. What is at stake is no less than the $100 billion transfer of wealth *annually* from your pocket to theirs. Countries have gone to war and millions have died for far less wealth than that. Don't think for a second it isn't possible for an entire industry to warp reality in order to justify taking in that kind of money.**

With that kind of money it's possible to shout over anyone who is out there telling you that you can invest on your own. With that kind of money, you can hire the best PR firms, the best ad agencies, the best lawyers. You can hire authors. You can create bestsellers. You can have your guy on TV all day long on talk shows. You can come to define reality for millions. And that's exactly what the financial services industries have done. It's the lie they're going to *keep* selling, even after the economic disaster their so-called experts have helped create. Trust me, they're going to do whatever they have to do to keep investing your money. They don't want you doing this on your own. They want to keep you a captive client. They want you ignorant about the truth of investing. They want your money to keep coming in.

After writing *Rule #1,* I began to see how hard it is for people to break away from the clutches of mutual funds and managed IRAs and 401(k) plans. Never mind that the system is set up as if it were for your benefit but actually results in guaranteed poverty if you manage to live more than about seven years after retirement. By the way, that's *your* poverty, not theirs. Yours. *They* got rich on your money. They should. They took about 60 percent of it (I'll explain how this happens in Chapter 2).

But let's be fair. Surely not all those in the mutual fund industry have blood on their hands. Surely there is some reason to believe mutual funds are a reasonable alternative for individual investors. There are some funds that do very well, right? Well, 4 percent routinely beat the market. But if the market lost 40 percent of your money, those funds could have lost 39 percent and still beaten it. What good is that to you? I did an analysis to see how many fund managers could achieve a consistent 15 percent return over ten years.* Out of 5,900 broad market funds, *three* managed a consistent 15 percent return. That's right: three, or .05 percent of those funds.

This is probably the reason Warren Buffett does not endorse mutual funds. Mr. Buffett believes there are only two kinds of investors: good and ignorant. Good investors can invest on their own and make a lot of money. Ignorant investors, on the other hand, should either learn to be good investors or just buy an index fund and forget about it. Not mutual funds. An index is like a mutual fund but doesn't come with exorbitant fees. I'll explain more about what these are and how to buy them in Chapter 2.

I agree. If you're not going to invest the way the best investors invest, then you should just buy an index fund and be done with it. Accept your 8 percent maximum investment return and be happy you got that instead of the 6 percent you'd be getting if you paid the mutual fund fees. That 25 percent change in return on investment will triple the money in your retirement account . . . in sixty years.

For some of you, that's all you're going to need to know. But most of you have a problem that's going to require reading this book and

---

*By "consistent" I mean they were compounding at 15 percent over ten years, eight years, five years, and three years—not just an average of 15 percent over that ten-year period. The reason consistency is important is that a lucky manager could have a huge year and bring up his average while most years he's getting killed. By applying a consistency requirement, you are left with the rare manager who can average that return every three years or so, consistently for long periods of time.

taking more aggressive action. Because most of you don't have sixty years. Some of you don't even have ten. And so you're going to have to stop being an ignorant investor and start becoming a good investor.

GET READY TO STAND UP

The process starts with understanding what stockpiling means for you, and then understanding why you must stockpile stocks, or pay a huge price in your life and the lives of the people you love. Prepare to be horrified by your potential fate if you don't take what I teach seriously, but also prepare to be inspired by how easy it really is to get rich.

CHAPTER

1

HOW the WEALTHY USE DOWN to GO UP

There are risks and costs to a program of action. But they are far less than the long-range risks and costs of comfortable inaction.

—JOHN F. KENNEDY

The best investment strategy I know is so counterintuitive, so shockingly upside down, such a crazy way of thinking about investing that hardly anyone who uses it wants to even try to explain it. It's not at all hard to *do,* but it is hard to explain. It just sounds so . . . impossible. But smart investors do it all the time and, man, does it work! I mean it really works. It's an "I can do whatever I want the rest of my life" kind of works. It works so well, it's the secret to the investing success of the best and richest investors in the world. Seriously.

I know that sounds like hype, but honestly it's impossible to overstate the effectiveness of this strategy. It really is the basis of the biggest fortunes in the world, including those of quite a number of Forbes's World's Billionaires list. For example, #3 is Carlos Slim Helu, the Mexican telecom entrepreneur who is worth $35 billion and is currently buying into cheap media, energy, and retail assets, including the *New York Times,* using this strategy. Lakshmi Mittal, #8, of India, created a $19 billion fortune and now runs the world's largest steel company, ArcelorMittal. He built ArcelorMittal using this strategy in

Eastern Europe in the 1990s after the Berlin Wall came down. Number 15 is Bernard Arnault of France, who built a $16 billion fortune by acquiring Christian Dior with this strategy. Number 16 on the World's Billionaires list is Li Ka-shing of China, who made $16 billion acquiring energy, banking, and utility companies with this strategy. Charles Koch and David Koch are ranked #19 with $14 billion each, which they got by using this strategy to build Koch Industries — one of the largest, privately held corporations in the United States. Michael Otto of Germany is ranked #23 and is using this strategy to take advantage of weak markets in the United States to buy up shopping centers in America. Donald Bren is #26. He used it to become the sole owner of the Irvine Company and bank $12 billion. The Irvine Company is one of the largest construction companies in California and the developer of about a fifth of Orange County.

The list of billionaires who used this strategy to become mega-wealthy goes on and on but wouldn't be complete without mentioning that the world's second wealthiest man, Warren Buffett (worth $37 billion), the world's best investor, used this strategy of investing to build his immense fortune and to increase his ownership and compounded return in companies like American Express, Washington Post, GEICO, and Coca-Cola.

This strategy is also the basis of thousands of little fortunes, including mine. In fact, as any of the billionaires I mentioned above would agree, it's much easier to use the strategy if you are a *small* investor. Being a big investor is actually a huge disadvantage in using this strategy. Mr. Buffett once said, "Anyone who says that size does not hurt investment performance is selling. The highest rates of return I've ever achieved were in the 1950s. I killed the Dow. You ought to see the numbers. But I was investing peanuts then. It's a huge structural advantage not to have a lot of money."*

I used this strategy to build my wealth by buying shares of bioscience, software, and other private companies. And soon, if you pay

---

attention and are willing to do a bit of fun work, you'll discover that this incredible strategy can be the basis of your fortune, too.

STOCKPILING

I call this amazing strategy "stockpiling" . . . as in "stash," "accumulate," and "collect." It means exactly as it sounds — stockpiling, as in piling up stocks. Not just any stock at any price, though. The essence of stockpiling is to buy stock in a business you'd be excited to own all of, then hope the price goes *down* so you can "stash," "accumulate," and "collect" as much as you can afford at as low a price as possible. Sounds strange, I know. But again, all of the billionaires I listed above and many more on Forbes's World's Billionaires list are stockpilers of businesses. (Note: This list might have changed by the time you read this but not the stories behind these guys' wealth-building strategies.)

Buy a Business, Not a Stock

"Buy a Business, Not a Stock" was a chapter title in my first book. It's such a key way of thinking that I can't reiterate it enough: You must stop thinking that stock investing is any different from buying a business. When you buy a business you're buying shares of the business. If you buy some percentage of the total shares, you become a part owner. Buy all the shares and you own the whole business. *There is no difference between that process and buying public stock in a business.* As long as you treat owning shares of public stocks as different from owning a piece of a business, you will fail to understand and execute the stockpiling strategy. A typical stock investor is unhappy when the price of his stock goes down, because he has no understanding of the true value of the business that stock represents. But that's because typical stock investors are not *investors* at all. They don't understand stockpiling, so they inadvertently have become speculators and outright gamblers.

The unfortunate truth is that the financial services industry has conned many millions of people into their game of stock speculation via mutual funds. I'll have a lot more on that in the next chapter. For now, let's just remember that for this book and for the rest of your investing career, you must think of stocks as shares of a business, and yourself as the owner of that business. So if you buy just ten shares of Coca-Cola, you're a part owner of Coke — not a stock investor in Coke. Got that? When you begin to think like this, you're joining some truly great investors like Mr. Buffett, and you're on the first step toward becoming a solid stockpiler of stocks, er, businesses.

"The basic ideas of investing," Mr. Buffett says, "are to look at stocks as a business, use a market's fluctuations to your advantage, and seek a Margin of Safety. That's what Ben Graham taught us. A hundred years from now, these will still be the cornerstones of investing."

From the late 1990s until 2008, Warren Buffett bought very few public stocks. He mostly just sat on about $45 billion of Berkshire Hathaway's cash, waiting patiently for Mr. Market to become fearful enough about the future to bring the prices of wonderful public businesses down to levels at which he was willing to buy. In May 2008 Mr. Buffett told his fans at the annual Berkshire conference that he hoped the stock market would drop 50 percent so he could finally put all his cash to work. Then the market crashed, and in October 2008 he invested $20 billion in public companies.

But here's the classic part of the story: As prices of the businesses Berkshire owned—and still owns, as of this writing—

plummeted, and the Berkshire stock price dropped accordingly, Mr. Buffett was attacked, again, for being over the hill and out of touch. The proof? The prices of businesses he owns were going down.

This is not the first time he's been accused of losing his touch. In the late 1960s he was sitting on a lot of Buffett Partnership cash. His unwillingness to chase high prices disturbed enough Buffett Partnership partners that Mr. Buffett dissolved the partnership, gave his partners back their money, and shifted his stockpiling strategy to Berkshire Hathaway, where he would no longer be required to deal with limited partners whining about his lack of investing activity. Of course, he turned Berkshire into the world's most successful investment vehicle. Ten thousand dollars invested in Berkshire in 1969 is now worth $40 million. Again in the late 1990s, as mutual funds racked up big gains by buying technology stocks, Mr. Buffett was accused of being behind the times. His ideas became more popular after the Nasdaq plunged 85 percent during the dot-com bust.

The fact is, stockpiling is something people either get right away or never understand at all, no matter how much sense the strategy makes or how much money the people who practice it make.

The Secret to Risk-Free Stockpiling Is Knowing Price Is Not Value

Okay, there's obviously more to stockpiling than just buying a stock and hoping the price goes down. What Warren Buffett and a lot of other billionaires know is that the price of a stock doesn't always have a whole lot to do with how much that business is actually *worth*. To put it another way, you have to learn how to look beyond stock price and at a business's *value*.

The one and only secret to stockpiling is to make sure the *value* of the business is substantially greater than the *price* you are paying for it. I swear to you that's all there is to it. If you get this right, you cannot help but get rich. Most investors make the mistake of thinking the price they paid has some necessary connection to the value of the thing they bought. I don't know why stock market investors think that when it's so manifestly and obviously not true in any other sort of market they buy in regularly. Surely they bought a used car sometime in their lives. They wouldn't confuse the price being asked for a used car with the value of that car, would they? Just because a guy is asking $5,000 for his old Toyota doesn't mean it's actually *worth* $5,000. If you're reasonably smart, you go look the car over; you make sure its got an engine that works and the body isn't a disaster. You check to see what similar cars are going for and use that price as a guideline, but only if it's reasonable.

Why wouldn't investors do something similar when they buy stock? Because they don't know how to calculate the value of a business the way they do with cars. Well, we're going to fix that in this book.

I'm going to show you how to calculate value—and make sure it's higher than price—in Chapter 4, but for right now just understand this: price is just the amount you paid. That's *all* it is. It doesn't mean a damn thing other than that. If you want to know the *value* of the thing you bought, well, that's an entirely different question. Price is what you pay but value is what you get. Those two things can be and often are quite different. We'll start our lessons on how to stockpile undervalued companies and make millions with that: Price is not the same as value.

Since I haven't taught you how to figure out the value of a business yet, allow me to make my point with an example from my horse farm. I wasn't a very good rider but I wanted to learn, so I was looking for a horse that knew a lot more than I did about what I'm supposed to do.

My partner, Melissa, got a lead on a Level-4 dressage horse that was for sale because the owner died. The family was wealthy, so they were just looking for a good home for the horse. Melissa called and found out they'd bought the horse for $60,000 plus shipping from Germany. They wanted $35,000 for a quick sale. She told them we weren't interested but they should call us back if they didn't find a buyer at that price. Two weeks later they called and offered us the horse for $10,000. We drove over for a look. We could see why they were having a problem selling him. He needed to get his feet trimmed and reshod. He needed to be fed better. And he hadn't been ridden for months. I got on him and he tried to toss me, but he was too out of shape to get into it. I wasn't impressed. A big, bony, out-of-shape, cantankerous horse wasn't what I was in the market for.

Melissa, however, is the former owner of a horse-importing and -training business and she's been a national champion rider several times. She knows horses. She took a ten-minute look at this guy moving around the arena, pulled me aside, and said, "Let's take him home. He's amazing."

Where I just saw the superficial problems, she saw a $60,000 horse and a great horse to teach me to be a better rider. We paid $2,000, and he's in our barn now with new shoes, getting fat. What's his value? I'm sure even in this market, if we sell him, we'll get more than we paid. Maybe a lot more. The lesson? In a bad market, superficial problems that have nothing to do with value can have a big impact on price.

Before we get back to businesses and the details of calculating value, I want you to notice one more thing about the purchase I made: It was essentially risk-free. There was no way I could lose money on that horse. Even if he died, I'd make money on the insurance.

Think about that for a second. If we know the price of a thing is less than what it's worth (its value), then something remarkable becomes possible: We can buy it and be certain we will make money.

"Certain?" you ask. "Come on. There's no way to be certain you're going to make money."

Yup, there is a way to be certain and it's really simple. Just put on your logical, rational hat and follow me: If the value of the thing you bought is greater than the price you paid, you are *guaranteed* to make money. You have gotten rid of the risk of making the investment. The only question is how long you have to wait for the price to come back into line with the true value.

In the case of our horse, Sherman, we bought him so cheaply we could sell him for a profit immediately after doing some basic mainte-nance. If we want to sell him for the maximum amount—his full value as a Level-4, 17-hand, beautiful dressage horse with amazing action— we'll have to be more patient and wait for a better market when the price will come up to the value.

The same thing applies to owning shares of a business. If you buy at a price well below the long-term value, you may not be able to sell for a profit immediately. In fact, the price may go down before it goes up. There's no guarantee that the short-term price for Sherman won't fall lower. But in the long term, the price will come up to the value. True for a horse. Especially true for a business.

I want to make another distinction between investing in things like horses, real estate, and art versus investing in businesses. The for-mer have no real "floor" to their price. Their value is based on nothing more than fashion, history, and the greater-fool theory. (The greater-fool theory is the basis of all investment price bubbles: that a greater fool will come along who will pay more for this thing than you paid.) Therefore, it's difficult to determine the value. A Picasso might sell for $20 million one year and $10 million the next. Which was the true value? Who knows? Businesses, on the other hand, have real value based on future cash. We'll talk about that more in a later chap-ter as well. The point here is this: You don't know exactly when you'll make money, because you have to wait for the price to come up to the value. But because it's a business that produces cash, it inevitably will someday. So that's pretty cool, huh?

But it raises an important issue: How long might it take before the price gets back to the value? What good is "someday" if we can't cash out when we need to? Well, here's where my 10–10 Rule comes into play: We don't buy a business for even ten minutes unless we are willing to own it for the next ten years. We do the 10–10 Rule for two reasons:

1. It forces us to think long-term.
2. We may be in such a bad stock market that we actually don't expect to see the price come back up to the value for ten years, and we want to be totally okay with that.

This puts quite a strong requirement on us that we know our businesses the way Melissa knows horses. You'll learn what to look for in Chapter 3. In the meantime, in case all this is scaring you, just remember: I've done valuations with both businesses and horses, and businesses are a lot easier. When you find a business with the price lower than the value, you can't lose if you don't have to sell. That's just for openers. But it gets way better than that.

The Secret to Riches Is Compounding Returns by Stockpiling

If you know the value of the business and you're intending to keep investing your money, then the more the price goes down, the better it is for you. If you keep buying as the price goes down, the average cost of your investment per share goes down, too. When the price goes back up to the value, stockpiling the stock at ever lower prices will massively increase your overall return. Stockpiling accelerates your compounded return.

According to Albert Einstein, one of the hardest things in the universe to understand is the power of compounding returns. So don't feel bad if the fact that you can become a millionaire simply by buying something as its price goes down doesn't seem to make sense. I told you before that stockpiling is not intuitive. It's easy and it's intensely rational but it's not something that just leaps out at you with a big YES. So let's take this compounding thing slowly.

Let's say you're willing to have Vinnie pay you $100,000 five years from now, in return for lending him $60,000 today. You lend him $60 large today; the deal is he pays you back $100 large in five years. The reason you're willing to do that deal is because your financial calculator tells you that if you want to get at least a 10 percent compounded return on the money you lend Vinnie for five years, you'll have to get back close to $100,000. You get your sixty grand back plus interest—*plus interest on the interest* when he pays you about $100,000 in five years. Simple. I mean compounded. (Sixty grand compounded at 10 percent over five years equates to just under 100 grand; at 10.8 percent, however, you reach 100 grand.) As a lender, the less you lend him up front for the same backend payoff, the higher your compounded return. If you lend him $50,000 and he pays you $100,000 in five years, your compounded return jumps up to 15 percent. Lend him $25,000 and get paid $100,000 in five years and your compounded return explodes to 30 percent per year. The less you lend him for the same payoff down the road, the higher your compounded return and the quicker you get rich. (By the way, this is the way zero coupon bonds, like U.S. Treasury bonds, work: you pay a price that is discounted off of the face value of the bond, in return for getting the face value of the bond back in a fixed amount of time. The size of the discount determines the compounded rate of return you're getting paid to lend your money to the bond's issuer.)

You do exactly the same thing when you stockpile stock at a big discount to its value, only better. There's a limit to what you can get a borrower to pay you for a loan, unless you're ready to get violent. But there's no limit to how high your compounded returns can get by stockpiling. The less you pay to buy a set value, the higher your compounded rate of return. The lower the price goes as you are stockpiling the stock, the more your compounded return goes up and the faster you get rich.

EXPLODING RATES OF RETURN

Assume that you find a business you know is worth $20 a share but is selling for only $10. You have $60,000 to invest. You decide to stockpile the business rather than lend the money to Vinnie. You start by using $20,000 to buy 2,000 shares at $10. A few months later the price is $5. There is no change in the long-term value. (How do you know that? Well, you've done your homework, which I'll be showing you how to do later.) It's still worth about $20. You invest another $20,000 at $5 per share for 4,000 more shares. The stock market keeps dropping like a brick and the stock drops to $1. The business hasn't changed at all. Things have slowed down some but the business will pick up again with the economy. It still has a $20 per share long-term value. So you invest another $20,000 at $1 per share and buy 20,000 more shares.

You now own 26,000 shares (2,000 plus 4,000 plus 20,000) and have invested $60,000. The average price you paid per share is $2.31. Five years later it's selling for its value of $20 per share, $520,000. Let's compare this with the loan to Vinnie:

With Vinnie you turned $60,000 to $100,000 in five years and made a 10.8 percent compounded return. Not bad, right? But in the second example, because you kept investing in the business as it went down in price, your $60,000 investment is now worth $520,000, and your return is 54 percent per year.

Instead of having $100,000 you have $520,000 because you learned how to stockpile.

And your risk went down, too. What do you do if Vinnie doesn't pay? You gotta deal with it. Go get some muscle. But as a stockpiler you don't have to strong-arm anyone. You just let the inevitable market forces deal with the price. You know eventually the price and the value will be the same, as sure as you know the sun will rise.

Stockpiling lowered your risk and exploded your return. You gotta like that. So what's the catch?

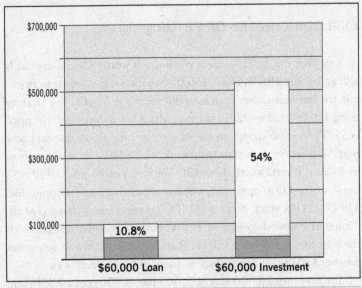

Investment Available	Value/Share	Price/Share	Shares Purchased	$ Invested	Sale
$20,000	$20	$10	2,000	$20,000	
$20,000	$20	$5	4,000	$20,000	
$20,000	$20	$1	20,000	$20,000	
5 years later	$20	$20	26,000	$60,000	$520,000
Return on Investment					54%

THE CATCH?

The example I just used must have a catch in it, right? You probably saw one issue immediately. The stock dropped like a brick from $10 to $1 and you're still buying it like it's diamonds? How could you do that if everyone else is selling? Are they really that stupid and you're really that smart? You have to be a genius to do this stockpiling stuff. Maybe that's the catch.

No, you don't. And no it isn't. The guys who are selling aren't stupid, and you aren't that smart. It isn't about stupid versus smart. If you've got a reasonable IQ you're going to be fine with this, because it isn't about being clever. It's about being *reasonable*. If you are a reasonable person you can rock the financial world. As crazy as that sounds, it's so true. Making big money stockpiling stocks is about their emotions versus your reason.

We'll deal with our very emotional partner, Mr. Market, in another chapter. For now just understand that if you can keep your head when all about you are losing theirs, you are going to become very rich. You don't have to be real smart. I'm not. (By the way, I stole that "keep your head" and "losing theirs" line from Rudyard Kipling's famous "If . . ." poem.) You just have to be calm. Can you chill out when the Big Guys — the mutual fund managers who control more than 85 percent of the money in the stock market — are freaking out? Of course you can. You already are. Trust me, as I write this, they are tearing out their hair and some of them are ready to commit suicide. Meanwhile, you've gone about your life, dealing with the financial issues the way reasonable people do. You've been through financial problems before. You know you'll find a way through this one.

But the fund managers have never been through anything like this. They're terrified of losing their cushy jobs, big Manhattan co-ops, limos, private schools, special tables at restaurants, box seats at Yankees games, pictures in the society pages, and all the other perks these people kill themselves to get so they can impress the other guys who are trying to impress them. They buy stuff with your mutual fund money and they pray the price will go up. If the price doesn't go up in a short time — like in a few weeks — fear starts to set in.

They deal with that fear by buying lots of stocks. Hundreds of stocks. Do you think each of the 5,900 fund managers can keep up on hundreds of companies in dozens of unrelated industries? Not a chance. They buy all these stocks not because they are experts in the businesses behind them but because they think surely *some* of them will go up. Enough to keep up with the other guys who are doing the same thing. For a guy like this, it's all about the price, not the value. The price has to be higher than the price he bought at within a few months at the most. Has to. Or he's going to dump it and buy something else. That's why a long-term down market is like a death sentence to these managers' entire way of life. When nothing is going up for months, their "buy and hold" advice starts to wear thin. They don't see anything but price. They can't buy more and hope it goes down like you can. If they did that, their ignorant clients would pull the money so fast the fund would be history in a month. In a long down market like this one, they have no answers and they are panicking.

They let fear get in the way of making rational decisions. When they get scared, they almost always do exactly the opposite of what they should. When they should be buying, they're selling. When they should be selling, they're buying. If it were otherwise, your fund manager would be on the Forbes 400 Richest list. But he isn't. None of them are, because they inevitably are dominated by their emotions: fear and greed.

This fact makes our job much easier: If we control our fear with knowledge and reason, we win. And that makes stockpiling simple. We are ready to buy when the dominant emotion is fear. We are ready to sell when the dominant emotion is greed.

Speaking of the Forbes 400 List, the richest people in America all own shares of a business. This is great news for the vast majority of us. If owning a business is one key element in getting über-rich, we're off to a pretty good start, because 66 percent of us say we want to start or own our own company someday, and another 15 percent of us own one now.* That means four out of five Americans already have the necessary basic urge toward business ownership that can lead to huge wealth.

Strangely, not nearly so many of us think we're capable of making a good decision about owning a piece of *someone else's* business. This fact accounts in turn for the fact that 50 million of us pay mutual fund

---

* 2006 Yahoo! Small Business and Harris Interactive survey.

managers outrageous fees (see Chapter 2) to do what amounts to nothing rather than make our own decisions. When President Bush suggested individuals be given control of the investing decisions for their Social Security money, more than half the congressmen and senators spoke out about the need to keep critical retirement funds out of the hands of their constituents for fear they would lose them.

Most of us seem to think it's a great idea to invest in our own business but a bad idea to make an investment decision about someone else's business. But what if it were just as easy, interesting, and fun to learn about someone else's business as our own? And what if learning about someone else's business and investing in it could be outrageously rewarding financially?

Of course, that's exactly what Ben Graham said for forty years and what Warren Buffett has been saying for fifty years: "Look at stocks as businesses."

THIS ISN'T THEORY, IT'S FOR REAL

The cool thing about all of this is that it isn't theory. It's proven. I've done it, but if I were you I wouldn't be impressed that some ex–river guide made some money. Big deal. Even a blind dog gets a bone once in a while.

But if the best investor in the world used stockpiling to become one of the richest people in the world, well, that would be another story altogether, right? So let's hear about stockpiling from Mr. Buffett in a letter written to Berkshire shareholders in 1997:

How We Think About Market Fluctuations

A SHORT QUIZ: If you plan to eat hamburgers throughout your life and are not a cattle producer, should you wish for higher or lower prices for beef? Likewise, if you are going to buy a car from time to time but are not an auto manufacturer, should you prefer higher or lower car prices? These questions, of course, answer themselves. But now for the final exam: If you expect to be a net saver during the next five years, should you hope for a higher or lower stock market during that period? Many investors get this one wrong. Even though they are going to be net buyers of stocks for many years to come, they are elated when stock prices rise and depressed when they fall. In effect, they rejoice because prices have risen for the "hamburgers" they will soon be buying. This reaction makes no sense. Only those who will be sellers of equities in the near future should be happy at seeing stocks rise. Prospective purchasers should much prefer sinking prices.

So smile when you read a headline that says "Investors lose as market falls." Edit it in your mind to "Disinvestors lose as market falls—but investors gain." Though writers often forget this truism, there is a buyer for every seller and what hurts one necessarily helps the other. (As they say in golf matches: "Every putt makes someone happy.") We gained enormously from the low prices placed on many equities and businesses in the 1970s and 1980s. Markets that then were hostile to investment transients were friendly to those taking up permanent residence.

When Down Is Up: When does the price going down make the profits go up? When you stockpile a great investment.

As Warren Buffett points out in that letter, a down market is the best time for a stockpiler. A down market creates so many opportunities for the creation of wealth that even a little effort on your part will make you richer than you ever imagined you could be. This is, and I say this without any intentional hyperbole, the opportunity of a lifetime. Right now is like it's 1848 and you are standing at Sutter's Mill in California and dang if that isn't a bunch of gold lying right there on the ground. All you have to do is know the difference between fool's gold and real gold—and any idiot can learn that—and then go pick it up. That's all. It's right there in front of you. JUST PICK IT UP!

A Stockpiling Rate of Return

Even a small piece of a gold mine can make you rich, and that's exactly what a wonderful business is—a gold mine. But a special kind of gold mine. Wonderful businesses convert small amounts of money into real gold by compounding it consistently for long periods of time. When you buy a wonderful business on sale, however, you increase the rate of return dramatically. And when you *stockpile* a wonderful business at ever lower prices, your rate of return becomes golden. Amateur investors, little guys like you and me, who stockpile properly, get long-term compounded returns of 17, 20, and 24 percent and higher. I'm talking returns over twenty years. You compound $50,000 at 24 percent for twenty years and you've made millions. Believe it. The numbers are right. And yes, you can.

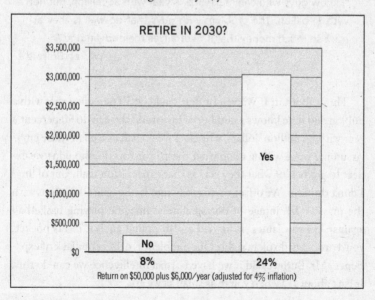

RETIRE IN 2030?

Return on $50,000 plus $6,000/year (adjusted for 4% inflation)

The mutual fund industry will scream *"Impossible!"* but it isn't. Professors at Ivy League universities will "prove" that no one can do it, much less a bunch of amateurs. But the truth is, amateurs like us do it all the time. And you can do it, too. As stockpilers, the little guy, you and me, have all the advantages entirely because we are little. When Mr. Buffett was first starting out, he made 100 percent a year. Then as he got bigger his returns dropped to a mere 36 percent per year. And as the capital he was managing got into the billions, his return dropped to 24 percent per year. Size matters and small is *all.*

"Anyone who says that size does not hurt investment performance is selling. The highest rates of return I've ever achieved were in the 1950s. I killed the Dow. You ought to see the numbers. But I was investing peanuts then. It's a huge structural advantage not to have a lot of money. I think I could make you 50% a year on $1 million. No, I know I could. I guarantee that."

"I know guys who can make 50% a year with $5 million, but not with $1 billion. The problem with guys that do well is they attract so much money that it neutralizes their advantage."

—Warren Buffett

Think about it: If Warren Buffett could do 50 percent a year with a million and if he knows a number of investors who can do 50 percent a year with $5 million dollars, why can't we do half as well as those guys? Assuming we're willing to do what these investors do, shouldn't we expect to get half of what they get? Is that expectation really out of line? I don't think so. We offset their genius and Ivy League educations with the massive advantage of our smallness. Imagine playing basketball against LeBron James. If he had a 400-pound anchor in his pocket, you'd probably do okay, right? Our nimbleness offsets our lack of experience. Mr. Buffett said if we have normal intelligence we can do this. It isn't about IQ when you're as small as we are.

Bottom line is, I expect 24 percent per year compounded annually from my efforts as a stockpiling investor and that's what you should expect, too. Don't listen to the people who tell you it can't be done. The moment you believe you can't, you won't.

And remember, they *are* going to tell you it can't be done. They can't do it. Look at what the experts have done with their own money. Half of Wall Street went bankrupt in one year. This happened five years after Warren Buffett was on the cover of *Forbes* telling the world that the derivatives market was a great black hole that could swallow up billions. He was off by three zeros. It swallowed up trillions. So do you really have to ask yourself, "If the pros can't do it, why can I?" That might have been a tough question in 2007, but by the end of 2008 the question of the value of professional money managers had been answered once and for all. They are worthless. You want the gold, you're going to have to pick it up yourself. Those mercenaries don't care about you and they never have. You should know that by now. They're bankrupt, and so are their "buy and hold" and "diversification" sales pitches. You did what they said. How's that working for you?

Okay, you say, the pros aren't going to help. But, you say, I've got the federal government on my side now. A woman in Atlanta said, "Now that the government is finally on my side I'm going to get my gas paid for and I'm going to get my medical bills paid for." Well, maybe not. If you're thinking like that — that Big Brother is there for you — I've got some bad news. Right now our politicians are throwing everything they have at an economic system that got overheated from twenty years of borrowing and overspending. To soften this necessary and required contraction, they've borrowed about $2 trillion, and they're going to borrow at least $2 trillion more. But let's think about that for a minute: The entire stock market is worth about $9 trillion at this writing. They are *borrowing* almost 50 percent of the value of all of the businesses in America. Do you think all that debt might have a devastating effect on the ability of the government to pay Social Security and health benefits in the future? Oh, you'll have Social Security and Medicare, but you won't like it. If you want to live a good life, you're going to have to pick up the gold yourself. Big Brother is going to be too busy writing bad checks. And your financial advisers and 401(k) managers? Well, let's just say you aren't going to like what you read next.

GET READY TO BE UPSET

In the next chapter I'll explain why you haven't been introduced to the strategy of stockpiling before now—and how your financial advisers are using your ignorance to rip you off and keep you poor while making themselves rich.

Then I'll take you through the steps of stockpiling businesses that will make you rich.

TAKEAWAYS AND ACTION ITEMS

To get rich, learn to value companies and build a portfolio of businesses at a discount to their true value.

Follow the Stockpiling Strategy:

1. Determine the true (intrinsic) value of a business and buy stocks in those companies when they go on sale.
2. Continue to stockpile as long as you can buy them on sale.
3. Follow the 10-10 rule and don't own a business for ten minutes that you wouldn't own for ten years.
4. Make a significant profit by selling your businesses at or above their true value.

Only buy businesses that you can understand and have meaning for you. Find businesses that are right for you by taking my investor profile test at **PaybackTimeBook.com**. This is a cool personal assessment tool to quickly review your investments and find instant savings. It is a step-by-step questionnaire designed to help you better manage your money, and best of all, it's free.

MUTUAL FUND INVESTING MAKES NO SENSE

A long habit of not thinking a thing wrong gives it a superficial appearance of being right.

—Thomas Paine

I f what happened to your retirement money in the last couple of years wasn't enough to prove to you the futility of the mutual fund industry, let me state the fact: You have been systematically brainwashed out of your rightful retirement by the very system into which you are putting your trust. The 401(k) you're using to stockpile your excess capital or the managed IRA you're pouring your retirement money into was set up for the benefit of *other* people — not you. They are not catering to your retirement out of altruistic concerns. Like sheep, you are being cared for only so you can be sheared.

The main beneficiaries of the investments in your retirement plans are the very people who created these funds: the fund administrators and managers. They've set up the system so that, in the end, they'll wind up with half to two-thirds of your money. You didn't know that, did you? You thought they were only taking a little piece. Not so. (Hang tight; I'll explain how this happens shortly.)

These fund managers are in the mutual fund business because it makes them rich without having to be talented. They either don't have the skill set necessary to successfully stockpile businesses or they don't have the luxury of time to wait for a great opportunity to stockpile. Either way, they are not business stockpilers. Yet you give them your capital—your hard-earned money. And they, in turn, eviscerate that pile of money.

YOU DON'T GET WHAT YOU PAY FOR

Your 401(k) fund managers and administrators are charging you, on average, 25 percent per year of your expected Return on Investment. And they take that money whether they made *you* any money or not. In 2008, they took about $100 billion in fees and commissions while lowering the value of your retirement account by over 40 percent. And if you think that's bad, consider this: What they take when they rip you off for 25 percent of your gain is far more than 25 percent. Over your investing life, that 25 percent fee off the top robs you of 60 to 70 percent of your expected gain by the time you reach retirement . . . and continues to rob you thereafter.*

I repeat: 60 percent of what you should have gotten from your investments is gone by the time you are sixty-five, taken by fund managers and fund administrators.

How is this possible? When you set up these accounts and signed on the dotted line, they certainly never told you they'd be putting 60 percent of your lifetime gains in their own pockets. It's a sneaky scam based, just like its polar opposite—*stockpiling*—on the power of compounding. As I mentioned before, Einstein said the most difficult to

---

*This figure is a general estimate that reflects most people's experience. The range depends on time—how long you stay invested in mutual funds. Less time, less rip. More time, more rip. It can be as much as 70 percent over a long life invested in mutual funds. For the purposes of this book, we'll stick with 60 percent as a conservative figure.

understand and yet most powerful force in the universe is compounded interest. While your eyes glossed over those itty-bitty fees and numbers, your fund manager figured out that they add up big-time.

Let's say Jane puts $1,000 into a 401(k) account when she starts earning money in her first real job at age twenty and keeps adding $1,000 a year until she's eighty-five. The money is invested in a broad-market mutual fund. The fund performs in the top 30 percent of all funds and achieves an annual rate of return that matches the S&P 500 index for all the years she is invested. For the last hundred years the S&P 500 index has averaged 8 percent. Her fund carries normal fees as follows: management fee of 1 percent, marketing fees of .05 percent, and an administration fee of .05 percent.

Jane accumulates $1.3 million in her retirement account and congratulates herself upon her retirement on doing such a disciplined job of investing.

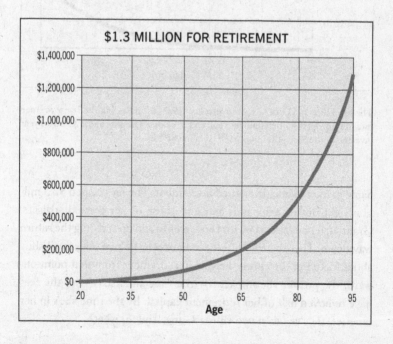

What she doesn't realize is that if she hadn't been stuck paying that tiny little fee, she would have $3.7 million in her account (the gray line).

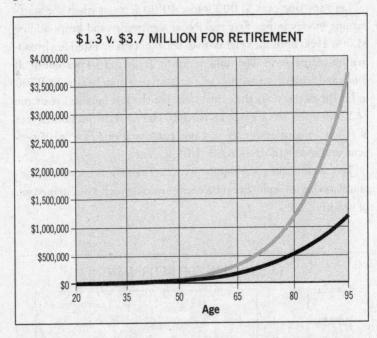

$1.3 v. $3.7 MILLION FOR RETIREMENT

The black line is $1,000 a year invested at S&P 500 index hundred-year average rate of return less mutual fund fees and commissions. The gray line is $1,000 a year invested in the S&P 500 index itself (symbol: SPY).

Same market. Same diversified investment. The fees ripped $2.5 million right out of her hands and into those of her trusted advisers. Granted, it does take time for those fees to add up and drag the return way down. There's little difference between the two lines until she's about forty, but the closer she gets to retirement from that point onward, the greater the impact. By the time she's sixty-five, the fees have removed half of her retirement capital. By the time she's in her nineties, they've taken two-thirds. Gone. And for what?

Since you're paying these fees, you should know what they cover. You're paying for the privilege of *active management*. That means that you're paying someone to use his best judgment every day to put your money to work and give you a high return in the long run. Your fund manager is supposed to get you out of overvalued stocks before they go down, and get you into great stocks if they are available at a good price. After all, that's the whole purpose of active management. If all he was going to do was match market returns, then there is no real purpose to active management, right? You'd be spending your money on something and getting nothing for it.

Now here comes the other half of the scam: *These highly paid fund managers can't outperform the market index.* More precisely, a recent *Forbes* study found that only 4 percent of fund managers beat the market over a fifteen-year period. Another study proved that the pension fund managers were no better. Only 4 percent of pension funds beat the market over a fifteen-year period, too. These facts might have been what Warren Buffett was referring to when he said, "People get a lot for their money when they hire a professional, like a plumber or a dentist. But people get nothing for their money from professional fund managers."

So maybe "active mutual fund management" is a waste of their time and your money. If that's so, then what does your money *really* buy? You pay for the fund's sales force, you pay for the fund's slick marketing, you pay for the Super Bowl halftime ads, you pay for their trading costs, you pay for their big offices on Madison Avenue, you pay for the fund manager's two-martini business lunches, you pay for the fund manager's kid's tuition at Dartmouth and his weekend home in the Hamptons. You pay for his first-class airfare to visit a potential investment in Hawaii. You pay for the Four Seasons hotel room and his $300-a-round golf match with the CEO of the business that he's thinking of putting your money in. You pay for his company's massive propaganda campaign to keep you convinced that only [insert the name of any mutual fund organization here] can get you the results you're looking for in your retirement.

FINANCIAL PORNOGRAPHY

Here's a verbatim quote in an ad from the largest fund-management company in the world: "Our funds are . . . managed by some of the most experienced professionals in the business. Maybe that's why we offer you more 4- and 5-star funds than anyone else." Note the word "maybe." Well, maybe not. The reason they offer more top-rated funds than anyone else is that they have more funds than anyone else. Actually there are several fund companies that have more highly rated funds as a percentage of their total funds than these guys. In fact, these guys have one of the most dismal records for highly rated funds as a percentage of total funds of all the fund-management companies. But it sure doesn't read that way in their advertising.

Here's a lovely example of seeming to claim good performance without the track record to do so: "Growth Investing is making a comeback. At [mutual fund company] it never went out of style." This ad ignores the fact that their flagship fund peaked in 2000 and eight years later was down 40 percent from the peak. How does a -40 percent return for eight years equate with "Growth Investing"? What's so stylish about losing 40 percent?

Yet another ad from a huge mutual fund company claims you should just stick with them because in three out of every four of the last hundred years the stock market went up. True, but massively misleading. On average, the one year the market went down, it often went down so far that it took three years of going up to recover. Wow! Look, Dorothy! The market goes up three out of every four years!

Those are just a few examples of the statistics that are used to mislead you.

Mad yet?

Get this into your head: **Mutual fund companies are not in the stockpiling business or even the investing business.** They are in the asset-collection business. They call it AUM and, like the yoga mantra *om,* they repeat it endlessly to assure a happy life. AUM means "assets under management" and that's the name of the mutual fund game. The value of a fund to the owners of the fund, in cash, is about 20 percent of the AUM. If you are a fund owner and get $50 billion AUM, when you sell the fund (or take it public), you get to take home about $10 to $18 billion, with a *b*. If you kept 20 percent of every dollar you raised, would you be in the *stockpiling* business or the dollar-raising business?

Gathering AUM requires heavy spending on advertising and marketing to sell the dream. But there's nothing in there about *delivering* on the promises they make. They just have to sell the hell out of themselves and then not do too much worse than the other AUM boys. There's always some hardworking, ignorant, and trusting soul looking for a place to put a bit of extra money who is clueless about how the game is played.

Peter Lynch, former manager of Fidelity Magellan, the largest mutual fund in the world, thinks you should absolutely be managing your money. In his book *One Up on Wall Street,* he writes, "The amateur investor has numerous built-in advantages that should result in outperforming the experts and the markets." (But then he became the spokesperson for a huge mutual fund company and stopped saying that heinous stuff.)

They're going to sell you every way they can, and if that includes hiding facts and twisting statistics, they'll do that, too. Some of these people are the ones who brought you the derivatives-market meltdown and still paid out bonuses in 2008 in spite of the fact their wisdom, experience, advice, and management lost you a huge portion of your retirement.

And consider this: Do you really want to trust your investment decisions to a company that can't keep its own boat afloat? In 2008, three of the Big Five investment banks—Merrill Lynch, Bear Stearns, and Lehman Brothers—went bankrupt or had to be sold to avoid bankruptcy. The other two—Goldman and JP Morgan—have been in critical condition, hooked up to IVs delivering much-needed capital from outside sources like taxpayers and investors. These are the same guys whose analysts—who you'd think should have a better pulse on the market than the average person—were encouraging buying stocks when things were about to get ugly. In 2000, for example, Merrill Lynch analysts said there were 940 wonderful stocks to buy and only 7 to sell. Salomon said you should buy 856 and only sell 4. First Boston analysts were more negative. They only found 791 stocks to buy and all of 9 to sell. And Morgan Stanley said there were 780 wonderful businesses to buy and exactly none to sell. This, right before the market plunged as much as 90 percent in some of these recommended stocks. The week that Enron went bankrupt, nine of the fourteen investment banking companies who were covering the stock had a "buy" rating on it. None said to sell it. And how many were shouting "Get out!" in late 2007? None. Why? Because they aren't in the business of investing. They are in the business of AUM. The investment banks that failed deserve what they got. They were greedy and they paid the price. **Too bad they are taking your retirement down with them.**

Oh. Did I mention that it gets worse? Well, it does.

YOUR "NUMBER"

In his book *The Number,* Lee Eisenberg tells us that "the Number represents the amount of money people will need to enjoy the active life they desire, especially post-career." He describes four types of people and how they might approach the Number. A Procrastinator has no sense of the Number and no plan for retirement and is in denial. A Plucker picks the Number out of thin air and has a plan based on a wild-ass guess. The Plotter has a rationally determined Number, a defined plan to plod toward it, and no sense of what life is all about. The Prober is all about what life is all about, has a Number and a plan determined by downsizing everything, and chants "I'm okay, you're okay" while watching *Oprah.* Because of all the variables in these four types of people, Lee doesn't tell us what the Number is. But fools rush in where angels fear to tread, so I'm going to give it a shot:

Let's take an average couple, mid-forties, who want to retire at sixty-five. They figure they had better plan to be around for a while in retirement. And they realize that it's going to take some money for two people to live comfortably for thirty years without an income and be able to handle the inevitable medical bills and eventually the nursing home.

They figure that they could live comfortably for the balance of their lives if they can spend $50,000 a year after taxes in 2009 dollars. That doesn't seem like so much. Between the two of them they're making double that now. Of course they don't actually bring home $100,000. They pay out about $30,000 in taxes, between Social Security tax, federal income tax, and state income tax. So they are really living on $6,000 a month after taxes today.

These people have $50,000 to invest. They intend to add $10,000 a year to it for the next twenty years. Yes, Lee, they procrastinated. They are guessing about the Number. They are now plodding dutifully toward it while reading *The Secret*.

If they keep their money in mutual funds and the markets manage to do 8 percent average for the next twenty years, they might accumulate $690,000 by the time they retire. At age sixty-five, they will begin drawing down that amount while keeping it invested at 5 percent a year in bonds. They will spend $50,000 a year in 2009 dollars. Because of inflation they will run out of money in five years.

This is terrible news. So terrible that right now you're thinking it can't be true. That I've somehow played with the inflation rate to make it massively expensive to live in 2029. I haven't. I've assumed an average inflation rate of 4 percent per year. It's actually expected to be quite a lot higher than that by a number of professionals, so the situation could be much worse than this, but it's unlikely to be any better. The alternative scenario is deflation . . . and the depression that goes with it, in which case their dreams of putting away $10,000 a year will go up in smoke. They'll be lucky to have enough left over after payday (if they have jobs) to cover the cost of living. Think 1934. Believe me, the inflationary scenario is prettier, even if it is rather grim.

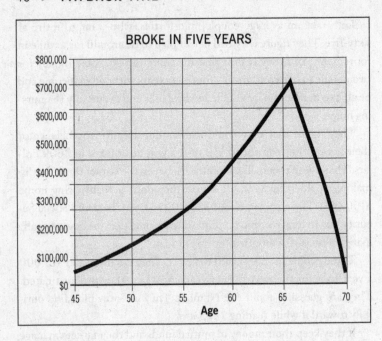

So in 2029, the equivalent of $109,000 a year will buy what $50,000 buys today. Our hypothetical couple have $690,000. Invested in a 5 percent bond, this amount is going to earn about $25,000 after tax their first year in retirement. They'll have to supplement the bond income by withdrawing $84,000 from their 401(k). But wait. There's more. The money they pull out of their 401(k) is also fully taxed. In order to have $84,000 *after tax,* assuming a 25 percent tax rate overall, they'll have to pull out a total of $112,000. Their $690,000 goes down by $112,000. That leaves $578,000. They will do that again the next year and they will then be down to less than $460,000. By the time they turn seventy they will have burned through the $690,000 and be broke. Five years.

If they win a nice lottery or have a rich old uncle and somehow get a million dollars in 2029, they'll last seven years.

Okay, so here's my best guess for the Number if you want to retire in 2029 on $50,000 a year in 2009 dollars, plan to live to be ninety-five, and don't want to rely on anyone else: **$3,600,000.** That's a lot. But it's going to take that to get you to the end without going broke.

If you're a Baby Boomer and you want to retire today, your number will drop to about $1.6 million, because $50,000 today is still $50,000. Inflation hasn't yet taken its toll. Of course, you have to already *have* that $1.6 million and that could be a problem for some of you right now given the fact that the stock market just chopped your IRA and 401(k) in half. If you're looking for retirement in ten years, inflation will have kicked in somewhat, but not horribly, so the Number is a nice middling $2.3 million. How close are you to that?

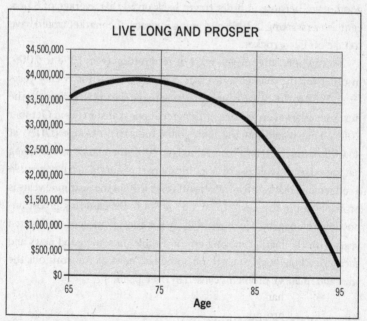

The above chart shows what would happen if you accumulated $3.6 million in your 401(k) between now and 2029, at which point you retire, buy a 5 percent bond, and pay taxes on your withdrawals at a 25 percent overall rate. Assuming a 4 percent inflation rate, you can live the rest of your life on $50,000 a year in 2009 dollars.

MAKING MONEY WHEN THE MARKET GOES CRAZY

As I'm writing this, my prediction at the end of the summer in 2007, when I told people to get out of the market, is ringing true: By March 2009 the Dow Jones stock market index melted down from 14,500 to below 6,600—a loss of over 50 percent from the high of October 2007. I told my readers to get back in at 6,600 and, as I'm writing this, the market rebounded to 9,500, where it was in 1998 when Bill Clinton was president and just beginning to tell Fannie Mae to push banks to make subprime loans. That means your retirement account has pretty much gone nowhere or worse for eleven years. That's not good news, because in order to get back up to that average of 8 percent a year starting in 1998 and going forward, the market would have to take off like a rocket.

For example, after eleven years of zero return, from 1998 to 2009, in order for the market to average 8 percent a year for twenty years (from 1998 to 2018), we're going to have to see the market go up for the next nine years at an average of 19 percent per year starting in October 2009. That would put the Dow Jones Industrial Average (DJIA) at 45,000 in nine years. Of course, in late 2009 the market is still being hampered by the collapse of a significant part of our financial system, so a sudden bull market that rockets off to 45,000 in the next nine years is probably not in the cards. In fact, it's *so* not in the cards it's almost impossible to imagine. Much more likely is a continuation of the last ten years with the market moving up for a while on some good news and then crunching back to earth on some bad news as we work out the wars and financial problems caused by overspending.

The Bulls and the Bears

If we define a "bear market" as a market that has not yet reached the previous "bull market" high point, we get a very interesting pattern of bull/bear markets.

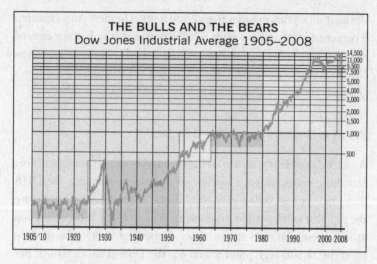

THE BULLS AND THE BEARS
Dow Jones Industrial Average 1905–2008

The bear markets are all in dark gray. The bull markets are light gray. Sometimes we might not know we're in a long bear market until we can look back on it. But sometimes it's pretty obvious. Like right now. The bear market that started in October 2007 as the Dow came off the peak price of 14,500 follows the longest bull market in history. We partied hard. And now we're going to pay the price.

In my opinion, this pattern points to a strong possibility this market will not rise above 14,500 for many, many years. Maybe fifteen or more. Maybe it'll match the record set between 1929 and 1955 — the market peaked in 1929 and didn't get back to that level for twenty-six years. Whatever happens, chances are a return to a bull market will take longer than most of us would like, and an investing strategy that's counting on a broad move upward may not produce much of a return on investment.

If, for example, it takes the Dow eighteen years to move permanently above 14,500 from, say, 9,500, the thirty-year average rate of return from 1998 to 2028 will be about 1 percent per year. Not so great. Not really what your financial adviser expected either.

Maybe I'm being too pessimistic, but that's a whole lot more likely than the market holding on to a 19 percent per year bull market for the next nine years in order to give you mutual funders your expected 8 percent compounded return. I halfway expect it to bounce upward in big, hairy explosions of unwarranted optimism and then crash as Mr. Market gets completely depressed. But hold on to the gains? Let's get crazy and just say, "It ain't gonna happen."

What a Bear's Trampling Can Do

A much more likely scenario is that the market will get some really big economic shocks from a worldwide slowdown, yo-yoing the DJIA down between 14,000 and 6,000. Maybe lower. Here's why: Notice the range of stock market prices from 1965 to 1983. You can see that at its lowest, the market lost about 45 percent. A 45 percent drop from the 14,500 high point would put the Dow at about 8,000. But the Dow already hit below 6,600, *so we've blown through that floor already.* The 1970s were a tough time economically but the consensus of economic professionals suggests that we're in way worse shape now. That isn't good news because it implies the bottom could be lower than 6,600.

During the Great Depression, the stock market dropped to about 55 from its peak price of 375. That's a little more than an 85 percent collapse. I doubt we'll see things deteriorate that far, but they could. Japan has been in a severe recession for years and its stock market has dropped 85 percent. An 85 percent drop from 14,500 would put the Dow at 2,175.

All this is horribly depressing, I know. But remember, if you're a *stockpiler* of stocks, none of it will matter to your investments. You can get off the Dow Jones hamster wheel. If the market goes up from here, we're going to make money on the stocks we stockpile, because their prices will rise to their value in a rising market. And if the market goes down, we're going to be even happier, because we'll have lots of opportunities to stockpile more great businesses at great prices, which will make us even richer when the market does go up. A long-term down market like we had from 1965 to 1983 is a time for planting lots of seeds. When the fear finally dissipates and people start investing again, we'll have ample opportunity to reap the harvest. Stockpilers make money in a good market, but we make fortunes in a bad one. In both cases we do well. So in the words of the old Nike ad, "No Fear." We just follow the example of the best investors in the world. Ben Graham made hundreds of millions in the 1930s and 1940s in the midst of the Great Depression and World War II. His student, Warren Buffett, made *billions* in the 1970s and 1980s when we lost a war, had years of stagflation, and suffered a national loss of pride and confidence. Lucky for us, we've got all of the above on the table for consideration for the next fifteen years!

The need to learn how to prosper as an investor in any sort of market—but especially in times of trouble and turmoil—is the whole reason for this book. We have to get you investing on your own so you can take advantage of the volatile market in ways your fund manager just can't.

WHAT YOU CAN DO RIGHT NOW

Many of you are investing in mutual funds now and are going to keep your money invested in the market while you learn to stockpile stocks on your own. But even if you're not ready to invest for yourself, there *is* an alternative to paying those mutual fund fees. If I were going to keep my capital in the market but not invest it on my own yet, I'd put my money into Spyders—the exchange-traded fund for the S&P 500 (symbol SPY). The average fund charges about 1.3 percent fees. SPY charges .08 percent. It's a big difference—you'll pay 16.25 times less for SPY. If you have $10,000 invested in your 401(k) in the average mutual fund, you're going to pay about $200 in fees. You'll pay only $8 for SPY. You save almost the entire management fee. That's the first good thing, because it's a 2 percent return just for knowing

(continued on next page)

a little thing about your money. And even better, today that 2 percent represents a significantly better return than you would get in a one-year U.S. Treasury bond. Again, just for having a little knowledge. The second is SPY is going to do the market rate of return because it *is* the market. It's a stock that mirrors the S&P 500 index by buying the index stocks. If the S&P 500 index goes up 20 percent next year, SPY will go up 20 percent, too. Same with going down 20 percent, of course, but SPY eliminates the mutual fund fee and then achieves what the vast majority of mutual funds fail to achieve—a market rate of return. This one change in your investing will solve the problem of being ripped off for fees. It doesn't solve the problem of making nothing for the next ten years if the market goes nowhere. But then again, you'd have made nothing in your mutual funds either and you'll be ahead the fee money.

I just read an article about what to do right now on Yahoo! Finance titled "5 Ways to Fix Up Your 401(k) Plan." Here's the gist of what those five tips are:

1. Save 'til it hurts and invest in mutual funds.
2. Save some more and invest in mutual funds.
3. Don't touch the money—leave it in the funds.
4. Pay attention to fees.
5. Get your coworkers saving more, too.

I'd laugh at the naïveté but I don't think the author meant it as a joke. With a little knowledge you can do better than just "leave it in the funds" even if the market goes nowhere.

You can make money on SPY by trading it using a simple computer tool called a Moving Average (you'll find this computer tool on investment and trading sites and many others. For my favorites, visit my website at PaybackTimeBook.com or read my first book, *Rule #1*).

Here's a real-world example: In mid-January 2009, the Dow was at 8,000, which meant it had gone nowhere for the previous ten years. This meant SPY went nowhere for ten years, too. The chart shows the price of SPY as the thick line and the Moving Average as the thin line. The gray arrows show the date when you would have bought; the black arrows show the date when you would have sold. Using this tool you would have bought and sold twice during those ten years.

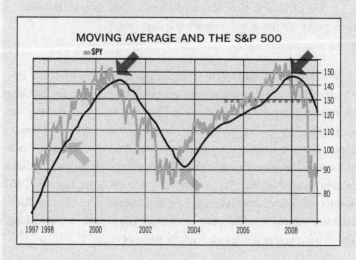

MOVING AVERAGE AND THE S&P 500

Had you done so, your compounded return in SPY over those ten years would have been 7 percent and you would have doubled your money. Nothing to write home about, but it's a lot better than a zero return for the same investment. And maybe even better, if you had used this tool it would have forced you to sell and avoid the big nauseating price drops in your retirement account. Notice that you would have been out of the investment before the big drops could have done any significant damage to your profits.

(continued on next page)

This is just a bare-bones introduction to the fun of Moving Averages—don't worry if all this doesn't quite make sense yet. You can get lots more information on my website at PaybackTimeBook.com or in *Rule #1*.

If SPY is not offered in your 401(k), demand it. Representative George Miller, a California Democrat who is chairman of the House Education and Labor Committee, is trying to pass legislation requiring all plans to offer at least one index fund.

The other way to make money on an index fund in this market is to stockpile it. But that's the next chapter.

What makes this all so gut-wrenching is that in a market like this, it's easy to believe that *nothing* can get you financial security. Nothing short of winning the lottery, anyway. The good news is that there *is* an alternative. *Stockpiling* businesses can get you to financial independence. But you have to get going on it *now*. And you can't just stockpile any old business that you think looks cheap. The mere fact that a certain stock has lost 50 percent in price since its high in 2007 doesn't mean it's 50 percent off. Like the people on the Forbes Richest List, you must know what businesses you *should* be stockpiling. That's what you're going to learn how to do next.

TAKEAWAYS AND ACTION ITEMS

Since 96 percent of mutual fund managers cannot beat the market, stop paying for active management and the fees that can rob you of more than 60 percent of your return by retirement.

- At minimum, invest in ETFs or a market index to avoid paying for active management.
- Review my website **PaybackTimeBook.com** to see how to calculate the amount you'll need to retire.

THREE Ms EQUAL NO-RISK INVESTMENTS

Successful and unsuccessful people do not vary greatly in their abilities.
They vary in their desires to reach their potential.

—JOHN MAXWELL

This book is all about buying shares in wonderful businesses whose stock is wildly undervalued. Stockpiling businesses you understand is the key to taking control of your money and compounding it the way the rich guys do. So now I'm going to tell you how to find these wonderful businesses step by step.

Let's start by taking Plato's advice. Plato said that if you want to find the best example of something, you should start off by thinking about the perfect "form" of that thing—some ideal version that exemplifies perfection—and then look for things in the world that conform to that perfection as closely as possible. Let's see if we can use that notion of a perfect business "form" to help us find a wonderful business.

Here are the top ten qualities that make a business *perfect* from a stockpiler's point of view.

1. It's a simple, easy-to-understand business.
2. It has some form of durable monopoly.
3. It sells a universal product.

4. It sells a habit-forming product.

5. Its products are cheap to make.

6. Its products are cheap to sell.

7. It has huge profit margins.

8. It can raise its prices with inflation.

9. Its products and processes make the world a better place.

10. Management is owner-oriented, passionate, dedicated, and honest.

Let's look at each of these qualities in a bit more detail:

1. *It's a simple, easy-to-understand business:* A simple, easy-to-understand business is easier to manage than a complex business. Fewer things can go wrong, and if they do, they're easier to fix. It's also easier to forecast future cash flow, and that makes it easier for an investor to put a value on it. And remember, knowing the value is everything.

2. *It has some form of durable monopoly:* A perfect business would last forever. To do that it needs protection against competition. In the real world, competitors see a business making a ton of money and they move right in. A perfect business needs to have products that potential competitors, for some reason, can't copy well. It could be a secret formula, a brand, the prohibitive cost to switch off the product, a government-awarded monopoly, or just low cost.

3. *It sells a universal product:* A perfect business sells something everyone wants, worldwide.

4. *It sells a habit-forming product:* A perfect business makes a product that compels the user to purchase it again and again even when money is tight.

5. *Its products are cheap to make:* A perfect business has very low costs to make the product and the costs go down, not up, over time.

6. *Its products are cheap to sell:* A perfect business has products that almost sell themselves.

7. *It has huge profit margins:* A perfect business can sell the product for much more than it costs to make it, and it can keep the profit margins high forever.

8. *It can raise its prices with inflation:* A perfect business doesn't concern itself with inflation. If its suppliers raise their prices, it just raises the product price.

9. *Its products and processes make the world a better place:* A perfect business cleans up after its manufacturing processes. It doesn't pollute. It doesn't take advantage of people to increase profits. And its products make its customers better, more productive, and happier. It doesn't violate the Golden Rule (i.e., "treat others as you would like to be treated").

10. *Management is owner-oriented, passionate, dedicated, and honest:* A perfect business has a management team and, in particular, a CEO who are all about the success of this business for all the stakeholders — investors, employees, suppliers, customers, community. They live and breathe this business. The last thing they would do is take a payday to the detriment of their honor and obligations to the people they lead.

That, to me, is the perfect business. I would love to own a business that meets all ten qualities. The only problem is that such a business probably does not, and maybe even cannot, exist in the real world. For instance, isn't it a logical contradiction to sell an addicting product that makes customers better people? Does it make sense to insist on "addicted" and "Golden Rule" in the same mission statement? The mere fact that the product is habit-forming, like tobacco or alcohol, probably makes customers less in control of their own lives.

And are huge profit margins in harmony with not taking advantage of people? Aren't huge profit margins, by definition, taking advantage? A business with huge profit margins can stay in business quite well even if it sells its product for a lower price, because it will still make a comfortable profit. So does "huge profit margin" violate the Golden

Rule, too? Are you doing your best for all your stakeholders, including your customer, by jacking the price as high as you can get away with?

And where are we going to find honest managers to run this thing? At Harvard Business School? Not a lot of classes are offered on honesty at HBS or any other B-school, for that matter. And owner-oriented managers? Some professors teach that the shareholders are not the owners. If the CEO doesn't know who the owners are, then how can he be "owner-oriented"? Most people at these elite business schools have outcompeted their peers to get there and are spending a small fortune primarily to get the credibility of an MBA from a top school. Learning something is secondary. After they graduate most of them will find out that a kid with five years in the Procter & Gamble management program knows everything HBS teaches and knows it better. If they're honest, they'll tell you they went for the prestige, because that degree gets better jobs, faster advancement, and mo' money, mo' money. These future CEOs are not the Bill Gateses and Steve Jobses of the world. Jobs and Gates are college dropouts who wanted to change the world. Your average Ivy B-school grad wants to climb it. That's why we get these financial debacles. Boards of directors put these people in charge — people who live their lives chasing the almighty dollar for the prestige it brings. It used to be that $5 million a year was a lot of money. Now these guys aren't happy unless they're making $20 million. If your average B-school grad is running your company, you are probably a long way from perfection.

Face it. If we're going to invest, we're going to have to settle for less than perfect. And anyway, our list is too long. Let's tighten it up a bit.

Some of our ten requirements for perfection will be the natural outcome of others on the list. For example, if a business has durable barriers to competition, typically some form of monopoly, it will also have big profit margins and can raise its prices with inflation. These latter two qualities follow directly from having control of a market. Also, I think I'll just combine all of the product qualities, except habit-forming, which is too good to let go of quite yet, and, of course, we must have great managers.

So a perfect business:

1. is as **simple** as a lemonade stand (#1)
2. is **protected** by some form of monopoly (#2, #5, #6, #7, #8)
3. has **universal** appeal (#3)
4. is **habit-forming** (#4)
5. makes the world a **better** place (#9)
6. is run by people who are **owner-oriented,** passionate, dedicated, and honest (#10)

Take the illegal drug business, for example. The business is **simple** (#1); they shoot competitors, so their market is **protected** (#2); plenty of people love to get high, so it's **universal** (#3); the customer is **hooked on the habit** (#4); it makes the world a . . . whoops. And it's run by honest. . . . Well, four outta six ain't bad and there's no such thing as perfection, right?

Except, according to at least one very smart guy, the soda pop giant Coca-Cola. Coke sells carbonated, caffeinated sugar water, so the product is **simple** (#1), **universal** (#3), and **habit-forming** (#4). It's **protected** from competition by a secret formula, brand awareness, and its quasi-monopoly on shelf space (#2); and it's run by **owner-oriented,** passionate, dedicated, and honest people (#6). Is it the perfect business? Well, there's that pesky #5 thing about making the world a better place. Maybe the world would be worse off without Coke. I'm hooked, so I'm the wrong guy to ask. (Charlie Munger, Warren Buffett's longtime investing partner, gave a talk on the perfect business to Harvard Business School students and used Coke as the example. So if you want to argue about this, talk to Charlie. He's a lot smarter than I am.)

Okay, those six items make for a perfect business. The problem is there are very few of those perfect businesses around, and even fewer of those around for the right price. We might have to settle for less than perfect. We might have to look for merely wonderful.

A WONDERFUL BUSINESS

A wonderful business has many, but not all, of the six requirements. We're going to hope for, but not demand, a product that is habit-forming and universal, so we're dropping those two as requirements. Consider them recommendations and add them to your requirements later when you're no longer a novice at this. We're going to hang on to "makes the world a better place," but we're going to let you decide what that means or if you even care, by combining it with "understanding the business."

We're keeping three critical parameters: Our business must: (1) be simple to understand and sell a product you're okay with, (2) be protected from competition, and (3) have owner-oriented, dedicated, passionate, and honest management. Therefore, a wonderful business:

1. has great **Meaning** to you (i.e., to *you* it's simple)
2. has a big **Moat** (i.e., because it's protected from competition, it's durable and profitable)
3. has owner-oriented, dedicated, passionate, and honest **Management** (i.e., you don't have to be watching it every day and can, therefore, go play)

Let's dig deeper into these three M requirements. If you read my first book, this will be a refresher course for you. And it's probably much needed. A lot has changed since *Rule #1* first came out. Companies that people once trusted, like Lehman Brothers and Washington Mutual, don't even exist anymore as we once knew them. We've watched old guards fall hard. Were those wonderful businesses that just disappeared? Not at all. There was nothing simple about Lehman, so unless you happened to think you understood their world, you never would have had money in that industry. And WaMu was making subprime loans. Did you really think real estate was going to go up forever and that subprime borrowers were wonderful credit risks? If you knew the industry, you knew it was a business that was addicted to the money, no matter the risk. Any WaMu loan officer could have told you things were out of control. And what was their Moat? There wasn't one, as it turned out. They were in a commodity business without any form of protection, so competition was driving them to do the wrong thing. No reader of mine would have made the mistake of going deep with WaMu.

Fannie Mae is another story.

Fannie Mae might have caught a good investor. It was appealing because it had a government monopoly and it had awesome Big Five numbers. You'll learn more about those shortly. The CEO was taking huge paydays, however. Big red flag. And fortunately for us, it was also massively overpriced (a subject we'll cover in plenty more detail later). Those two issues were enough to keep us safe even from a business that was faking its numbers.

Some skeptics argue it's impossible to ever know what's really going on inside a company. But that's because they don't know how to invest. Great investors laugh at that statement. We hope they keep teaching that sort of nonsense at business schools so we can continue to buy great businesses at fantastic prices. If we apply these three Ms, today's stock market stops being a hand-wringing nightmare and becomes the opportunity of a lifetime. And I say that with no exaggeration. You just follow the three Ms and do your homework.

It's critical to fully understand Meaning, Moat, and Management and go through them each and every time you evaluate the wonderfulness of a company you think might be a good one to stockpile. The three Ms will protect you from getting burned by some not-so-wonderful business that goes to zero value. Later on in this chapter and the next, I'll cover other specific red flags to watch out for, which will further reinforce the significance of these three Ms.

Now let's dive into each of the three Ms in detail so I can show you how to be sure the business is at least wonderful and maybe actually perfect.

MEANING

"Meaning" is about knowing the industry. If the *industry* has Meaning for you, then you understand the environment in which the business competes. If you love computers—not just what they do but how they do it—then the computer industry may be a group of businesses that you can come to understand well. If you're a chef, then the restaurant industry may be more up your alley. If you're a (guilt-ridden) fast-food addict like me, you might find the fast-food industry is your bowl of beans.

To get a grip on what industries you might already be knowledgeable about, try the 3-Circles exercise. It's real simple and fast. Just draw three circles that slightly overlap one another. Label the top circle "Passion." Label another circle "Talent," and label the third circle "Money." In the Passion circle, write a list of all the things you're passionate about. In the "Talent" circle, list the things you are talented in. In the "Money" circle, list the places you make or spend money. Now see if there is anything that's in all three circles.

This exercise took me less than five minutes, so I'm sure I could do better and be more exhaustive if I needed to. But I don't. As you can see, I've already got plenty to explore.

I bolded the six things I found in all three circles:

1. Investing
2. Writing
3. Speaking
4. Guiding
5. Traveling
6. the Outdoors

These are all parts of my life that I know I'm passionate about, think I'm somewhat talented in, and either spend or make money in.

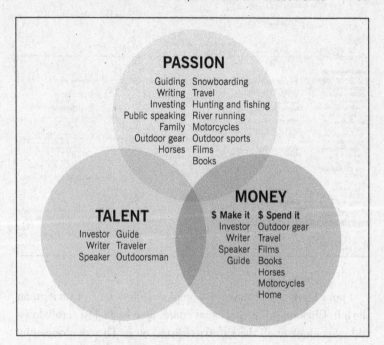

PASSION

Guiding	Snowboarding
Writing	Travel
Investing	Hunting and fishing
Public speaking	River running
Family	Motorcycles
Outdoor gear	Outdoor sports
Horses	Films
	Books

MONEY

$ Make it	$ Spend it
Investor	Outdoor gear
Writer	Travel
Speaker	Films
Guide	Books
	Horses
	Motorcycles
	Home

TALENT

Investor	Guide
Writer	Traveler
Speaker	Outdoorsman

Now, let's see if any of these six correspond to industries I can invest in. Get on your computer and follow me. We're going to check out Yahoo! Finance and take a look at Industries.

To get there, go online and put "yahoo.com" into your URL bar. When Yahoo! comes up, on the left you'll see a list of web pages you can click on. The third one is Finance. Click on it. Bookmark this page. You'll be going here a lot in the future, because Yahoo! is my favorite place for industry information and we stockpilers are really good at getting industry info.

Near the top of the Finance page there are several tabs. The second tab from the left is Investing. As you put your cursor on it, it will present a drop-down menu with a list of additional web pages. Slide on down to Industries and click on it. The Industry page will come up and look like this:

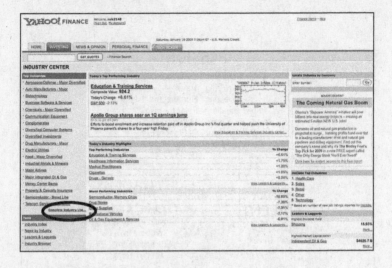

I put a black oval around the Complete Industries List, an item on the left. Click on it. The page that comes up is huge. Just scroll down and take a look at all the industries listed on it. They're grouped by similarities that someone at Yahoo! Finance decided on. These groups are called Sectors and they vary by website or brokerage. Yahoo! decided on nine Sectors:

1. Basic Materials
2. Conglomerates
3. Consumer Goods
4. Financial
5. Health Care
6. Industrial Goods
7. Services
8. Technology
9. Utilities

Every one of the dozens of industries and thousands of companies on Yahoo! is found inside one of these nine Sectors.

Okay, now back to my 3-Circle list. I'm an investor and passionate about it, but as you may have guessed from the preceding pages, the financial industry isn't my first choice for owning a business. Among other things, I believe the people who run those businesses are pretty much just in it for the money. I'd rather the people who run my business are passionate about what they sell.

I write, so that's the publishing industry. As a writer, I create the raw product, and my editor helps me refine it. I know that part of publishing. But the business of selling books is a whole 'nother world that I don't know much about. I could learn and might be interested. I'll keep "publishing" as a possible industry to own something in. It might be fun to own my publisher.

Speaking? Is there a "public speaking" industry? Maybe entertainment? Something to consider.

Guiding? I love guiding river trips, horse-packing adventures, travel adventures, and guiding you guys through the investing world.

Outdoors. Ahhh. I *know* there is an "outdoor gear" industry because I buy their stuff all the time. I can almost list them. I have gear from Garmin, Life-Link, Burton, Harley-Davidson, Arc'teryx, Ruger, Weatherby, Buck, Ka-Bar, Cloudveil, The North Face, REI, Patagonia . . . just off the top of my head. I wonder if any of them is public? Let's go find out.

I can look up each one, of course, but let's come at it from the top down rather than the bottom up. It doesn't matter in the end, but I want to show you how to find a business even if you don't have anyplace to start. Begin by taking a look at those nine Sectors and the industries under each Sector. Just open each Sector and look at the Industries listed under it. We can eliminate a bunch of Sectors where the outdoor gear companies couldn't possibly be hiding. First one, Basic Materials. Looks like the industries listed are all about chemicals and stuff in the ground. Next. Conglomerates. Big companies full of smaller companies. Next.

Consumer Goods. Maybe outdoor gear is hiding in here. Let's go down the list of industries until we find one that looks likely. Down near the bottom of the list is Recreational Goods — Other, followed by Recreational Vehicles. Then a couple of industries later is Sporting Goods, then Textile–Apparel, then after that a bit is the Trucks industry. Let's check these out. I'm just going to pick one and dive in. No particular reason. It's like shopping and picking a likely aisle to walk down.

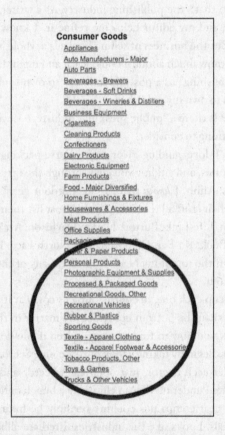

Consumer Goods

Appliances
Auto Manufacturers - Major
Auto Parts
Beverages - Brewers
Beverages - Soft Drinks
Beverages - Wineries & Distillers
Business Equipment
Cigarettes
Cleaning Products
Confectioners
Dairy Products
Electronic Equipment
Farm Products
Food - Major Diversified
Home Furnishings & Fixtures
Housewares & Accessories
Meat Products
Office Supplies
Packaging & Containers
Paper & Paper Products
Personal Products
Photographic Equipment & Supplies
Processed & Packaged Goods
Recreational Goods, Other
Recreational Vehicles
Rubber & Plastics
Sporting Goods
Textile - Apparel Clothing
Textile - Apparel Footwear & Accessories
Tobacco Products, Other
Toys & Games
Trucks & Other Vehicles

Click on Textile–Apparel Clothing. A list of the top businesses in this industry appears in the center box, Industry Top Performers. If you aren't sure what kinds of businesses you're looking at just from the names, then this probably isn't the industry for you at this time. The first thing you'll notice when you get into an industry that's going to be easy for you to understand is you'll recognize the names of businesses because you buy from them, or want to. I see Ralph Lauren and Columbia are listed under Market Capitalization, meaning they're some of the big guys in the business. Okay. I'm walking down an aisle that has stuff I like. Let's go deeper and see who else is in this industry.

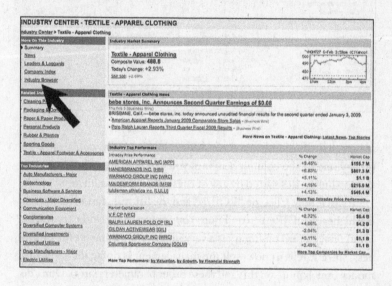

Click on Industry Browser in the upper left box. This tool lists all the businesses in the industry along with several key ratios for comparison purposes. These ratios give you some information about which companies in the industry are the strongest and best competitors. In the old days we'd have to go get reference books, look up industry codes, and dig for hours in the library to get this information. Now we just click a button. You should see a page that looks like this one:

					Industry Center	Industry Index	Leaders & Laggards	

Click on column heading to sort.

Description	1 Day Price Change %	Market Cap	P/E	ROE %	Div. Yield %	Long-Term Debt to Equity
Sector: Consumer Goods	-1.74	1702.8B	16.06	21.95	3.45	0.97
Industry: Textile - Apparel Clothing (More Info)	-5.68	20.5B	24.70	8.60	2.57	0.72
				Companies		
American Apparel, Inc. (APP)	-9.81	169.2M	18.39	11.32	NA	0.88
Bebe Stores, Inc. (BEBE)	4.37	574.1M	9.86	12.51	3.20	NA
Bernard Chaus Inc. (CHBD.OB)	-10.00	3.4M	NA	-50.52	NA	1.52
Brownie's Marine Group, Inc. (BWMG.OB)	0.00	0.4M	1.83	750.52	NA	6.12
Carters Inc. (CRI)	-7.60	978.8M	13.26	19.67	NA	0.83
Columbia Sportswear Company (COLM)	-4.07	1.1B	9.38	12.96	1.90	0.00
Crown Crafts Inc. (CRWS)	-1.73	21.1M	4.99	11.12	NA	0.67
Delta Apparel Inc. (DLA)	-4.35	26.2M	15.25	1.64	0.00	0.85
Eddie Bauer Holdings, Inc. (EBHI)	-1.25	24.4M	NA	-22.81	NA	1.37
Ever-Glory International Group (EVK)	-5.71	12.2M	1.97	29.28	NA	0.31
Execute Sports Inc. (EXCS.OB)	NA	NA	NA	NA	NA	NA
Frederick's of Hollywood Group (FOH)	-2.63	9.7M	NA	NA	0.00	0.78
G-III Apparel Group, Ltd. (GIII)	-12.97	104.4M	5.60	10.47	NA	0.88
Gildan Activewear Inc. (GIL)	-3.12	1.4B	9.93	19.59	NA	0.07
Hanesbrands Inc. (HBI)	-4.12	1.2B	7.84	52.97	NA	6.27
Jeantex Group, Inc. (JNTX.OB)	0.00	1.0M	NA	NA	NA	NA
Joe's Jeans Inc. (JOEZ)	4.44	28.1M	4.39	26.02	NA	0.08
Liz Claiborne Inc. (LIZ)	-14.84	309.7M	NA	-26.22	5.90	0.71
Lululemon Athletica Inc. (LULU)	-5.01	530.4M	12.34	36.67	NA	NA
Maidenform Brands Inc. (MFB)	-11.52	215.0M	7.80	28.13	NA	0.73
Nitches Inc. (NICH)	4.35	1.4M	NA	-19.48	0.00	1.42
Oxford Industries Inc. (OXM)	-8.35	123.5M	24.04	NA	8.50	0.60

It lists all the businesses in the industry alphabetically, and by clicking on any one of the column headings you can rearrange the list to see the top businesses sorted by any of these different parameters.

Try that now. Click on "ROE %" and the list will rearrange itself so the highest ROE (Return on Equity) businesses in this industry will be listed first. Return on Equity is a very important parameter for a business, since it tells us how well the management is doing investing our money (much more on this and these other parameters later). Don't be too concerned about what these parameters mean or even if you have them arranged correctly. All you need to do at this point is play with the toys like a kid at Christmas. Click on stuff. You can't break it. And you'll get an idea of what these tools can tell us about an industry.

Click again and it reverses the list, putting the worst ROE performers on top. Click on some of the other parameters. Try Price to Book Value and then click on Price to Free Cash Flow. You'll start to see that for any industry, a few businesses keep showing up at the top of all these ratio lists. Those are the ones we want to focus on. As you'll learn below, wonderful businesses have wonderful numbers.

Sectors > Consumer Goods > Textile - Apparel Clothing (More Info)

— Industry Index | Leaders & Laggards

Click on column heading to sort.

Description	1 Day Price Change %	Market Cap	P/E	ROE %	Div. Yield %	Long-Term Debt to Equity
Sector: Consumer Goods	2.28	1631.7B	11.00	18.39	3.57	NA
Industry: Textile - Apparel Clothing (More Info)	2.96	20.4B	19.10	7.50	2.59	NA
Companies						
Brownie's Marine Group, Inc. (BWMG.OB)	0.00	0.4M	1.74	750.52	NA	NA
Hanesbrands Inc. (HBI)	6.83	807.3M	6.44	53.65	NA	NA
True Religion Apparel Inc. (TRLG)	0.99	299.2M	7.29	38.13	NA	NA
Lululemon Athletica Inc. (LULU)	4.13	546.4M	12.71	36.67	NA	NA
Ever-Glory International Group (EVK)	-5.26	11.1M	1.79	29.28	NA	NA
Maidenform Brands Inc. (MFB)	4.15	215.5M	7.61	26.13	NA	NA
Joe's Jeans Inc. (JOEZ)	-9.68	16.8M	2.62	26.02	NA	NA
Carters Inc. (CRI)	3.76	948.3M	12.85	19.67	NA	NA
Gildan Activewear Inc. (GIL)	-2.04	1.3B	8.87	19.59	NA	NA
Polo Ralph Lauren Corp. (RL)	4.06	4.2B	9.23	18.25	0.50	NA
VF Corp. (VFC)	2.72	6.4B	10.03	18.01	4.00	NA
Phillips-Van Heusen Corp. (PVH)	3.05	1.0B	6.71	14.54	0.70	NA
Bebe Stores, Inc. (BEBE)	0.49	543.8M	9.34	12.51	3.30	NA
Under Armour, Inc. (UA)	4.12	886.2M	23.76	12.50	NA	NA
American Apparel, Inc. (APP)	9.45	155.7M	16.92	11.32	NA	NA
Crown Crafts Inc. (CRWS)	0.00	19.6M	4.64	11.12	NA	NA
G-III Apparel Group, Ltd. (GIII)	-1.40	81.7M	4.39	10.47	NA	NA
Warnaco Group Inc. (WRC)	5.11	1.1B	13.03	9.97	NA	NA
Columbia Sportswear Company (COLM)	2.49	1.1B	11.44	9.03	2.00	NA
Quiksilver Inc. (ZQK)	-1.04	242.5M	NA	6.82	0.00	NA
Perry Ellis International Inc. (PERY)	-0.51	59.0M	3.21	6.78	NA	NA
Superior Uniform Group Inc. (SGC)	-0.53	49.4M	14.89	6.16	6.60	NA
Delta Apparel Inc. (DLA)	1.41	36.6M	7.12	4.97	0.00	NA
Sport-Haley Inc. (SPOR)	0.00	1.0M	NA	-11.71	NA	NA
Niches Inc. (NICH)	0.00	1.1M	NA	-19.48	0.00	NA
Eddie Bauer Holdings, Inc. (EBHI)	0.00	21.6M	NA	-22.81	NA	NA
Liz Claiborne Inc. (LIZ)	-0.77	244.3M	NA	-26.22	8.70	NA

You can dig around in Yahoo! Finance and MSN Money and find lots of information about every industry, and I encourage you to do that. You just never know where digging around will lead you. But I want to show you the most streamlined, fastest way to get up to speed on a business.

Here's one nice trick: The CEO of any public business is going to get asked industry-related questions during the quarterly conference call he holds with analysts. You can listen in or, if you missed it, you can listen to the recording on the company's website. Some of the more enlightened CEOs, like John Mackey at Whole Foods, publish a transcript of the call on their website. A transcript makes it easy and quick to scan for new information.

Here's the page from the Whole Foods website that gets you access to years of these quarterly calls. If you wanted to understand Whole Foods as a business, a couple hours of reading or listening to this stuff would teach you a whole lot about how the company works. This is way cool, because only a few years ago it was impossible to do this. As in, no matter how much money you had to throw at it, you couldn't do this sort of backdated research. Now you can with the click of a mouse.

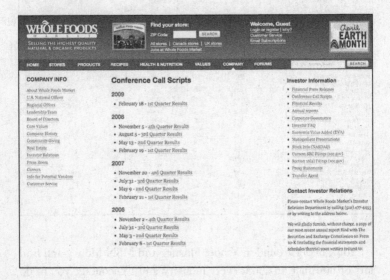

Another good research target is a company's annual report, also available (usually along with five years' worth of past reports) right on the company's website. Warren Buffett's research consists primarily of reading annual reports. If Mr. Buffett does it, and you want to be a successful and rich investor, perhaps you should do it, too.

Another great information source is a company's SEC quarterly and annual filing—the 10-Q (quarterly) and 10-K (annually). These reports are required for every public company and are supposed to disclose everything investors need to know to make an informed decision about investing in that business. In these reports you'll read about the risks inherent in the business, who the key competitors are, and what the business has to do to compete. Here's an example of a 10-Q filing from Whole Foods:

UNITED STATES
SECURITIES AND EXCHANGE COMMISSION
WASHINGTON, D.C. 20549

FORM 10-Q

x   Quarterly report pursuant to Section 13 or 15(d) of the Securities Exchange Act of 1934 for the period ended January 18, 2009; or

o   Transition report pursuant to Section 13 or 15(d) of the Securities Exchange Act of 1934 for the transition period from

Commission File Number: 0-19797

WHOLE FOODS MARKET, INC.
(Exact name of registrant as specified in its charter)

Texas
(State of
incorporation)

74-1989366
(IRS employer
identification no.)

550 Bowie St.
Austin, Texas 78703
(Address of principal executive offices)

512-477-4455
(Registrant's telephone number, including area code)

Indicate by check mark whether the registrant (1) has filed all reports required to be filed by Section 13 or 15(d) of the Securities Exchange Act of 1934 during the preceding (or for such shorter period that the registrant was required to file such reports), and (2) has been subject to such filing requirements for the past 90 days.

In the General section, Whole Foods says this about how it intends to compete: "We aspire to become an international brand synonymous with not just natural and organic foods, but also with being the best food retailer in every community in which we are located. We believe **our heavy emphasis on perishable products, along with our unparalleled customer service** [my emphasis], is helping us reach that goal, differentiating our stores from other supermarkets and enabling us to attract a broad base of loyal customers."

Use the 10-Q and 10-K filings to read about the industry and how your target business intends to compete. Then read the filings for a few other businesses competing in this industry. If you're willing to spend a few hours reading, you'll become pretty knowledgeable about an industry very quickly. The more you read, the more and more *meaning* the industry will have to you.

How do you know when you've read enough? When you aren't getting any new information. When it all starts repeating itself, you're there.

Does this sound like a lot of work? Oh, poor baby. Does it sound like more work than flipping burgers all day when you're seventy-five?

A lot of people apparently think so, because they don't seem to be willing to do it. I can't figure out why people are willing to work their butts off in some menial job but aren't willing to work a hundredth as hard to be rich. Go figure. (If you're one of those people, please shoot me an e-mail at phil@PaybackTimeBook.com and explain!)

To me it's real simple: If you'll do what others won't do, you'll get what others won't get. I did what other river guides didn't do. And I have a life they don't have. If you're willing to do the homework your friends won't do, a few years from now you'll live the life they can only dream about. That dream life begins with finding an industry that has *meaning* for you.

Once we have Meaning solved, we dig in on the best businesses in that industry. We're looking for a durable business that has a plan to keep competitors at bay. We call this quality a Moat, and it's the second of our three Ms.

MOAT

A Moat is about the durability of the business — the competitive advantage a company has over other companies in the same industry. Just as a Moat protects a castle from attack, a durable competitive advantage protects a company.

Let's say you own a company. If you don't have some way of blocking competition, some niche that you alone occupy or some way to make your product obviously better than the other guy's, what'll happen if your competitors suddenly lower prices? You'll have to lower your price as well or lose your customers. And there go your profits. Under no circumstances should you own a business that has to compete on price unless your business is the undisputed low-price monster. But I'd prefer you look for a business that's so durable it can pay its people well, raise its prices every year, and never be forced to lower them by a stalking competitor.

Whole Foods's plan is to make their perishable section huge. Perishables are really dangerous because they, well, *perish.* Quickly. If you can control your perishable losses better than the other guy, he can't compete with you on quality, quantity, or price, because he loses too many perishables and has to make up for the loss with either smaller quantities and variety, or lower quality that he gets at a lower cost, or he has to raise his prices to pay for the losses, none of which is going to help him keep customers. This is rather clever of Whole Foods and they pull it off well. Their stores have an overflowing-horn-of-plenty feeling. It's like you're in an urban jungle of delicious-looking food. No other market compares. If they keep learning how to do that better and better, they can make a Moat so wide their customers won't ever leave them and the competitors can never get near them. The perishables secret helps create Brand Moat—a wide Moat indeed.

Think about Coke again. These guys have been making sugar water for 150 years. In the early days their product was unique, but over the years science has advanced and now there are colas on the market that taste quite a lot like Coke, some would say *exactly* like Coke. But Coke still owns half the market and charges a premium price. How? Because they have such a strong brand that you don't think "I want a cola." You think, "I want a Coke."

There are five kinds of big Moats, any one of which can give you that kind of durability: Brand, Secret, Toll, Switching, and Low Cost (see sidebar for definitions).

Whole Foods is going for a Secret Moat with secrets about how to manage perishables from farmer to customer better than anyone in the world. And from that success, they're building a Brand Moat. Coke has a Secret Moat with its formula, a Switching Moat with its distribution system, and a Brand Moat that's so strong it's become a Toll Bridge: you want a Coke, you have to buy a Coke—nothing else will do.

Big-Moat businesses have numbers to back up the Moat, which in *Rule #1* I call the Big Five plus Debt. If a business has a big Moat, these numbers, as a group, are usually consistently high over long periods of time. With consistent financial numbers and a durable product, we can

THE FIVE MOATS

Type	Definition	Example
BRAND	A product you're willing to pay more for because you trust it	Coke, Gillette, Disney, McDonald's, Pepsi, Nike, Budweiser, Harley-Davidson
SECRET	A business that has a patent or trade secret which makes direct competition illegal or very difficult	Merck, Pfizer, 3M, Intel
TOLL	A business with exclusive control over a given market—if you want to use a road, you have to pay the toll	Media companies, utilities, ad agencies
SWITCHING	A business that's so much a part of your life that switching isn't worth the trouble	ADP, Paychex, H&R Block, Microsoft
LOW COST	A business that can price products so low no one can compete	Wal-Mart, Costco, Bed Bath & Beyond, Home Depot, Target

make a reasonably educated guess about what kind of cash this business will earn you well into the future.

The Big Five Numbers plus Debt are as follows:

ROIC: Return on Invested Capital (also called Return on Capital, ROC) is the amount of money that the business makes each year on the capital it has to invest. ROIC should be 10 percent or better.

The Four Growth Rates: earnings, sales, equity, and cash should all be growing at 10 percent or better.

Debt: Zero is best but in any case not more than can be paid off in three years of earnings.

For research on the Big Five Numbers, we're going to need long-term financial information. Yahoo! only goes back five years. We want ten years, so I'm going to send you to MSN.com. Click on Money.

Let's take a look at Polo Ralph Lauren. Type "RL" in the symbol box and hit enter. The left column has a list of menu items. About halfway down, under Fundamentals, is Financial Results. Click it. A button for Key Ratios will appear. Click that. Now, in the center of the page is a menu with seven items, starting with Growth Rate. The fifth item on the list is Investment Returns. Click that. We're going to look at the most important number of all — Return on Invested Capital, aka Return on Capital.

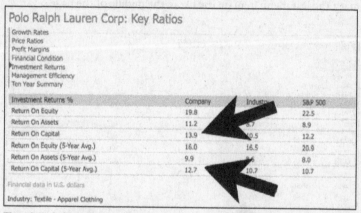

Polo Ralph Lauren Corp: Key Ratios

Growth Rates
Price Ratios
Profit Margins
Financial Condition
Investment Returns
Management Efficiency
Ten Year Summary

Investment Returns %	Company	Industry	S&P 500
Return On Equity	19.8		22.5
Return On Assets	11.2	5.7	8.9
Return On Capital	13.9	10.5	12.2
Return On Equity (5-Year Avg.)	16.0	16.5	20.9
Return On Assets (5-Year Avg.)	9.9	8.6	8.0
Return On Capital (5-Year Avg.)	12.7	10.7	10.7

Financial data in U.S. dollars

Industry: Textile - Apparel Clothing

Throughout the book, I'll be showing you corporate financial information so you can learn how to use this data. It doesn't matter that this data is outdated or changed. It's the way you use the data that is important, and that's what this book is about.

Return on Capital is 13.9 percent. Excellent. Over the last five years it's averaged 12.7 percent. Even more excellent. I love the consistency. The consistency and size of the ROIC is hugely important — consistency because it tells us the CEO is investing shareholder money well and growing the business. He's giving shareholders a 13 percent return on their capital, including borrowed capital. And he's doing it consistently over the long term without seeing ROIC drop. This tells us that he's paying attention to our interests. With interest rates at 1 percent, I'm quite happy with a 13 percent return on my capital.

Now let's take a look at the long-term growth numbers: sales, earnings, equity, and cash.

The most important growth number is Equity. If you owned a company and, for some strange reason, it suddenly stopped doing business, collected all the money the business was owed, sold off everything it owned, and then paid off all its debts, the amount of money you'd have left would be its Equity (also known as "book value"). I like the Equity growth rate the best, because it's the hardest number to manipulate and is going to be the closest we can get to the real rate of growth of value. So now let's click on the Ten Year Summary, the last menu item on the list in the middle of the page.

Polo Ralph Lauren Corp: Key Ratios

Growth Rates
Price Ratios
Profit Margins
Financial Condition
Investment Returns
Management Efficiency
▶Ten Year Summary

	Avg P/E	Price/ Sales	Price/ Book	Net Profit Margin (%)
03/08	19.30	1.24	2.40	8.6
03/07	18.40	2.21	3.93	9.3
04/06	17.30	1.73	3.12	8.2
04/05	20.20	1.21	2.36	5.8
04/04	16.80	1.34	2.50	6.4
03/03	12.80	0.91	1.83	7.2
03/02	14.60	1.	2.87	7.3
03/01	33.20		3.30	2.7
04/00	12.50	0.95	2.36	7.5
04/99	25.90	1.13	2.96	5.2

	Book Value/ Share	Debt/ Equity	Return on Equity (%)	Return on Assets (%)	Interest Coverage
03/08	$24.02	0.31	17.6	9.6	25.4
03/07	$22.45	0.19	17.2	10.7	30.2
04/06	$19.45	0.14	15.0	10.0	41.3
04/05	$16.25	0.17	11.4	7.0	27.2
04/04	$14.07	0.20	12.0	7.4	21.3
03/03	$12.24	0.29	14.5	8.6	15.2
03/02	$10.16	0.32	17.3	9.9	15.4
03/01	$8.33	0.47	7.3	3.6	4.7
04/00	$7.93	0.56	19.1	9.1	17.6
04/99	$6.60	0.24	13.7	8.2	56.4

We want the Book Value/Share column. Remember, Book Value is the same as Equity; by viewing it "per share," we're looking at it even more accurately.

You can see that back in 1999, BVPS was $6.60. That means there was $6.60 of equity for every share of stock. As of March 2008 there was $24.02 per share. Look at the growth from 1999 to 2008. Is BVPS growing consistently? Yes. Are there any years when it didn't grow or went negative? Even in great businesses there can be bad years. (In *Rule #1* we go through an analysis of the growth rate for ten years, seven years, five years, three years, and one year to be sure of consistency. You can do that if you like. But it's okay to get good enough at looking at numbers to see that the growth is consistent. If you're not sure, dump the numbers onto an Excel spreadsheet and look at them on a graph.) In that ten-year period, RL grew its equity at about 15 percent per year. Quite good.

Before you get too comfortable with what you're seeing on the Ten Year Summary, you should check the most *recent* book-value numbers. And to see that, you'll have to look at the Balance Sheet. Click on Financial Results: Statements: Balance Sheet. Click the Interim button; this'll give you the most recent batch of quarterly reports. Look at the most recent quarterly balance sheet, and near the bottom you'll see the line for Equity. That's the same as book value but it's not per share.

Total Equity	**2,694.4**
Total Liabilities & Shareholders' Equity	**4,385.3**
Total Common Shares Outstanding	98.7

Luckily, right below the Equity line is the Shares line. Just divide the shares into the Equity. In this case, $2,694.4 divided by 98.7 is $27 book value per share. Still growing.

Calculating Growth Rates

I didn't guess at that 15 percent number for the growth, by the way. To get that number you can use an Excel spreadsheet formula or, even better, go to my website at PaybackTimeBook.com and use the calculator designed to do it for you. Alternatively, you can get good at the Rule of 72 and approximate it.

The Rule of 72 is a handy shortcut for estimating growth — more precisely, it helps you figure out when your money (or any number) will double at a given interest (growth) rate. First, it helps to understand that it's called the Rule of 72 because at 10 percent, money doubles every 7.2 years and when you divide 7.2 by 10 percent, you get 72. For example, if you want to know how long it'll take to double your money at 9 percent interest, divide 9 into 72 and you get eight years. You can also do the reverse, and solve for the interest (growth) rate.

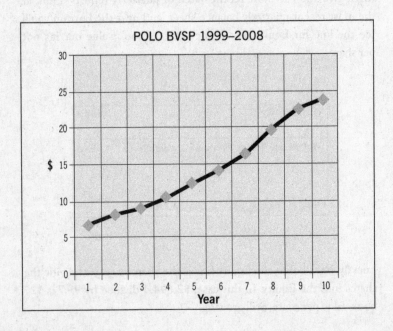

For example, if your money has to double in two years so you can buy a trip to Europe, you'll need 72 / 2 = 36 percent rate of return on your stash. So the Rule of 72 is an approximation, but it's a remarkably accurate one. Let's try it here using Ralph Lauren's BVPS numbers.

RL's BVPS goes from $6.60 to $24.02 in nine years. Follow along: Take the $6.60 and roughly double it to $13 (that's one double). Then double again to $26 (that's two doubles). The most recent BVPS is $24, which is less than the $26 we reached with two doubles, so we don't quite have two doubles in nine years. One more year of growth, though, and we'd have two full doubles, so let's say it has doubled once every five years. Divide 5 into 72. You get 14.4 percent. Round up to 15 percent and you get the same answer as you would have in Excel or in my online calculators.

And we can see from the graph that it's also quite consistent over most all time periods. This is what we're looking for.

Now let's see if RL holds that level of consistency through the other growth numbers: Sales, Earnings, and Cash.

On the left side of the page, under Financial Results, click on Statements. Click on the tab Ten Year Summary.

On this page we can look at the growth rates for both Sales and Earnings. Earnings per share, EPS, grew from 91 cents to $3.99 in nine years. I'm not going to worry about getting the latest earnings. I'm looking for the five-year view, not the six-month view. Calculate that growth rate using the Rule of 72 again. Let's go step by step.

1. First, let's round $0.91, the EPS from 1999, to just $0.90 for ease of calculation.

2. Now double $0.90 as many times as you can and still not go over the 2008 EPS of $3.99. $0.90 to $1.80 is one double (.9 x 2). And $1.80 to $3.60 is two doubles (1.8 x 2). So it takes more than two doubles to get to $3.99 in nine years.

3. So how many years does it take to double one time? Well, if two doubles in nine years is 4.5 years per double, and we have more than two doubles, we can call it four years for one double.

| Income Statement | Balance Sheet | Cash Flow | 10 Year Summary |

Financial data in U.S. Dollars
Values in Millions (Except for per share items)

Income Statement - 10 Year Summary (in Millions)

	Sales	EBIT	Depreciation	Total Net Income	EPS	Tax Rate (%)
03/08	4,880.1		201.3	419.8	3.99	34.62
03/07	4,295.4		144.7	400.9	3.73	37.68
04/06	3,746.3	02.	127.0	308.0	2.87	26
04/05	3,305.4	297.8	102.1	190.4	1.83	
04/04	2,649.7	263.1	85.6	169.2	1.68	35.69
03/03	2,439.34	276.82	80.6	175.68	1.77	36.54
03/02	2,363.71	276.0	83.9	172.5	1.75	37.5
03/01	2,225.77	97.95	78.6	59.26	0.61	39.5
04/00	1,955.53	248.89	69.98	147.46	1.49	40.75
04/99	1,713.07	152.83	48.01	90.55	0.91	40.75

Balance Sheet - 10 Year Summary (in Millions)

	Current Assets	Current Liabilities	Long Term Debt	Shares Outstanding
03/08	4,365.5	1,975.8	546.0	99.5 Mil
03/07	3,758.0	1,423.1	445.9	104.0 Mil
04/06	3,088.7	1,039.1	0.0	105.4 Mil
04/05	2,726.7	1,051.0	292.9	103.1 Mil
04/04	2,297.55	882.11	277.35	100.6 Mil
03/03	2,038.82	830.06	248.49	98.7 Mil
03/02	1,749.5	751.3	285.41	98.2 Mil
03/01	1,626.09	816.78	296.99	97.2 Mil
04/00	1,620.56	848.13	342.71	97.4 Mil
04/99	1,104.58	445.68	44.22	99.8 Mil

4. Now we use the Rule of 72, which says if you know the number of years it takes to double once, divide the years into 72 and you get the growth rate. So now divide 4 into 72 and you get 18 percent for the EPS growth rate.

Check that with my calculator on the website, and you'll see we're correct.

Now let's check the consistency. The year 2001 was a bad year and 2003 and 2004 were flat. What was going on then? The year 2001 was a recession year. It might be that RL doesn't do so well when we're in a recession, and that would make sense, of course. People cut back on luxury goodies and stick to necessities when money is tight. Something to keep in mind for now.

THE "CHEAT SHEET" TABLE FOR THE RULE OF 72	
Years to double once	**Growth rate**
1	72%
2	36%
3	24%
4	18%
5	15%
6	12%
7	10%
8	9%
9	8%
10	7%

Do Sales the same way. Sales grew from $1,713 million to $4,880 million in nine years. Again, I'm not going to worry about getting the latest sales.

1. First, let's chop $1,713, the sales from 1999, to $17 for ease of calculation.

2. Now double $17 as many times as you can and still not go over the 2008 sales of $50 (rounded and chopped). From $17 to $34 is one double, and $34 to $50 is a half double. So it takes 1.5 doubles to get to $50 in nine years.

3. So how many years does it take to double *one* time if we have 1.5 doubles in nine years? Divide 90 by 15. That's a double every six years.

4. Now again we use the Rule of 72, which says if you know the number of years it takes to double *once*, divide the years into 72 and you get the growth rate. So now divide 6 into 72 and you get 12 percent for the Sales growth rate.

Then do Cash Flow, too. MSN doesn't do long-term cash-flow summaries, unfortunately. We have to dig it out. Click on the Cash Flow tab. Look at the line Cash from Operating Activities (sometimes called OPS if you have the Operating Cash Flow on a per share basis). Read from right to left. Cash grew from 213 to 695 in five years.

Income Statement	Balance Sheet	Cash Flow	10 Year Summary		
⊙ Annual ◯ Interim				Financial data in U.S. Dollars Values in Millions (Except for per share items)	
	2008	2007	2006	2005	2004
Period End Date	03/29/2008	03/31/2007	04/01/2006	04/02/2005	04/03/2004
Period Length	52 Weeks	52 Weeks	52 Weeks	52 Weeks	52 Weeks
Stmt Source	10-K	10-K	10-K	10-K	10-K
Stmt Source Date	05/28/2008	05/30/2007	06/15/2006	06/15/2006	07/01/2005
Stmt Update Type	Updated	Updated	Updated	Restated	Restated
Net Income/Starting Line	419.8	400.9	308.0	190.4	169.23
Depreciation/Depletion	201.3	144.7	127.0	102.1	85.64
Amortization	0.0	0.0	0.0	0.0	0.0
Deferred Taxes	-7.7	-112.4	35.5	10.1	-5.1
▶ Non-Cash Items	80.9	70.4	63.3	118.1	34.94
▶ Changes in Working Capital	1.1	292.5	-84.7	-38.7	-71.1
Cash from Operating Activities	**695.4**	**796.1**	**449.1**	**382.0**	**213.61**

Don't bother looking at Cash from Investing Activities, Cash from Financing Activities, or Net Changes in Cash. Focus just on Cash from Operating Activities. The reason I prefer to use Cash from Operating Activities is that it comes from the business itself. Companies burn up Investing cash by buying companies or capital items or even just T-bills. When that happens, you get a drop in that form of cash. That can mess up your view of the business if you count it as a drop in Cash Flow when all that happened is they put the cash into a safe investment. Same thing with Financing cash. That section is about money going out the door to retire debt, buy back stock, or pay dividends. You'd hardly count that as a negative on Cash Flow, but Cash gets deducted for each of these. So for our purposes we're going to just keep it simple and look at how much cash the operations of the business are producing. Then we have something stable from year to year to compare with previous years and we'll get a better Cash Flow growth number because of that.

You can do this in your sleep it's so easy.

1. First, chop $213, the cash flow from 2003, to $200 for ease of calculation.

2. Now double $200 as many times as you can and still not go over the 2007 sales of $800 (rounded and chopped). From $200 to $400 is one double, and $400 to $800 is two doubles. So it's a tad less than two doubles to get from $213 to $795 in five years.

3. So how many years does it take to double *one* time if we have two doubles in five years? Divide 5 by 2. That's a double every 2.5 years.

4. Now we use the Rule of 72, which says if you know the number of years it takes to double *once,* divide the years into 72 and you get the growth rate. So now divide 2.5 into 72 and you get 29 percent for the EPS growth rate. I always try to do the dividing in my head, so I just ask myself what 2.5 goes into easily that's close to 72. Answer: 75 (25 goes into 75 three times). So 2.5 goes thirty times. And it's not 75, it's 72 and I rounded up for the 2.5, so I'm going to ballpark this at 26 percent. Close enough.

So let's review our four growth numbers. BVPS is 15 percent, EPS is 18 percent, Sales is 12 percent, and Cash is 26 percent. And 15, 18, 12, and 26 are all good. All are past 10 percent and going up. Actually, let's see if they are. Let's put the numbers on a graph using Excel Charts. (If you want to see how to do this, go to PaybackTimeBook .com and look at more exercises in the online addendum for this chapter.)

Cash is starting to decline after a fast run-up, but at a 26 percent growth rate, that's to be expected. And with the recession that started in 2008, I'd expect to see these numbers headed south.

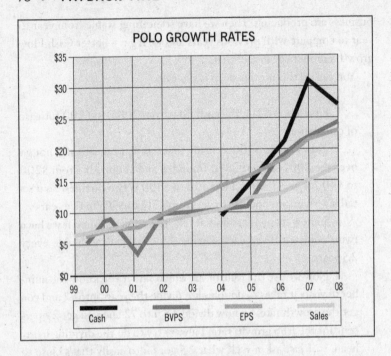

POLO GROWTH RATES

Legend: Cash | BVPS | EPS | Sales

Now check the debt. Especially considering all the problems businesses are having getting credit these days, let's be sure we're buying companies that have their debt covered. That means they can pay it off in three years or less from earnings. Go to Company Report on the RL Main Menu and you'll see RL's Interim Trailing Twelve Months of Earnings: RL produced $465 million in the last twelve months.

Financials	Last 12 Months	5 Year Growth
Sales	5.0 Bil	14.9%
Income	465.0 Mil	19.0%
Dividend Rate	0.20	NA
Dividend Yield	0.54%	0%

Now look up the current debt. To get that number go to the Balance Sheet and click Interim so you get the most recent quarter's Balance Sheet. Balance Sheet numbers are not like Income and Cash numbers. Income and Cash numbers accumulate through the year, so one quarter of Cash is not the same as a year of Cash. But the Balance Sheet numbers are always accurate for the entire business right up to the date of the Balance Sheet. So Debt for the third quarter is the total company obligation, not just a piece of it.

| ▶ Total Long Term Debt | 419.6 |

Debt is about $420 million. Divide debt by earnings, and you get 1. So debt can be paid off in about one year from earnings. Check.

In general, what we're looking at here is a well-run company that's been doing a good job achieving consistent growth but is going flat because of the recession. This looks like some sort of Moat to me, and also like opportunity. One way to think about this is to ask yourself: *If it has Moat, will it fare better than its competitors and emerge from recession even stronger? And can I buy it cheap because of the recession?* More on that in the next chapter.

First, it's time to find out about the people who are running it.

MANAGEMENT

With Meaning and Moat checked off, a business is pretty certain of making money in the long term . . . *if* Management doesn't screw it up. If our great business isn't being run by a traitor and for his own benefit, not for the benefit of the owners (us), the employees (also us sometimes), the environment (also us), the community (also us), or anything else.

Here are some ways to spot traitors:

• They pay themselves a ridiculous amount of money: When I started investing in 1980, the average CEO compensation for public companies was about 40 times the lowest-paid employee in their business. If the lowest guy on the totem pole made $30,000, the CEO made about $1.2 million. Today that ratio is up to 500 times, or a CEO salary of $15 million. I wouldn't trust my financial future to a CEO who plays like that. (Note: In 1993 Congress passed a law limiting CEO pay to $1M. Anything more than that had to be incentive-based or it wasn't deductible as an expense. The unexpected consequence of their meddling was to encourage CEOs to take large stock options as "incentive" pay. This led directly to CEOs manipulating the option dates to maximize their compensation, manipulating the stock price with manipulated earnings, and finding other ways to max out those options. And that is what led to the massive disparity between paychecks. We need to get rid of income tax codes so Congress isn't tempted to mess with the marketplace. Check out our website for information on a very interesting alternative that over a hundred congressmen already support.)

• They set up a golden parachute so if you fire them they get paid off massively. What kind of employee can do a crappy job, get fired, and make out like a bandit? Only a CEO or someone who has pictures of somebody on the board doing something they shouldn't have been doing. This is just so wrong on so many levels. And CEOs wonder why employees want unions?

• They treat company assets like their own and use business assets for nonbusiness. One CEO I know sent the company-paid Gulfstream jet to pick up a board member on the East Coast and fly him, by himself, out west to go on a hunting trip. The hunting trip and the jet were paid for by the company owners. What right does the officer of a corporation have to take money out of the stockholder's pocket? If I owned that company I'd be furious the CEO just ripped me off for $60,000 for the flight and another $20,000 for the hunting trip. That's *my* money, you traitor! What are you doing spending it like that? (Actually what he was doing was schmoozing a key member of the CEO compensation committee. Hmmmm. I wonder why?)

• They buy other businesses to make a bigger business rather than a *better* business. Watch what's happening with ROIC. If the CEO is stockpiling businesses and the ROIC is going down, then the CEO might be creating an empire with a lot of sales and a terrible return on invested capital. Well, the capital he invested badly is *my money!* I don't want him to buy things just to get so big that he "needs" a big private jet for his outsized ego. He only should buy things if the return on the investment is excellent. If he isn't going to acquire a business with a great return, I want my money out so I can invest it properly.

What we're looking for in a great CEO is the following:

• Service-oriented, not ego-oriented: She is all about serving the stakeholders of the business — the owners, the brand, the employees, the community, the suppliers, the customers. Like a good infantry officer, she eats last.

• Passion: She is all about this business. Everything the company creates and stands for is her passion, and her passion is contagious. The entire company is caught up in it.

• Honor: She would never risk their honor and reputation for a buck or power or prestige.

• BAG: Big Audacious Goal (adapted from Jim Collins's Big Hairy Audacious Goal concept outline in his book *Good to Great*). A CEO who's driven to change the world and can inspire her employees to help. This zeal drives the whole organization, and that's where outsized profits come from.

While we can make a lot of money with just Meaning and Moat, when we add in good Management, we're less likely to suffer through a period when a traitor is running the show poorly and costing us all money.

These three qualities together constitute a wonderful business. You get these right, you're buying a really good company.

HOW TO CHECK OUT MANAGEMENT WITHOUT HIRING A PRIVATE EYE

So how do you know if the CEO has these qualities? John Templeton, a great investor in the Rule #1 tradition and founder of Templeton Funds, called the solution to this problem "scuttlebutt." His goal was to gather all the latest gossip and loose talk about every business he was interested in. Yes, it's a lot more work than the late shift at McDonald's. Oh. Wait a minute. No it's not. And besides, there's a great tool called the Internet.

If your CEO has been around awhile, there will be a tremendous amount of info written on him or by him linked on the Internet. Start with Wikipedia.com, a great summary of information including links to other sources, and go where it leads. Cross-check facts, however, when you use a site like Wikipedia, which can occasionally contain false information. Try Googling the CEO's name. Read all the articles written about him or her in all the trade magazines. Your CEO is the subject of scrutiny by reporters, some of whom are going to write the truth as they dig it out. You'll find articles in *Forbes, Fortune, Barron's, Wired 2.0, Success,* and the *Wall Street Journal.* Next, go to the *New York Times* web page and do a search on your CEO.

See the *New York Times* search results on Ralph Lauren on page 83. I can get articles back into the 1800s. Not on Ralph, of course.

Another great source of information about both your target company and the manager is the competitors. Everybody likes to dish dirt, right? Go to their websites and blogs. John Mackey wrote a blog bashing his competitors at Wild Oats for a few years leading up to the Whole Foods acquisition of Wild Oats in early 2007. In fact, Mackey began posting a blog under a pseudonym on Yahoo! Finance in the late 1990s, and quickly became known as a cheerleader for Whole Foods stock. In 2000 he wrote, "I admit to my bias. I love the company and I'm in for the long haul. I shop at Whole Foods. I own a great deal of its stock. I'm aligned with the mission and values of the company. . . .

The New York Times
Tuesday, April 14, 2009

Times Topics

WORLD | U.S. | N.Y. / REGION | BUSINESS | TECHNOLOGY | SCIENCE | HEALTH | SPORTS | OPINION

TIMES TOPICS > PEOPLE > L > LAUREN, RALPH

Ralph Lauren

Updated: Feb. 13, 2009

In 2007, Ralph Lauren had a year to go on his contract to run the design empire he founded, Polo Ralph Lauren. But Mr. Lauren, the indefatigable fashion icon, re-upped through March 2013, when he will be 73. His five-year extension could be worth much more than $100 million, and that's not counting the reimbursement for the mandatory use of private jets and helicopters for all of his business and personal travel.

Mr. Lauren, the chairman and chief executive, was to receive a salary of

Blog
On the Runway
Cathy Horyn posts about Ralph Lauren.

Ralph Lauren Navigator
A list of resources from around the Web about Ralph Lauren as selected by researchers and editors of The New York Times.

· Ralph Lauren fashions
  Official site
· Home and lifestyle products

Is there something wrong with this?" No, I don't think there's anything wrong with that! Look at how he justifies owning stock: "love the company," "in for the long haul," "shop," "aligned with the mission and values." Could hardly tell you better myself what you want to feel like when you own a piece of a business.

Read the CEO's annual letter to shareholders. One way to spot hot air is to compare the numbers on a company—the strength of its growth rates and ROIC—with what the CEO says in his letters to shareholders. Are they synching up? Or is the CEO telling you everything is fantastic and the numbers speak another language? This is actually so common as to be laughable. Clearly, some CEOs assume their shareholders are idiots. The CEO of one large firm wrote in his 2001 annual letter that in three years the company would be doing $10 billion in business from the "new businesses" he was investing in today. But in the 2005 annual letter he makes no mention of the fact his business is only doing $5 billion in sales. It was as if his previous prediction never existed, even though it was sitting right there on the website for all to read. Not only did he completely ignore that prediction, he then had the nerve to make a similar prediction for three years hence. If that's how your CEO plans on keeping you informed, better to stockpile a different business.

Red Flags

I can't tell you how many times people have asked me recently, "Phil, I get it—I get the three Ms and how to identify a 'wonderful company,' but seriously, how do you really *know?* How can you ever really *know?* Look at all the people who got ripped off in the last couple of years when they thought they owned solid companies?"

To that I always say, "No, they didn't know. They were speculators. They weren't Rule #1 stockpilers."

I have a list of Biggest Mistakes people make when it comes to investing. Anyone who has ever experienced substantial losses has committed one of the following Big Mistakes.

No grip on the industry: If you don't understand the business's industry, then you can't possibly have a good enough grip on it to own stock in it. For example, let's say you're a high school teacher and one of your students keeps raving about his dad's company—a pharmaceutical giant. You just read about this company in the paper because the FDA approved one of their hot new drugs. But you know zilch about pharmaceuticals. You don't even take aspirin because you're so healthy (this new drug is for an ailment you don't understand either). And every time you try to read something about Big Pharma, you get bored because it doesn't interest you in the least (yeah, you're not even a science teacher—you're in the English department). Should you even consider this drug company? No way. Stay away.

Too optimistic: Be careful of this one. It's easy to assume big numbers will continue to be big numbers. Big numbers, as you will learn in the next chapter, lead to big valuations. And big valuations can get you in trouble if you're a stockpiler. It's far better to be realistic. Make conservative assumptions about the future.

No real Moat: Moats can be deceiving, but this goes back to understanding the business well enough to distinguish between a real and fake Moat. Something that looks like a Moat may actually fall to new technology, unions, new trends and fads, or a dwindling customer base. A company that makes typewriters doesn't look so good with the advent of computers. Similarly, a company that produces hardcopy encyclopedias will find it hard to compete now that the Internet brings people up-to-date information for free. Some businesses don't even pretend to have a Moat. I call these "commodity businesses." A commodity business is any company that produces a product that anyone else can similarly produce. If you're a grocery store just like the other grocery store, you're going to be competing on price. I'm a regular on MSNBC's *Your Business,* a TV show about solving problems for small businesses, and this issue of owning a no-Moat business comes up all the time. People who invest time and effort in a business that's easy to copy almost always end up with a not-so-wonderful business. True for small business. True for big business. Do not invest in a business without a real Moat.

Failed to keep up: If you don't have passion and enthusiasm for your business, then you have no business owning a piece of it, because you're going to have to keep up with it once you own it. And if you aren't into the business, you won't keep up with it. It's a huge mistake to buy it and forget about it. You want to see the problem coming and get out. If you aren't keeping up on the industry changes and your business's quarterly reports, you could get run over. And if you do, shame on you. These big changes unfold over time. You'll see them if you're paying any kind of attention. Don't be like the stupid henchman in the movie *Austin Powers* who got run over by a steamroller moving two miles an hour.

Pay a little bit of attention. If you were to look at the companies

that have recently fallen or, in some cases, disappeared, you'd discover that there were plenty of red flags waving well in advance of their fall. Take AIG, for example, the insurance giant that was bailed out by the government. The chairman of the company was forced out in 2005—*big* red flag. If I had been invested in AIG then (which I wouldn't have because it's not an industry that meets the first M for me), I would have been out, because it would have failed the Management test.

Meaning, Moat, and Management—the three Ms. Get these right and you'll be targeting a wonderful business. When to start stockpiling it is the next question, and that depends on the three most important words in investing—"Margin of Safety." It's the all-important fourth M.

THE RICHES IN CREATIVE DESTRUCTION

Technology is a great destroyer of businesses and jobs and even entire industries. But that's not just a good thing, it's a great thing. It might not seem like it to the investor who gets wiped out or the worker who loses her job, but it's exactly this kind of destruction that is at the very heart of the creation of wealth. Real wealth is just the elimination of labor. Let's say it takes five guys a month to build a car, so the cost of labor for the car might be about $25,000. And let's say all the other stuff in the car—all the parts—cost $15,000. If we own a car business, we have to sell the car for $40,000 just to break even. But we won't be in business long if we don't make a profit, so we decide to charge $50,000 for the car. We're doing fine making cars and making money. Then along comes a competitor who figures out how to make a car with only one guy and a big car-making machine he built for almost nothing. Now he can build a car for $7,000 of labor (the smartest and hardest-working laborer got a raise) plus $15,000 in parts: $22,000. If he sells it for $32,000, he's just as profitable as we are when we sell the same car for $50,000. Except we aren't profitable anymore because all of our customers went to our competitor and bought the $32,000 car and saved $18,000. The money the customers save by buying a car from our competitor is real wealth that was created out of thin air. Each car buyer has both the car and $18,000 to spend on something else. All these car buyers are suddenly made richer by our competitor's destructive technology. Then we either get a one-man machine, too, or we're out of business. Or we put in a tariff law that forces our competitor to charge $52,000 for the car because our government taxes them $20,000 at the port they ship their cars to. If our government does that, no wealth is created. Every $20,000 they take is $20,000 that would have been in the pocket of a car buyer. Wealth is, in fact, confiscated by our government. Of course, four workers keep their jobs, which is nice, but eventually they will lose them to that machine anyway. You can't stop progress but you can push wealth overseas.

America has been successful because it didn't attempt to block the pain and suffering caused by innovation. The net effect has been the rapid creation of wealth for everyone in a capitalistic society. Today in America, for example, there are people who live in apartments with running water, flushing toilets, working electricity, a refrigerator, a washing machine, a

(continued on next page)

stove, an oven, multiple rooms, and glass windows who, by our standards, are living in poverty. But *real* poverty is nothing like that. People who live in poverty are on the edge of starvation and live in wretched hovels. You don't believe me? Keep in mind that most of our "poor" are unhealthily overweight.

Creative destruction destroyed real poverty in America. Today, American "poverty" is more about having limited education, opportunity, or intelligence. Our poor have a relatively low standard of living (relative to Americans—not to, say, Pakistanis) because something about their circumstances keeps them from rising out of their environment. They are not poor by any world standard of poverty. As a thinking member of our society you must embrace this process of creative destruction. Every vote to protect prices or wages by decree is a vote against the future well-being of our country and a step toward making our poor *really* poor.

TAKEAWAYS AND ACTION ITEMS

Companies that can make you money are those with a big Moat that are managed by passionate and trustworthy people. Find companies with the three Ms and you have the recipe for making money.

- Find businesses that relate to your passions, talents, and how you make and spend your money.
- Conduct the three Ms analysis—only own companies that have Meaning, Moat, and capable Management.
- Do your homework. Review my articles at **PaybackTime Book.com** to learn how to use a variety of *Rule #1* and Payback Time tools to scan the market for acceptable stockpiling candidates and to analyze their management teams.

CHAPTER
4

PAYBACK TIME MEANS "NO FEAR"

Too many people today know the price of everything and the value of nothing.

— ANN LANDERS

What to stockpile is the harder question than when. There aren't many (or any) perfect businesses, and there aren't going to be thousands of wonderful businesses that you'll be able to understand well enough to stockpile them. Once you've found that right business, knowing when to start stockpiling it is easy: You buy shares when they are on sale.

We call "buying on sale" *buying with a Margin of Safety (MOS)* in Rule #1 investing. Those are the three most important words in investing. They are especially important when it comes to stockpiling. All you have to do to get a big MOS is to know the value of the business you are buying—as a business—and then wait to buy it until the market drops the price quite a lot lower than the value. Be forewarned: just because the market drops from 14,000 to 7,000 doesn't mean everything that went down is suddenly "on sale" and priced below its value. Some companies can still be overpriced even after a market meltdown.

Think of buying stock as you would buying a car. You can buy a beautiful Maserati and get a super deal or get cheated. You ask: Are the fundamentals good? Is the drivetrain in good shape? Is the body rusting out? Essentially, if you get those kinds of questions answered correctly, you can put a value on the car. Sure, there are superficial problems to consider, too — cracked windshields, dings in the body, torn seat covers, blown tires, or a bad radio, for instance — but you can put a solid cost estimate on those cosmetic problems, adjust what you'll pay for the car, and still get a really good deal. If the fundamentals are bad, however, if the engine or tranny is shaky, and the body has a lot of rust, the potential cost to you for the car might be much more than you can ever sell it for in the future. If you buy a fundamentally unsound car at any price, you lose. But if you get a fundamentally sound car on sale, you can make money in days.

This is why understanding how to arrive at value is so critical to stockpiling. Investors have gotten very rich buying companies, but unless they were very lucky they only got rich if they knew the value first.

Robert Shiller, author of *Irrational Exuberance* and a well-respected Yale professor of economics, contends, as I do, that emotion often determines the prices in the market, resulting in prices that are often far lower or higher than values. The graph he created on page 91 looks like an abstract of someone's nightmare, but actually it shows what happens if you buy when the market has a low price-to-earnings ratio (PE) versus a high PE ratio.

Dr. Shiller's graph shows that low PE ratios (left side of the graph) coincide with high returns (the top of the graph) and that high PE ratios (right side of the graph) coincide with low returns (bottom of the graph). Note that the bottom-right portion of the graph shows investors who bought at a 20–30 PE ratio got a -2 percent to 5 percent return for twenty years. Price is what you pay. Value is what you get. Don't let anyone tell you that you can't get a 0 percent return for twenty years by buying and holding the S&P 500 index. If you buy when the index has a high PE ratio, it's not only possible to get a bad return for twenty years, it's likely. (The original graph has much more

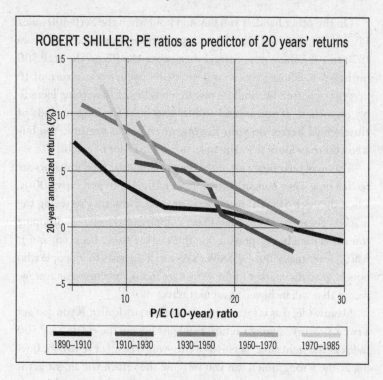

ROBERT SHILLER: PE ratios as predictor of 20 years' returns

20-year annualized returns (%)

P/E (10-year) ratio

| 1890–1910 | 1910–1930 | 1930–1950 | 1950–1970 | 1970–1985 |

information on it as Dr. Shiller created it—with colored dots. To see the original color graph, go to PaybackTimeBook.com. Or see another black-and-white version in his wonderful book *Irrational Exuberance*.)

The PE is a ratio of price to earnings (price per share divided by earnings per share). Sometimes the PE is referred to as the "multiple," because it shows how much investors are willing to pay for each dollar of earnings. If a company has a PE of 10, that means an investor is willing to pay $10 for every $1 of earnings.

On the other hand, if you buy and hold when the S&P 500 index PE ratio is low, your chances of a good return are excellent. From 1970 to 1985 there were several years when the PE on the S&P 500 hit below 8. Those years mostly yielded a twenty-year return of 10 percent or better. Dr. Shiller's research teaches us something incredibly important: **If you intend to buy and hold for long periods of time, you'd better do your buying when prices are low.** You buy when there's a lot of fear. You sell when there's a lot of greed.

This explains quite a lot of the pain that mutual fund investors are feeling now. They bought mutual funds in the 1990s and early 2000s, when the S&P 500 PE ratios were soaring. Now they're seeing the market going nowhere and their compounded returns dropping toward zero. They're praying for the market to go back up, and it will . . . eventually. But Dr. Shiller's research suggests that people who bought into the market in the 1990s are in for a twenty-year average return that will be hovering around zero.

Meanwhile, this is great news for a savvy stockpiler. If you can get a twenty-year 12 percent return from just buying the entire S&P 500 index at the right time (versus a twenty-year 0 percent return for buying at the wrong time), can you imagine the return you might get if you stockpile the best and most on-sale businesses, rather than just buying all of them? This is, of course, exactly what Mr. Buffett did to compound at 24 percent per year and make billions. And for the second time in my investing lifetime, we're seeing the S&P 500 PE ratio heading toward single digits. The first time was when I had just begun investing in 1980, and it made me rich.

So we have the opportunity of a lifetime in front of us, the opportunity to stockpile the right businesses in the right market environment at the right time.

Okay, now let's get down to some specifics. How do you figure out the value of the business you want to stockpile? Don't worry yet about how much you should be investing in those companies, or how many companies you should aim to have in your portfolio. I'll get to all those details in the next chapter. For now, we have to nail down the process of finding value and comparing it with price.

Take your time reading and rereading this chapter. You may also want to use my website to follow along with the analysis described below, because I've created more examples online than I could fit here. Check out PaybackTimeBook.com. Walking yourself through those examples will give you a pretty good idea how I get to the value—what I call "Sticker Price"—for a business. I've even included some examples of companies I *can't* get a Sticker Price for. If you like, you can make this more fun by choosing a company aligned with your passions and interests (a business that passes the first M test) rather than the ones I've chosen here or on the website and seeing how your numbers match up to my view of a wonderful company.

Remember: price and value are two entirely different things. It's not hard to understand why everyone gets value and price mixed up. The two words are confused and misapplied almost every day. Flip on the television and you'll hear experts who are discussing the price of a stock refer to it as the stock's value. "What's the market say the value of AT&T is today, Bob?" "How is the market valuing Apple right now?" If the experts are confused about the two words, is it any surprise that most investors are, too?

Professional investors are under pressure to perform quarter to quarter. They can't take the long view. They can't buy into a business and focus on its long-term value. They have to focus

(continued on next page)

on the price *today.* If the price goes down after they buy, the paper loss has an immediate negative effect on their quarterly earnings report. That the value of the business may be far more than the amount they paid gives them no comfort at all. They know they're judged on how well they're doing against everyone else this quarter based on price, not value. Someday this stock's price will indeed shoot up, if they bought it at a discount against value, but that fact is absolutely worthless to them. They have to take the "price" view because if they don't, all you mutual fund investors are going to pull your money out and give it to some other fund manager. Being right about the value in the long term doesn't make you feel so great if you've lost your job in the short term because of the price.

Rule #1 stockpilers, on the other hand, know that price alone will not get us where we want to go. Since it's our money, we don't have anyone judging how we're doing except ourselves, and we can take the long-term view. If we know the value of the business we're buying and are happy with the price we paid for it, it's not a problem for us if the price goes down. In fact, it's an *opportunity.* If I buy $10 of value for $5, am I really feeling bad if the new price is $3? How could I feel bad? I got in at half of the value. I'm golden. And now I can buy more at one-third of the value. I'll be even more golden. The *last* thing I would feel is that I messed up!

Why this is such a difficult concept for some investors to comprehend is simply beyond my understanding. I've been teaching it for years, and some people get it right away while others never comprehend it at all. Those people get a glazed look in their eyes, like they heard me but just can't believe what I'm saying. That's because they still haven't grasped the distinction between price and value. So they believe that as the price goes down, so does the value of the thing they bought. If they could just learn to see it the other way, they'd be rich.

FINDING THE STICKER PRICE

There's a lot of Wall Street gibberish and jargon about what to call value. Some call it "intrinsic value." Some call it the "retail" value. Some call it "what it's worth as a business." Again, I call it the "Sticker Price," as in the Sticker Price on the window of the car you were thinking of buying. And just as we never pay the Sticker Price for the car, we never pay the Sticker Price for the stock. We always want a discount. Sticker Price is *retail value, intrinsic value,* and *what it's worth as a business.* And we never pay it. Ever.

In *Rule #1* I showed you how to calculate the Sticker Price of a business based on four key numbers:

1. Earnings per Share (EPS) for the last twelve months
2. EPS growth rate for the next ten years
3. Price-to-earnings (PE) ratio in ten years
4. Minimum Acceptable Rate of Return (MARR)

If you know these four things, you can get to the value of your business target quite easily with an Excel formula called FV (future value) or by using the calculators on my website, PaybackTimeBook.com.

Finding key numbers #1 and #4 is very easy: #1 is a number you simply look up online. MSN and Yahoo! both publish what's called a Trailing Twelve Months (ttm) EPS.

Fundamental Data	
Debt/Equity Ratio	0.17
Gross Margin	54.96%
Net Profit Margin	9.35%
Total Shares Outstanding	98.7 Mil
Market Capitalization	4.03 Bil
Earnings/Share	4.58
StockScouter Rating	8
	More financial ratios

On this MSN Money Company Report page, you can see the Earnings/Share for Ralph Lauren Polo is $4.58 (it doesn't say "ttm," but on this report Earnings per Share is a figure covering the previous twelve months). To arrive at this page you simply go to MSN Money and enter RL in the symbol box, then click on Company Report.

The MARR, #4 on our list, is a fixed 15 percent. That number never changes — it's what we demand as investors to be our minimum acceptable rate of return. Why 15 percent? Because it's a high enough return to cover the hidden cost of inflation, the bond rate, and taxes and still give us a return that justifies the effort. Don't ever forget that number: 15 percent. You can certainly demand more, but never go lower. Fifteen percent is our minimum. Use this percentage every time you valuate a company.

Finding #3, the PE ratio in ten years, isn't too hard. It's the multiple of earnings that the stock is normally priced at. We get this by looking at the range of PE ratios in the past. Not just in the last quarter, but over a long time — a decade, say. That makes us reasonably confident in estimating a future PE. Of course, here's where knowing the business comes into play: if, for instance, a new technology is about to make a company's product obsolete, then those old PEs aren't so great. But if you followed the three Ms, you'd know better than to be bothering with a soon-to-be-outmoded business in the first place.

The reason stocks always sell at a *multiple* of earnings is that no one will sell a business for one times the earnings. That would be stupid. The seller is going to get one times the earnings simply from holding on to the earnings themselves. If I have a lemonade stand that earned $100 last year, I'm not going to sell my stand for $100 (a PE of 1), because I'm going to get that $100 next year, even if I don't sell my stand. I might take $300, since it's going to take my stand three years to pay me that much at $100 per year. If I sell for $300, the multiple that I sold my stand for is 3. We also say the stand sold for a PE (price divided by earnings) of 3. Or the stand sold for "3 times earnings."

You can look up a stock's PE over time on MSN Money. Go to any stock, click the Financial Results menu item, click Key Ratios, and click Price Ratios; you see the high and low average PE for this business for the last five years. If you click "Ten Year Summary" you'll see the average PE ratio each year for the last nine or ten years. You can just add them up and divide by the number of years. Polo has an average PE of 18.4 over the last five years.

Polo Ralph Lauren

Growth Rates
Price Ratios
Profit Margins
Financial Condition
Investment Returns
Management Efficiency
▶Ten Year Summary

	Avg P/E
03/08	19.30
03/07	18.40
04/06	17.30
04/05	20.20
04/04	16.80
03/03	12.80
03/02	14.60
03/01	33.20
04/00	12.50

The other way to find a good PE or multiple to use is to double the estimated future growth rate. Look up professional analysts' average estimate of future growth of earnings by clicking Earnings Estimates, then click the Earnings Growth Rates tab.

If the estimated growth rate is 13 percent per year, then a PE of 26 is in the ballpark (13 x 2 = 26). Use the lower figure of these two methods. In other words, if multiplying the future growth rate by 2 gives you 26, but the average PE for the business over the last five years is 18, then use the number 18 — the lower of the two. Be conservative.

The last number we need to calculate the Sticker Price is #2 on

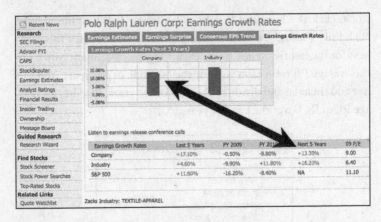

Research
SEC Filings
Advisor FYI
CAPS
StockScouter
Earnings Estimates
Analyst Ratings
Financial Results
Insider Trading
Ownership
Message Board
Guided Research
Research Wizard
Find Stocks
Stock Screener
Stock Power Searches
Top-Rated Stocks
Related Links
Quote Watchlist

| Earnings Estimates | Earnings Surprise | Consensus EPS Trend | **Earnings Growth Rates** |

Earnings Growth Rates (Next 5 Years)

Listen to earnings release conference calls

Earnings Growth Rates	Last 5 Years	FY 2009	FY 2010	Next 5 Years	09 P/E
Company	+17.10%	-0.50%	-8.80%	+13.30%	9.00
Industry	+4.60%	-9.90%	+11.80%	+16.20%	6.40
S&P 500	+11.80%	-16.20%	-8.40%	NA	11.10

Zacks Industry: TEXTILE-APPAREL

the list: EPS growth rate for the next ten years. And this is where the rubber meets the road for valuation. This number is our best estimate of the rate of growth of the *future* earnings of the business. Knowing how much cash this business *will* create is central to knowing what to pay for it today.

The value of a business is more dependent on its future earnings than what it currently holds in cash on hand, real estate, or net equity.

Figuring out a reasonable growth rate for your target business depends — and I can't overstate this — on knowing the industry and the business very well. You cannot bypass the first three Ms, skip directly to calculating MOS, and expect a return of 24 percent per year. If you haven't checked out Meaning, Moat, and Management, it's impossible to arrive at the true value of a business.

In *Rule #1,* I cut you a ton of slack in this part of the process by showing you certain tools that help you follow the Big Guys (the institutional fund managers) in and out of the stock. In effect, I showed you how to avoid the problem of not getting the Sticker Price right.

It's simple: If the Big Guys start to get out, you get out. Getting the value right is important to making money in Rule #1, but trading it with the Big Guys will help you avoid *losing* money if you're wrong about the value, because it gives you a reliable way of getting out before it crashes. Therefore, we can get away with a lot of error in our estimate of value. *We can't do that when we're stockpiling.*

When we *stockpile,* we're not going to use those tools to get out. Rather, we're going to be like owners of a private business. Our only reasons to bail out are if the business is no longer wonderful, and if the price is so high we can't refuse the opportunity to cash out (I'll take you through knowing when to sell in the next chapter), and if we must have the money now—one or more of these three reasons. We're not going to get out because the price is going down. Just like the Forbes Richest, we're going to take advantage of price drops to increase our compounded rate of return. When we stockpile, we're going after the big money. We really are in this for the long term.

But for those reasons, *stockpiling* means we need to be a great deal more certain about the value of the business than we need to be if we're trading. And that means a *stockpiler* of a business has to be a lot more certain about the growth rate of future earnings than a trader of a stock.

Why Not Just Trade?

If Rule #1 trading strategies will keep you out of trouble, why should you bother with the extra research of the stockpiling strategy? Because of the way the market is right now—I'll get to that in a minute—and because the technical tools of a trading strategy aren't free. There's a price to be paid for using them. They're like an insurance policy: they protect us but they do so at a cost. The reason is something called trading friction: even the best traders aren't always going to get out at the top and get in at the bottom. Sometimes we miss big jumps up or get caught in big drops. By getting caught up in this trading game, we minimize our short-term losses, but this friction also cuts into our rate of return. If we do a good job trading, we can expect a solid 15 percent return for our trouble. But if we know a stock's going to go up over the long run, we'll make more money by *stockpiling* it than by trading it. If we want the biggest returns with the least work, we have to stockpile. Stockpiling eliminates the friction of trading and accelerates the compounded rate of return by lowering your overall cost of acquiring the business. The highest returns you can get as a novice come from stockpiling. And now, for the first time since I started investing twenty-nine years ago, we're experiencing the best time to be a stockpiler.

Right now we're faced with a once-in-a-lifetime opportunity to get rich with very little effort and very little risk if we do our homework and stockpile. During the next few years some of the best companies in the world, companies with monopolies, companies that'll be around for the next fifty years or longer, are going to see their profits dry up and their businesses shrink, and they will be offered to us at increasingly better prices. Nothing is changing long-term, but the short term looks bad and creates fear. Stockpiling a wonderful business as it drops in price sets you up for a huge return when the price returns to the company's proper value.

So if you want easy money and guaranteed wealth, stockpile in this market. Certainly you can trade, and you'll do well on the run-ups. But if you trade you'll also have long periods of time when you are buying into undervalued companies only to see them go down in price even further. This stock market is tough on traders but nirvana for stockpilers. And all it requires is nailing down the growth rate.

Nailing the Future Growth Rate of Cash

Warren Buffett bought about $6 billion (representing over 64 million of the 342 million available shares, or about 20 percent) of Burlington

Northern railroad in 2007–2008 in a price range of $79 to $84 a share. I decided to use this company, BNI, as an example because it's not perfect. It doesn't have the greatest numbers. It's not massively on sale. But isn't that the way the real world of investing works? You'll find there are very few perfect companies, and if you ever find one, chances are good it won't be on sale. Because it's perfect. So you do your homework and understand the business, and you start to see the beauty of the business. It's like finding a wife or husband: if you wait for Mr. or Ms. Perfect, you might be waiting a long time if not forever. But get to know someone who has some flaws, and you just might find out they're perfect for you. In that sense, Burlington Northern was perfect for Mr. Buffett.

Let's see if we think he got a good deal or not.

Warning: As noted in the beginning of this book, the numbers and data retrieved during the writing phase have changed by the time you read this. Companies update and republish their information routinely. As you follow this example in the upcoming pages, please be aware that you won't find the exact same figures online—including historical data. This evaluation is for educational purposes only.

We start with the Big Five Numbers and Debt: (1) *Return on Invested Capital*, (2) *Sales Growth Rate*, (3) *Earnings Growth Rate*, (4) *Equity Growth Rate*, (5) *Cash Growth Rate, and Debt.* We want all of these growth rates to be 10 percent or better for many years in the past. The most important number is the Return on Invested Capital (ROC or ROIC). This tells us how the company is doing at investing the money it's getting from investors and from borrowing. And in looking at BNI's Investment Returns, we get an immediate red flag:

Burlington Northern Santa Fe Corp: Key Ratios

Growth Rates
Price Ratios
Profit Margins
Financial Condition
➤Investment Returns
Management Efficiency
Ten Year Summary

Investment Returns %	Company
Return On Equity	17.9
Return On Assets	5.8
Return On Capital	6.5
Return On Equity (5-Year Avg.)	14.4
Return On Assets (5-Year Avg.)	4.6
Return On Capital (5-Year Avg.)	5.1

Financial data in U.S. dollars

Industry: Railroads

Check out the five-year average Return On Capital: 5.1 percent.

What in the world is Warren Buffett doing buying a business with a 5 percent Return on Capital? Simple answer: He's buying it because he believes the Return on Capital is going up and will probably be going up more in the future. According to the annual report, Burlington poured $24 billion into new track and equipment to prepare for a doubling of freight tonnage in the next two decades. If management is right about the demand for rail freight, and obviously Warren Buffett thinks it is, then it's likely that investment in infrastructure will result in an increase in ROC over time.

A secondary indication of which way ROIC will go is Return on Equity (ROE).

Think of ROE as Return on Capital's younger brother. Same family, but ROE isn't quite as grown up as ROC. ROE is calculated without considering *borrowed* money. When you remove debt from the equation, then the managers suddenly look like better managers: 14 percent average for five years and 18 percent last year. Those are good

In the 10 years that ended in 2007, BNSF spent nearly $24 billion to improve our infrastructure. That includes maintaining a strong infrastructure through strategic investments in expanded track, yards and terminals; track renewal; technology; and acquiring more than 2,700 new, high-efficiency locomotives. All of our investments in infrastructure, equipment, asset utilization, people and technology help ensure we have the capacity to meet current and future freight transportation needs, while also improving our operating reliability and efficiency.

From BNI's 2007 annual report and Form 10-K

numbers. That fact means there might be more to the low ROC than meets the eye.

There is one time when it's fair to buy a business with low ROC: if whatever they spent the borrowed money on is *about* to produce a good ROC. For example, if Burlington borrowed the money to build a new line from L.A. to Chicago so they could double the amount of stuff they could move from the ports in L.A. to shippers in Chicago, the borrowed money would produce no return until the track was completed. That construction might take years, and during all that time the debt is calculated as part of the ROIC calculation without any corresponding return at all. It looks bad for the managers, but only if you don't know your business. If you understand Burlington — and if you know enough about the business to agree with their prediction about freight demand — you would expect the ROIC to go up.

This is one of those things you'll start to spot when you know the business you're buying. If management is borrowing to build new track, you can decide if you think it's a good investment. If they're borrowing to buy companies, maybe they're using debt to fund acquisitions that produce zero value to the investor but which get them a nice private jet so they can fly in style to visit their new factories. I agree with Warren Buffett that Burlington is building for the future, and I believe we'll see ROIC rise as the new track and equipment get used. Will it happen in five years? Maybe. Maybe not. But it will happen. We don't have to know *when* it will happen if we're stockpilers. Most of us are net savers and investors for the next twenty years, so we can be patient.

We'll give Burlington a pass on the low ROIC number. But let me warn you: If you're going to let a low ROIC slide because the ROE is big, you had better know *why* the ROIC is low. Don't let a traitor in the CEO seat fool you.

The second most important number to examine is the Equity Growth Rate, or Book Value Per Share (BVPS) Growth Rate — same thing. Book Value grows from earnings that don't have to be spent to maintain the business. Its rate of growth is ultimately reflected in the rate of growth of the stock price, since the stock price will increase with the growth of real owner value. Here's the page to look at for BVPS:

Book Value/ Share	
12/08	$32.82
12/07	$32.05
12/06	$29.42
12/05	$25.59
12/04	$24.71
12/03	$22.87
12/02	$21.11
12/01	$20.35
12/00	$19.10
12/99	$17.98

You can see it's nearly doubled in the last nine years. (Growth is calculated from some starting-point year that isn't counted as a year in the calculations — you have to have a baseline. If there are ten years of data, there are nine years of growth data; 1999 to 2000 is the first year of growth on this chart.) Growing from $17.98 to $32.05 is about an 8 percent growth rate. (See Rule of 72, page 72). And it's very consistent in a range around 8 percent. I don't have to run ten-, seven-, five-, three-, and one-year analyses. I want to see how it's doing over five-year chunks of time. It's not so important what's happening in one year. I can run the numbers if I need to, but after some time of doing this, I can just see it. So can you. Look. It's obvious it's growing its equity steadily. Good sign of consistency. Even though it's 2 percent below our usual minimum of 10 percent, consistency is far more important, because consistent earnings in the past are a good indicator of consistent earnings in the future. It turns out there's a very good reason for that consistency: Burlington shares a monopoly on shipping coal out of Wyoming with Union Pacific. Every day these two businesses load 30 miles of coal cars and haul them east far cheaper than any alternative. A good bet is that energy will cost more tomorrow than it does today. Forever. So Burlington Equity will grow as coal from Wyoming becomes more and more valuable down the road. We can't say when exactly, but someday for sure. Check. (For the record, BNI is not just about shipping coal. In fact, the company transports an enormous variety of goods using its rails. These include consumer, industrial, and agricultural products.)

Now we look at this web page (see top chart on page 106) — the ten-year summary of financial statements. Sales were flat for several years but have been accelerating consistently at 14 percent over the last five years. I had to use the calculator on my website for that one.

EPS was also flat and then shot up. The long-term rate of growth is 11 percent, but over the last five years the growth rate is 24 percent. I had to use the calculator on my website for that one, too.

Let's switch the page to Cash Flow and get the last five years. Do the calculation. Remember the first year is the zero year. Cash is

| Income Statement | Balance Sheet | Cash Flow | 10 Year Summary |

Financial data in U.S. Do
Values in Millions (Excep

Income Statement - 10 Year Summary (in Millions)

	Sales	EBIT	Depreciation	Total Net Income	EPS
12/08	18,018.0	3,368.0	1,397.0	2,115.0	6.08
12/07	15,802.0	7.0	1,293.0		5.1
12/06	14,985.0	2,996.	1,176.0	1,889.0	5.11
12/05	12,987.0	2,453.0	1,111.0	1,534.0	4.02
12/04	10,946.0	1,273.0	1,012.0	791.0	2.1
12/03	9,413.0	1,231.0	910.0	777.0	2.09
12/02	8,979.0	1,216.0	931.0	760.0	2.0
12/01	9,208.0	1,173.0	909.0	731.0	1.87
12/00	9,205.0	1,585.0	895.0	980.0	2.36
12/99	9,195.0	1,819.0	897.0	1,137.0	2.44

| Income Statement | Balance Sheet | Cash Flow | 10 Year Summary |

◉ Annual ○ Interim

Financial data in U.S. Dollars
Values in Millions (Except for per share items)

	2008	2007	2006	2005	2004
Period End Date	12/31/2008	12/31/2007	12/31/2006	12/31/2005	12/31/2004
Period Length	12 Months	12 Months	12 Months	12 Months	12 Months
Stmt Source	10-K	10-K	10-K	10-K	10-K
Stmt Source Date	02/13/2009	02/15/2008	02/15/2008	02/15/2008	02/15/2005
Stmt Update Type	Updated	Updated	Reclassified	Reclassified	Updated
Net Income/Starting Line	2,115.0	1,829.0	1,889.0	1,534.0	791.0
Depreciation/Depletion	1,397.0	1,293.0	1,176.0	1,111.0	1,012.0
Amortization	0.0	0.0	0.0	0.0	0.0
Deferred Taxes	417.0	280.0	316.0	219.0	237.0
▶ Non-Cash Items	135.0	5.0	-82.0	-101.0	444.0
▶ Changes in Working Capital	-87.0	85.0	-110.0	-57.0	-107.0
Cash from Operating Activities	3,977.0	3,492.0	3,189.0	2,706.0	2,377.0

growing at 11 percent per year and consistent. (I got that number using the Cash Flow Growth Rate calculator you can access free at my website; it's easier to use the calculator than the Rule of 72 when the numbers don't double.)

One final thing to check is Debt. Go to the balance sheet and take a look (see top chart on page 107).

| Total Long Term Debt | 9,099.0 | 7,735.0 | 6,912.0 | 6,698.0 | 6,051.0 |

| Net Income | | 2,115.0 | 1,829.0 | 1,889.0 | 1,534.0 | |

You can see the most recent Debt figure from the Interim Balance Sheet: $9,099 million. Can they pay that off in three years of net earnings? Let's see: Look at the bottom line of the Annual Income Statement. These numbers are quarterly income, so add up the last 4 quarters: Net Income (aka earnings) is $2,115 million in 2008. Divide the Debt by the 2008 Net Income: $9,099 / $2,115 = 4.3. That's the number of years it will take for BNI to pay off its debt out of Net Income. We want it to be three years or less, so Debt is a red flag. If you stockpile this one, you'd better know why they're carrying so much debt. Answer: "To help ensure we have the capacity to meet current and future freight transportation needs" (from the Annual Report). In other words, they're borrowing to get ready for the demand for rail freight to skyrocket. If you believe in the business plan, if you think the Debt load is a good idea, then you're going to give BNI a pass on Debt, and you're going to keep digging to see what other red flags you turn up. If you don't think it's a good idea, no free pass, and you don't buy this business.

Let's summarize:

- ROIC is low due to investment costs and ROE is high. Red flag.
- BVPS Growth Rate is consistent and 8 percent. Below the 10 percent minimum. Red flag.
- Sales Growth Rate is recently consistent and 14 percent. Excellent.
- EPS Growth Rate is recently consistent and 24 percent. Excellent.
- Cash Growth Rate is consistent and 11 percent. Good.
- Debt is payable in four years from earnings. Bad but maybe for a reason.

On first glance the Big Five plus Debt look mixed. Excellent growth of sales and earnings with solid consistency in cash and equity. And debt is steady, if high. This is not a bad-looking stock and it has two huge things going for it: It has a huge, unchallengeable Moat and it's got a great story for the future.

I can't overemphasize the importance of Moat to stockpiling. The Big Five in and of themselves cannot predict a great investment even when they're perfect. The Big Five are the view out the rearview mirror, and you can't buy a business looking backward any more than you can drive a car by looking at the road you just drove over. The past doesn't predict the future. It points but it doesn't predict. Lots of businesses have had good historical numbers only to be wiped out by competitors.

The Big Five point us in the right direction. But you have to know your business. In *Rule #1* I told you that all big-Moat businesses have good Big Five numbers. And here is BNI, a big-Moat business with some of the Big Five numbers excellent and some red flagging us. Which goes to show you, never say never. Or never say always. Stockpilers live in a less black-and-white world than Rule #1 traders; when you're trading, using the tools to exit with the Big Guys will protect you from the events the Big Five numbers can't predict. As a stockpiler, your only protection from those kinds of events lies in *understanding the future of the business*. You have to know you have a durable barrier to competition that will preserve your sales and profit margins. Fundamental to that understanding is knowing whether you have a big Moat.

Here's a test to know whether your business has a big Moat. If someone gave you a billion dollars to compete with Burlington Northern, could you do it? Could you open up a railroad to compete with BNI to deliver goods across land? No. Why not? Because you can't get the right-of-way to build the track. And if you could get permission to build, it would cost you $3 million per mile. With $1,000 million, you can build 333 miles of track. And then you're broke. No locomotives, no coal cars, no employees, no nada. You simply cannot compete with BNI. Even if you wanted to do it with trucks, you're out of luck. Over long distances, BNI railcars are much less expensive than trucking. Rail can deliver a ton of coal, for instance, from Wyoming to Georgia for $40. I can't send my 2,000-pound gun safe from Wyoming to Georgia for $40. I couldn't even get it from the sporting goods store to my house for $40. BNI has such a lock on the business that Bret Clayton, CEO of Kennecott Energy, said, "If there's one thing you don't want to do in this business, it's piss off the railroads."* Their first Moat is a Toll Bridge Moat and their second barrier is a Low-Price Moat. Nice.

How does the future look for BNI? Well, the cargo they carry is heavy on commodities, construction materials, Far Eastern goods, and coal, so if you think construction prices, food prices, coal prices, and shipping prices are going up in the long-term future, this is a good business to own.

Is BNI wonderful? I'd say so. But only long term. Short term, who knows?

Okay, so we've got a wonderful, long-term business we just might want to buy (assuming we've done our homework and know the industry well). What's it worth?

Plugging in the Numbers to Calculate Value—the Sticker Price

Here are the steps to calculating BNI's Sticker Price given all the homework we've done so far:

1. Look at the Growth Rates we got: 14, 24, 8, and 11 percent. I'd be okay with using 12 percent because I think things are heading BNI's way for the next fifty years.

Big Coal, by Jeff Goodell.

2. Look at what the analysts' consensus of growth is. Go to Earnings Estimates on the left menu and click the fourth tab, Earnings Growth Rates. This tells you the analysts are estimating 13.5 percent in the next five years. On average they're more optimistic than I am.

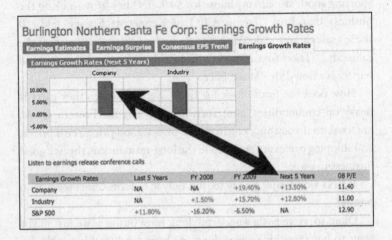

Burlington Northern Santa Fe Corp: Earnings Growth Rates

| Earnings Estimates | Earnings Surprise | Consensus EPS Trend | Earnings Growth Rates |

Earnings Growth Rates (Next 5 Years)

Listen to earnings release conference calls

Earnings Growth Rates	Last 5 Years	FY 2008	FY 2009	Next 5 Years	08 P/E
Company	NA	NA	+19.40%	+13.50%	11.40
Industry	NA	+1.50%	+15.70%	+12.80%	11.00
S&P 500	+11.80%	-16.20%	-6.50%	NA	12.90

3. Take the lower of the two estimates. Mine is lower, so we'll go with 12 percent.

4. Pick the PE ratio—a multiple of earnings that this company trades at. Go to Financial Results, Key Ratios, Price Ratios. The range from low to high BNI PE ratios is from 14 to nearly 34. Add them up. Divide by 2. You get 24 as an average. You can also look at the ten-year statements on MSN Money and see the average annual PE. The highest of these is 17 at this writing. So which do you use? For a big Moat business like BNI, I like to use an average "high" PE because the buyer is going to have to pay up to get that Moat. If the buyer wants to be in the railroad business in the parts of the country where BNI has track, they have to buy BNI. That's going to make the multiple of earnings higher, so I'm going to use a higher-than-"average" PE (as long as it doesn't go more than dou-

ble the growth rate and it's not out of line with the historical highs) and I feel good about it.

Burlington Northern Santa Fe Corp: Key Ratios			
Growth Rates			
▶Price Ratios			
Profit Margins			
Financial Condition			
Investment Returns			
Management Efficiency			
Ten Year Summary			
Price Ratios	Company	Industry	S&P 500
Current P/E Ratio	13.0	11.2	14.6
P/E Ratio 5-Year High	33.7		16.7
P/E Ratio 5-Year Low	14.0	1.9	2.5
Price/Sales Ratio	1.43	1.58	1.49
Price/Book Value	2.20	1.78	2.92
Price/Cash Flow Ratio	7.50	7.00	9.40

Financial data in U.S. dollars

Industry: Railroads

5. Double your estimated Growth Rate. We've chosen a growth rate of 12 percent per year. Double 12 is 24.

6. The two PE ratios are 24 and 24. We choose the lower one. That would be 24.

7. Find the TTM EPS. It's on the Company Report page: $5.76.

8. Pick a Minimum Acceptable Rate of Return (MARR). Ours is 15 percent. This is a key number. It tells me that if I pay the retail value of this business and everything goes as projected above, I'll make 15 percent a year.

9. Summarize the four numbers: TTM EPS = $5.76, Growth Rate = 12 percent, PE = 24, MARR = 15 percent.

10. Run the numbers through the calculator on my website (PaybackTimeBook.com) and you get a Sticker Price (the retail value) of $108 per share.

11. Calculate the Margin of Safety Price. If you are just starting out, I'd go **50 percent off retail** — $54. If you know this business and you know your railroad stuff, I'd go no more than 80 percent of Sticker Price, or $86. (See box about MOS on page 114.)

12. Check today's price (March 2009): $52.

13. Decision: This is buyable (in March 2009) even if you're a novice investor.

14. Action: Finish reading everything you can about this industry and company. Read *Atlas Shrugged* for a good railroad story. And then start stockpiling it whenever the price goes below $54. (More on that in the next chapter.)

In 2008, Warren Buffett bought billions of dollars' worth of BNI stock at prices ranging from $79 to $84. Why didn't he wait until it got into the $50s? I haven't had the privilege of asking him that question, but my best guess is that he'd say, "It's a great business and at a price in the range of $79 to $84 for a business worth over $100 a share, it's an attractive deal." And he might add Charlie Munger's advice. "It's better any day to buy a great business at a fair price than to buy a fair business at a great price." Remember, Mr. Buffett sat patiently on the sidelines with billions, waiting for an opportunity to move a huge sum of money into a great business. He began acquiring BNI in March 2008 and bought much of it in February 2009. Remember what he said about big investors having structural disadvantages? Well, it's very difficult to buy enough of a public business at a great price when you're investing as much money as Mr. Buffett. You simply can't do it all at once without seeing the price explode upward as everyone who follows you jumps on the bandwagon. He is the ultimate Big Guy. My guess is he was willing to start stockpiling at a price 20 percent below the Sticker Price, with the hope of buying more as the price dropped. He has done exactly that, of course, buying in again earlier last year at $63. And as of this writing, Berkshire Hathaway owns 20 percent of BNI — 70 million shares.

More than anything, seeing him stockpile BNI points to the advantages we have as small investors. He can't afford to wait and hope the price makes an extreme drop below value. He might never get in with the $5 billion he wants to spend. But we can wait. (More on how to do that later.) We have so many more opportunities to invest that we can insist on a great price for a great business rather than merely a fair price. Mr. Buffett has said many times that he knows quite a number of investors who can make 50 percent per year with a million dollars but can't beat the market with a billion. The reason, of course, is that size kills your ability to move your money in quickly when you get a great price, and forces you to take fair deals instead of waiting for great ones. I imagine he'd say there are many better deals out there than BNI for a small investor who knows what he's doing.

The above valuation exercise takes time and practice to get down, but once you do this a couple of times and get used to looking these numbers up and playing with them in your calculator, or online with mine, this methodical valuation technique becomes second nature. Go to PaybackTimeBook.com, where you can go through examples from several industries created by students of mine. You can put your best estimate into the calculators, get a valuation, and then see what we thought the value of the same stock is. Do this a few times and you'll get good at it. We critique one another on the site, so if you want to take a crack at doing a valuation on your favorite company, send it to my website, and if it's a decent job, I'll post it and your work will be evaluated by thousands of kind, sweet people. This is important because valuation is where the rubber meets the road. If you get the value right, you're going to get rich, because you'll be able to buy $10 of value for $5 over and over in this market. When the price goes back up to the value, you make huge returns.

If you want to know how to perform these steps using an Excel spreadsheet, go to my website and I'll show you how to do that, too. I encourage you, however, to learn how to apply this method as we just did above before you rely on a preprogrammed spreadsheet.

In addition to spreadsheets on my website, there are powerful automated tool sets available for you to use that save a great deal of time when making these sorts of calculations. For details, go to my website as well.

THE MOS

A Margin of Safety price is 50 percent off the Sticker Price, the retail price you calculate. For all you newbies out there getting used to this analysis, stick with 50 percent as your MOS. Only if you've been doing this for a while (i.e., have learned about MOS in the past and have bought into companies using this strategy), and you feel *very* confident about a particular business, can you let that MOS threshold go as high as 80 percent. This means that you've really nailed all four Ms down and are confident in your ability to find the correct Sticker Price. Remember that the MOS is your safety net. The more wiggle room you sacrifice by upping that MOS threshold, the more certain you need to be of the Sticker Price.

PAYBACK TIME—PLAYING WITH HOUSE MONEY

Stockpiling means we're buying a company for the long term. We're not going to sell it as the Big Guys get out. In fact, as you'll see, we're going to buy it as the Big Guys get out. So we better have a good grip on the MOS. When it's that important to get the MOS right, I want a second opinion. A second powerful way to arrive at the Margin of Safety Price is the "How Long Before I Get My Money Back" method, aka Payback Time. If you buy the whole business and pocket all the earnings, Payback Time is just the time it would take you to get your investment back. Once you get all your money out of the business, you have no risk. From that point on, you're playing the game with house money. This is often the way private business buyers determine what they are willing to pay because there is no liquid market to sell the business into. Once they have their money out, they don't need to worry about an exit strategy.

Let's take an easy example: A friend of mine bought a white-water river-guiding business that was earning $1 million a year. It can't grow, because the National Park concession rules won't let it. But it's also going to produce $1 million a year probably forever. So what's this sort of infinite $1 million worth to someone? Well, he got it for $5 million, and both parties thought it was a good deal. Why? Because he was laying out $5 million and he wanted his money back in some reasonable time. His "Payback Time" on this investment is five years. For my friend, five years seemed to be a long time to wait to begin making any money on the deal. If he'd put his $5 million into a risk-free bond, he'd have been making around 3 percent a year—about $150,000. Five years of that is serious money: $750,000. So he was giving up that interest income, plus putting the $5 million at risk. If he had to wait longer than five years to get his original capital investment back, he wouldn't do the deal. That's how a lot of people think when it comes to buying businesses.

Payback Time isn't a supersophisticated analysis of earnings, capital requirements, and working capital. In fact, it's downright simple. It's so simplistic it doesn't even consider whether the business will have any resale value down the road. It's purely a mental exercise about getting your money back. But you know what? Sometimes the simple beats the complex. Near the end of his career, Ben Graham, the author of the bible of complex analysis, *Security Analysis,* said, "I am no longer an advocate of elaborate techniques of security analysis in order to find superior value opportunities."

If the business is growing, Payback Time has to be adjusted for growing earnings. My brother just sold his private company to a public company. Steve's business had earnings coming in to the tune of $10 million a year, and the public company paid him $91 million in cash for it. If his business's earnings hadn't been growing, it would take the public company 9.1 years to get their money back. But his earnings were growing at 12 percent a year and were expected to be at $20 million in six years. At that rate, the public company would have its money back in six and a half years.

First, notice that the PE ratio for the river company was 5 and the PE for my brother's company was 9. Second, Payback Times were five and six and a half years respectively. Those PE and Payback Time numbers are about what buyers are willing to pay for private businesses. Now compare those PEs to those of the S&P 500 — the biggest and best 500 public companies. The PE on the S&P 500 has averaged 15 times earnings for the last ninety years, more than double what private companies sell for. If the earnings aren't growing, it will take fifteen years to get your money back if you buy out a typical S&P 500 company. In fact, according to Robert Shiller, earnings on the S&P 500 have averaged 2.7 percent since 1874, which means that the average Payback Time for an S&P 500 company is about thirteen years, almost double that of private businesses. Why do private buyers demand less time for payback?

The private-equity buyer is swapping a no-risk cash asset for a business asset with some risk. The risk he's taking is that he won't get his money back, which is why a private-equity buyer has a built-in psychological limit to how far out he's willing to go in a deal. He knows that finding another buyer might take a long time, and he doesn't know what that potential buyer might be willing to pay him for this business.

The only way he can be sure he's going to get his money out of this deal is from earnings, but the earnings road for a small business controlled by the National Park Service gets foggier the further into the future we look. Who can be comfortable projecting what's going to happen with the NPS twenty years from now? Because of this, the private business buyer doesn't want to pay more for this business than a few years' worth of earnings. My river-running friend would have liked to pay $1 million for a business with $1 million of annual cash flow and get out of the risk of losing his money in one year, but like the lemonade stand owner, the owner of the river-running business wasn't stupid.

The seller knows he's going to get this year's million-dollar earnings with a high degree of certainty, so if he can't get more than $1 million for the business he'll just keep it. But when $5 million was flashed in front of him, it was enough to get him to let go and move on.

Knowing why the seller of a private business will take $5 million in trade for an infinite annual million bucks is an important part of knowing what to pay for a business. The seller is getting a million a year from earnings, and he thinks it looks solid well into the future. But consider his risk: He knows there's no guarantee people will show up next year to go down the river. A drought could empty the river. A recession could cut into vacations. Gas prices could get so high people couldn't afford to get there. Someone might drown on one of his tours and the Park Service could pull his license (or give him a really bad reputation). Or maybe the Sierra Club lobbies the Park Service to cut the number of trips he can lead.

People who own even great private businesses sometimes sell because they want to retire or cash out outside owners. For this river-running business owner, getting $5 million cash meant he could pay off his two partners, get rid of a big personal debt, and still have enough to go sit on a beach in Margaritaville for the rest of his life and never work again. For him it was compelling to trade his at-risk future cash in exchange for no-risk cash at that $5 million price.

The range of Payback Times for private businesses is from three to ten years, with eight years as the average for venture-capital deals, and about six years for smaller deals.

Things are different when you buy public stock, because your investment is liquid—since it's actively traded, you can sell almost instantly. If you've made a mistake, or things start to take a turn for the worse, you can get out and cut your losses. This holds true for the Big Guys as well: they may not be able to get out as quickly as we can (because the Big Guys are dealing with so much more money and shares that they have to sell off in chunks rather than all at once), but they *can* get out. At least theoretically. That's worth a lot.

And you can see exactly *how much* that liquidity is worth by looking into those average PEs and Payback Times. The value of the liquidity of a public business gets translated, on average, into about double the price the same business would fetch if sold privately. Payback Time for a public company averages thirteen years, and can go much higher because the buyers aren't really worrying about how long it will take to get their money off the table.

Therefore, if we can buy stock in a wonderful public business at a private business Payback Time price, then we're getting a heck of a Margin of Safety.

BNI'S MARKET-CAP PAYBACK TIME

So with that in mind, let's see what happens when we look at a public business without adding in any value for liquidity—in other words, we'll evaluate a public business as if it were a private business and we were going to buy *all* of it. If you have only $20,000 to invest, it's a bit of a stretch to think of buying an entire $20 billion railroad, but hey, $20,000,000,000 is just $20,000 with a whole lot of zeros after it. Take away six zeros and you're buying a $20,000 railroad. Financial statements show the numbers in millions anyhow. If it helps to think of it that way, go for it. I'll use that financial standard below.

So how long will it take us before we're playing with just house money if we buy all of BNI at its March 2009 price of $52 per share? At $52 per share, BNI has a market price (called Market Cap on Wall Street) of $17,680 million. I found that by looking at the Company Report (MSN Money) online, but I could figure it out myself by finding the total number of shares outstanding on the Company Report. BNI has about 340 million shares outstanding and it's priced at $52. Do the math: 340,000,000 shares x $52 per share = $17,680,000,000. If I cough up $17,680 million out of my spare change and buy the whole enchilada at this price, here's how to figure out how long it'll take to get my money back out of earnings:

1. Find the Market Cap for the company on the Company Report: $17,680 million.

2. Find the last 12 months' earnings on the Income Statement

(add up all four quarters): $2,115 million. Or just look it up on the Company Report.

Net Income	➡	695.0	350.0	455.0	517.0

3. Grow it forward at 12 percent for ten years or until you get your investment back, whichever is first, using Excel (see box below) or by using the calculators on my website. Here's how the net income at BNI could grow for the next few years assuming a 12 percent annual growth (again, we didn't have to go to ten years because we surpassed the Market Cap in the sixth year). These dollar figures are in millions.

YEAR	PAYBACK TIME
1	$2,368.80
2	$2,653.06
3	$2,971.42
4	$3,327.99
5	$3,727.35
6	$4,174.63
NET INCOME	$19,223.26

4. Add it up. Is it more than the $17,680 million we are thinking about paying? Yes. In 5.5 years we've got our money back. Saaaaah . . . weeeeeet! We've got a Payback Time that's right in there with private-equity deals. Wow!

FIGURING OUT EARNINGS GROWTH THROUGH THE YEARS

Calculating earnings growth through the years is easy. We start with net earnings of $2,115 million if we buy today (year 0). We grow it at 12 percent in year 1 (0.12 x 2,115 = 254. Remember, we

(continued on next page)

decided on 12 percent growth for BNI earlier in the chapter. Add that to $2,115 million and we arrive at $2,368 million for year 1). Now do it again: 0.12 x $2,368 million = $284 million. Add that to $2,368 million and we get $2,653 million for year 2. And so on. Eventually you'll see that you surpass the Market Cap for this company midway through year 5—so you can stop there. If you're looking for a shortcut, my website also has a free Excel spreadsheet template, as well as a free tool designed to do Payback Time analysis.

If we can buy a wonderful public business at a private-equity price, then we are buying at, in Warren Buffett's words, "an attractive price." A Payback Time of ten years or less is an attractive price. The Payback Time of less than six years is very attractive. Very.

Again, Payback Time is not literally the amount of time it would take you to get your cash back. I'm quite aware there are ongoing capital items that must be replaced and that investment of capital is required to sustain a high growth rate. Payback Time isn't a shortcut to a Ph.D. in Finance. If you want to be able to put a value on a business you can defend in your thesis, you'll have to read Aswath Damodaran, not me. And he's a good read. But we're not trying to value the esoteric company. If the value of this thing doesn't leap out at us, either we don't know enough about it (in which case we can't buy it) or it's a complex business (in which case we can't buy it). We don't do complex. We do simple. We don't do gray. We do black and white.

Now put the two concepts together. We've got a wonderful company with a Margin of Safety price of $54 for the novice investor. And we have a Payback Time of less than six years at $52. That price is lower than the MOS Price and has an attractive Payback Time. Knowing the Payback Time is short takes a huge amount of emotion out of doing the deal. If you know the business is going to pay for itself in less than ten years, you know you can't get into too much trouble by buying it. Knowing the Payback Time gets rid of fear. If you remove the fear of investing, you can shout "LET'S GO BUY THIS THING!" when everyone else is shouting "THE SKY IS FALLING!" And that's how you get rich.

Why Bother Looking at Payback Time When You're *Not* Buying the Whole Thing?

Looking at Payback Time may seem like a meaningless or useless tactic for the small investor like you and me because we do not get to put the earnings in our pocket. We're going to have to sell some of our shares to get to where we're playing with house money. But it's actually helpful in giving us a new perspective on price. Even if we're just buying a small piece of a business, a check of Payback Time can help us spot price bubbles that MOS might not catch.

Price bubbles in public stocks can get so crazy that sometimes the stock price bears no rational relationship to the stock value. For example, on January 4, 2000, Yahoo! stock was selling for $500 per share. The business had a Market Cap of $505 billion at the time. The earnings were $47 million. The PE ratio was a mere 11,478. And real people — people who are supposed to be smarter at this than you — were actually buying Yahoo! on that day for $500 a share. Did they think about Payback Time at all? Assuming the earnings were growing at some astronomical rate, say 36 percent a year, how long before we'd get our money back? Sixteen years. Never mind that no company ever grew that fast for that long starting that big. Even if it could have a Payback Time of sixteen years, I'd stay away.

Oh, and if it did somehow grow that fast, the earnings would be over $300 billion. Exxon just had record earnings in 2008 of $45 billion. Earnings of all of the U.S. stocks traded regularly that year added up to about $300 billion, so Yahoo! all by itself would have to become pretty much the whole stock market to make sense out of that price. Yes, Professor, stocks do get mispriced from time to time. Just a bit.

Another way to think of the price you're paying for a business is to imagine that the earnings aren't going to grow at all. In that case, the PE or multiple will be the number of years it will take you to get your money back from your investment. The PE of a nongrowing business will be the same as the Payback Time. In the case of Yahoo! in 2000, if the earnings didn't grow, it would take 11,478 years to get your money back. That's longer than most investors are willing to wait to see a return and implies either an incredible expected rate of growth of earnings or a massive bubble in the price.

BUT *WHAT IF . . .*

I'm in front of big crowds about three times a month on a tour with former presidents and former secretaries of state, and after I talk about all this investing stuff, I usually stick around during lunchtime and answer questions. It's an open-mike format with thousands of people hanging out during the break, some of whom have some really tough questions. People write them down and send them up onstage, where I take my best shot at an answer. I always promise that if I don't get to their question, I'll try to answer it on my blog. Here's one that was sent to my website. It's a doozy but it gets right to the point of valuation:

> Isn't the big flaw in your analysis that your growth estimate is always, in some sense, a guess? Either it's a guess based on extrapolation from historical data points or on professional analysts' opinions. In the spring of 2007 I might have thought that AIG was a real steal, based on the numbers. Or Fannie Mae. Or Countrywide. Don't all investors commit the sin of assuming consistent company behavior, based on a false faith in homework? We now

know that the above-mentioned remarkable companies (or so they were portrayed — maybe — by the spring 2007 MSN.com numbers) were in fact booby-trapped. Because we'd seen nothing but white swans in the 9 years of numbers we searched through, we assumed a black swan wouldn't appear. So why can't a company that's heading down the center lane of a superhighway at 100 mph suddenly, for no rational reason, veer completely off the road and over a 1000-foot cliff? Nassim Nicholas Taleb would say, "It sure as hell can." What do you say?

I say that is one heck of a question. Nassim Taleb wrote an intriguing book about the potential for a completely unexpected event to occur. He calls these unexpected and totally disruptive events "black swans" (hence the name of his recent work *The Black Swan*). So the question is: How can we be certain we're buying a business that's not going to turn from a white swan into a black swan?

Well, I think the answer lies in the question itself. Mr. Taleb would insist that even a great business can suddenly veer off the cliff "for no rational reason." Charlie Munger and Warren Buffett are so right so often because they are, if nothing else, intensely rational. In his 1990 letter, Mr. Buffett wrote, "Optimism is the enemy of the rational buyer." In other words, after nine years of wonderful numbers, the rational buyer is still going to insist on a great price or he won't buy. Meanwhile the irrational buyer not only is expecting nothing but good news forever, but he also could be paying a high price, never mind a black swan; if good news doesn't come, he's going to lose money. If we are going to stockpile and still safely account for Mr. Taleb's black swans, we're going to do it by buying with a big margin of safety.

Let's start with valuation. We don't value the business based entirely on either historical data points or analysts' opinion. We value it based on our own opinion, which is constructed in part from historical data, but we also make sure to keep our view firmly out the front window rather than the rearview mirror. When we stockpile a business, we're buying it long-term, typically from the Big Guys who are running for the hills. To buy from fund managers as the stock price is going down requires a level of confidence that only knowledge of the business can create. You have to know your stuff.

Let's review what "knowing your stuff" means: It means you know the business well enough to be happy holding on to it for ten years, even if there is no stock market. It means you know it well enough to be happy buying all of it at the first MOS price you get in at. And it means you know it well enough to know, short of total fraud, that you are getting a good deal. And even fraud can be mostly avoided by investing only with a CEO you trust for good reason. If there is something you don't trust about the CEO, don't invest with him.

Let's look at some examples:

1. Enron: Nobody understood how Enron made its money. You don't understand, you don't invest. End of that story.

2. WorldCom: Did you understand telecom enough to buy the business? No? And did you love the CEO and his big parties and lavish lifestyle? Hey. Clue. If the CEO builds a mansion, make a quick exit.

3. Countrywide, Washington Mutual, and Fannie Mae: Did you really think real estate was going to just go up forever? I was waiting for the crash since 2005. Along with Robert Shiller from Yale and Jim Rogers (Investment Biker) and dozens of other investors I know. And if you ran the numbers at the time, you'd have seen that bubble pretty clearly. Those valuations were nuts. Real estate was in a bubble and these stocks were in a bubble, too. We don't buy bubbles. We sell bubbles. And the key executives of Countrywide were selling stock like there was no tomorrow. And they were right. There was no tomorrow.

4. AIG: This is about knowing your business, too. Mr. Buffett knows insurance and I didn't see him buying these guys. Not to mention they fired their chairman and founder—always a red flag. If you don't know the business, don't buy the business. Let's stick

to simple. Knowing how to evaluate the risk AIG was taking to insure derivatives based on mortgages wasn't something I know how to do. Heck, even their CEO didn't know he had a problem. Note to CEOs: Don't run a business you don't understand. Note to investors: Don't invest in a business the CEO doesn't understand.

Does the requirement to understand the business put too much responsibility on our shoulders? Some experts will say yes and use that as an excuse for telling you not to do your own investing. Some of *you* are going to say yes and use that as an excuse for not taking control of your financial lives. Never mind that your best alternative — buy the whole market by buying an index — can be shown to be invalid for about half the years of the last century. But some of you will do that anyway, for fear you might make a mistake. I can understand the feeling.

You might think of it like driving a car. Think of the risk: 50,000 people a year get killed on the highways. There are traffic accidents every day in every city. Why would anyone in their right mind want to take that chance?

But we drive anyway. And we deal with the fear of dying on the road by learning to drive properly. We practice with a coach — usually Dad or Mom. We don't take the wheel until we're ready. We drive slow when we start out. We might have a fender bender or two but we learn from our mistakes. And pretty soon, driving is not so scary or so risky. I hit a tree last week in my driveway. I learned that trees can jump out at me in my driveway. Now I watch them carefully.

So you get the point, right? The difference between just throwing money into Countrywide and hoping it goes up versus learning the industry and the business, knowing the business has a big Moat and then making a decision to trust the CEO, is as different as driving yourself to work versus letting a drunk without a license drive you. It's the same journey in the same vehicle, but one driver will get there with no problem while the other is sure to crash. Just like that, one knowledgeable investor makes millions while the ignorant investor goes broke. Getting where you want to go financially is similar to getting where you want to go in your car. In both cases, safety — avoiding the accident or the black swan — is all about not going faster than you can handle, staying out of bad situations, pulling over if you aren't sure. And if you refuse to become giddy when Mr. Market gets manic and you stay rational when he's depressed, you're going to do very well indeed — in spite of the occasional black swan.

Having said all that, let's ask the following question: Does this mean we will never lose money if we do everything right? The answer is: You will almost certainly not do everything right at first, and then you may lose money. But if you start off slow and *try* to do it right, you can correct your mistakes and learn from them, and *then* you will make money. In fact, you will make enough money to more than cover the mistakes. This has been the experience of every great investor I know. We all make mistakes. But we learn and then we make fewer mistakes.

One of the reasons I'm writing this book is to help you guys make fewer mistakes by showing you what works. It's why I have my website up for you to use — so you'll be able to learn in a few months what it has taken me twenty-five years to learn. Reducing the errors and the time to become expert is the whole point of an education. You and I are able to do that because we're standing on the shoulders of great investors. Great investors, men like Mr. Graham and Mr. Buffett, know this: if you learn how the best investors have done it for the last hundred years and then you go do what they did, you will reap the reward they got, too. The key is to recognize that if you do this right, if you do this the way the best investors have always done it, you will succeed.

FOR MAXIMUM PAYBACK, DOWN IS THE NEW UP

Even after you buy into a business — unless you own all of it — you want the price of the part you don't own (the part you haven't bought yet) to go down. That's right: *Down*. Not up. If it goes up, we do good. If it goes down, we get rich.

I know that sounds crazy. But remember, our net worth is not about prices, at least not in the short term. It's about value. If prices go down but we know what we're doing, our net worth is going to go up big-time. We're not expecting to cash out today or tomorrow. We know we're investing for many years into the future. Therefore we want the price of any business or stock we stockpile to stay low so we can buy more of that great company at ever better prices.

Assume that you find a business you really understand with great Moat and Management. Assume it has a conservative value of $20 a share, it's selling for a Margin of Safety price of $10, and it has a Payback Time of eight years. You have $10,000 to invest and you buy 1,000 shares. Six months later you've managed to save another $10,000 and are looking for something to invest in, so you reconsider this business you love. But now it's priced at $20, with a Payback Time of thirteen years. Nothing has fundamentally changed in its long-term value, but it no longer has a Margin of Safety, and Payback Time is too long. That means that you can't buy any more with your $10,000. You are priced out of this stock.

At the end of five years, the price is still at $20, and if you decide to sell you've doubled your money and made a 15 percent annual return on your 1,000 shares. Well done.

Now let's compare this result with another scenario. Same stock. You own 1,000 shares at $10 and now it's six months later and you have another $10,000 to invest. But in this case, let's say the price of the business has fallen to $5 per share (with no change in the long-term value of $20) and a Payback Time of five years, so now you buy 2,000 more shares. In both this case and in the previous one, by "no change in the long-term value" I mean you've double-checked your four M analysis to ensure the value of the company still stands as you first calculated it at the first buy-in. The only difference might be a better Margin of Safety.

In six months you've saved another $10,000 to invest, so you look around and discover that the price of your favorite business continued to fall to $1 with a Payback Time of two years. Again, we're assuming the business hasn't changed at all—you know it hasn't, because you've gone through the four Ms carefully. Why's the price down so low? Maybe the whole stock market has just fallen off the table, the Dow is down 85 percent, and no one wants to own stocks. But your company still has a $20 per share long-term value by virtue of its potential for future earnings. So you buy 10,000 more shares.

You now own 13,000 shares and have invested $30,000. The average price you paid per share is $2.30. Five years later, sure enough (and just as in the last example), it's selling for its value of $20 per share. But look at the difference to you: In the first example you doubled $10 to $20 and made a 15 percent compounded return. In the second example, because you stockpiled the stock as it went down, you have $30,000 invested, which you've turned into $260,000, with a return of 54 percent per year. Instead of making $20,000 you made $260,000 because you have trained yourself to stockpile stocks.

When Down Is Up: Remember, when does a drop in price make the profits go up? When you stockpile a great investment.

Every day there are wonderful businesses that you can buy on sale. You might not be able to buy the whole thing, but you can certainly buy a piece. And a small piece of the right business at ever better prices will make you rich.

Why This Isn't Dollar Cost Averaging

This process of buying more shares as the stock goes down might strike you as similar to the common investment strategy of Dollar Cost Averaging (DCA). It's not. DCA means investing a fixed dollar amount at fixed intervals **no matter what the price** of a given stock might be. Dollar Cost Averaging has been widely criticized by economists and academic finance researchers as more of a marketing gimmick than a sound investment strategy. Numerous studies have shown that in addition to lowering overall returns, DCA does not even meaningfully reduce risk when compared with other strategies — even a completely random investment strategy. In a sense, Dollar Cost Averaging is a refuge for scoundrels. If you bought some stock and it went down, a bad adviser can tell you, "The best thing to do is hold what you have and buy more at these lower prices. That way you Dollar-Cost-Average down the overall cost of your stock position." You bought at $20; it's at $10. You follow the scoundrel's advice and buy more. It goes to $5. You adviser has no idea whether this investment is ever coming back, because he didn't know the value of this thing in the first place. It might be worth $1, for all he knows. But he *also* knows that if you sell now, you'll blame him for your loss. He hopes that if he can keep you Dollar Cost Averaging, then someday the price of this dog will rise above your lower average cost. Sneaky. And effective in a bull market. But in a market like this one, Dollar-Cost-Average the wrong stock and you can throw good money after bad and lose it all.

Could that happen? Sure. Easily. Happens all the time. Surely it couldn't happen over a longer period, could it? The market can't misprice a stock for years, can it? Unfortunately, yes it can and often does. Stocks can be and often are overpriced for ten years or more. Eventually they get priced correctly and then they crash. Look at the tech stock run-up in price from 1999 to 2009. If you DCA'd the Q index, which is a popular tech index comprising a hundred companies listed on the Nasdaq, with $12,000 a year from 1999 to 2009, you would have invested $120,000 at an average price of $47. In March 2009, the Q index was priced at $27. Because of the genius of DCA you lost 43 percent after ten years. Okay, eventually Mr. Market will price the Q properly for the long haul, and if you can take the pain long enough, you will eventually DCA yourself into a 0 percent rate of return. Someday. In this market, "someday" could be a long way off. Meanwhile you're decimating your retirement.

Dollar Cost Averaging is stupid. It's a brain-dead way to buy into a business or an index. The fact that it *appears* to be a simple and effective way to avoid buying at a bad price makes it a great tool for clueless financial "experts."

Built into the DCA strategy is the same old mindless assumption that has messed up professional investors for thirty years—that price is the same as value. There is nothing about DCA investing that demands you know the value of the stock you're buying.

If you've liked DCA in the past, then you'll love stockpiling as a basic investing strategy. Think of stockpiling as DCA with a brain. It requires that you start buying with a big Margin of Safety and a good Payback Time, then continue buying as long as that MOS and Payback Time hold. If the stock price goes down even more, we get more shares for the same money. If the price goes above the MOS price or the Payback Time gets too long, we don't buy.

Instead of riding the market up and down through idiotic DCA, stockpiling gets you great returns by limiting your purchases to when the stock is undervalued.

BACK TO BNI: WHAT'S NEXT?

Now an important question: Once you buy some BNI at $52, what should you do from that point? Should you hope that the price of BNI will go up or down? Maybe answer this question first: If you're going to be buying hamburgers for a long time in the future, do you want the price of hamburgers to go up or down? (Answer: down!)

TAKEAWAYS AND ACTION ITEMS

Because they have uncertain earnings potential, some businesses may be overvalued at any price. Review the ten-year financial history and get a rear-view mirror look into businesses you understand. Gauge their future earnings potential and determine the Sticker Price. Buying investments at a significant margin of safety (MOS) will protect your minimum acceptable rate of return (MARR) when you eventually sell at or above retail value.

- Don't confuse price with value. Always determine the retail value of a business and never pay it.
- Calculate the Margin of Safety price by using the free stockpiling tools found at **PaybackTimeBook.com**.
- Determine the payback time to get your money back. It will help you find price bubbles that MOS may not catch.

EIGHT BABY STEPS to WEALTH

Learning is not compulsory . . . neither is survival.

—W. EDWARDS DEMING

The purpose of *stockpiling* a business is to maximize our return on investment with the least effort and least risk possible. We *stockpile* a business by investing in a piece of a business at a Margin of Safety price. If the price goes *down* without fundamental change in the business, we buy more. Investment at the lower cost reduces our average investment cost, and our overall rate of return goes up. This is how the poor get rich and the rich get richer.

Put simply, the essence of *stockpiling* is to turn a *down* price into an *up* return on investment. To turn your *down* into *up*, take these eight simple steps:

EIGHT STEPS TO TURN *DOWN* INTO *UP*

1. Find it.	5. Own it.
2. Value it.	6. Stockpile it.
3. Watch it.	7. Sell it.
4. Buy it.	8. Repeat until rich.

STEP ONE: FIND IT

You know what you're looking for: A wonderful business. (If you aren't sure what a wonderful business looks like, reread Chapter 3 and spend some time on my website.) *Finding it* is the first step to turning a down market into up returns. You're looking for something very specific: a business in an industry you understand (Meaning) with a durable competitive advantage (Moat) and a CEO you trust (Management).

Sometimes knowing what *not* to look for is the best place to start narrowing what *to* look for. I touched upon some of these red flags at the end of Chapter 3. But now that we're really ready to buy, let's recap that list and go into a little more detail. Remember, if you're going to stockpile, you really have to get all this stuff right. Which is why having a clear sense of all the red flags and being able to spot them quickly will save us a lot of time, effort, and of course, money.

Red Flags List—Part II

1. **No Meaning.** Remember, if you're not an expert in an industry, you don't have any business owning a company in that industry. If you don't understand the industry you are thinking of getting into, don't go there until you do. See Chapter 3.

2. **No Moat.** If there is no durable competitive advantage, don't even consider it. Without a Moat, a business has to compete on price. If their hammer is just about as good as yours except it's cheaper, you might find your customers buying theirs. That will force you to drop your price, too. If your competitor lives in China, he may be able to drop his price well below your cost. This is what happened to hardware stores in small towns all over America when Wal-Mart moved in. Because of their volume buying, Wal-Mart could sell the hammer for less than Mr. Smith's Hard-

ware, and before long, Mr. Smith's Hardware was gone. Do not own a business without a big Moat—public or private.

3. **No CEO.** Yes, there will be a body in the CEO chair with the title, but that does *not* mean the business has a real leader. Leadership is about vision and values. All public businesses have management. Fewer have *leadership*. As I'm writing this, Steve Jobs is overcoming health challenges. I've worked with Steve and I can tell you from personal experience that he can be a total son of a gun about what he thinks is right. He's like Simon on *American Idol.* He has absolutely no concern for your personal feelings. What you are doing is either "cool" or "@#%s%!" But it's that laser-like focus on what he sees as "cool" that allows his company to connect technology with consumers better than any company in the world. Thank God Steve recovered quickly. America needs every hard-core, iconoclastic, SOB like Steve Jobs it can get. But what happens, God forbid, if Steve doesn't stay healthy? It's an open question whether anyone else can keep Apple's products at the cutting edge of brilliant innovation.

Last time Steve stepped down, the company was turned over to a sugar-water salesman and Apple nearly went down the tubes. When Steve brought it back, he saved the company. We'll see if a real leader can step up to keep it saved now. (To that end, you also need to be careful about buying into a company that's so reliant on the brains of a single person. If that asset goes away, the entire business as an asset can go away, too.) Also be certain to not invest in businesses that have political climbers at the helm. They are not leaders. They are the polar opposite. They look to where the band wants to go and then get in front of it and wave their baton. The world has enough self-promoting grandstanders in politics. Be careful of investing with one.

4. **Big Debt.** No debt is best, particularly in this credit crunch. Debt implies the business needed to borrow money to finance either working capital or growth or both. When money gets tight, they might find their source of cash drying up. Then they have to either sell equity and dilute the existing shareholders or

slow down growth or even sell off parts of the business to get capital for the rest of it. Make sure you know that the debt load isn't too high for the business to handle even in a bad credit market like this one. As explained in Chapter 3, make sure a company can pay off its debt within three years by dividing total long-term debt by current earnings.

5. **Trade Unions.** I like the idea of an intracompany union because I'm all about the little guy, but I'm not a fan of trade unions. An intracompany union is a union of both management and employees within the same company, which gives employees a way to come to consensus and let the CEO know what they want, along with a forum for management to explain what it wants. It's a means of building consensus for all the stakeholders. A trade union, on the other hand, has no stake in any particular business. Its role is to advocate for the employees of all the businesses it covers. Like an attorney defending you in court, the trade union's job is not to arrive at a just conclusion but rather to win at all costs. Naturally, as in court, this creates a war between the union and the other stakeholders—shareholders and management, in particular. Sometimes the trade union is even at war with members of the trade union (employees) when employees believe the union's taking action to their personal detriment—like going on strike, for instance.

Trade unions, by their very nature, kill the goose that lays the golden eggs. The success of the auto trade unions in raising employee wages and benefits has killed all three American car companies, yet they refuse to bear one iota of responsibility. When there are profits, trade unions grab every cent they can get for their members by holding up management, suppliers, customers, bondholders, and shareholders with the threat of market-share-destroying strikes. In effect, their best weapon is the reality that the business means more to other stakeholders than it does to employees. Replacing a $50 per hour job is less daunting than rebuilding a billion-dollar business and everyone at the table knows it. Unfortunately, although intracompany unions are common in other countries, Congress outlawed them in 1935 as part of the National Labor Relations Act. This archaic law leaves modern employees with the evil choice of having no power in their company or joining an industry-wide union with their competitors — possibly to their own detriment. Walk carefully where there are powerful trade unions.

6. **Technology.** Technology companies are great for trading but dangerous for stockpiling. Technology is about destroying an existing way of doing things and replacing it with a new one. (The proper name for this phenomenon is "creative destruction".) In other words, the essence of tech is to wipe out someone's Moat. Castles with technological Moats are easy to defend until someone digs a tunnel underneath and undermines the entire defense. The biggest problem with technological Moats is the lack of warning of attack. One day you have the best computer. The next day you're obsolete. You have the fastest chip, but what happens if the future doesn't need chips? You've got a BlackBerry today. But here comes the iPhone, so what are you going to do tomorrow? The problem with owning a company that depends on developing new products is that it's so reliant on engineering talent and management's sense of the future. If you lose the top engineers and can't attract the new generation of marketing geniuses, you're going to be obsolete. For a passive owner that means a scary ride into the future. Leave technology to the venture capitalists and the speculators. Don't stockpile technology without being an expert, and even then, watch out.

Using Search Parameters Online

Once you know what *not* to look for, you still might have problems finding what you *are* looking for, particularly if you're not big on any particular industry. In Chapter 3, I took you step by step through the process of searching for potential candidates within a particular industry. I showed you how to navigate Yahoo!'s nine Sectors, and we honed in on apparel based on my own 3 Circles, and then we went further and looked at Ralph Lauren in particular. Now I'm going to show you an even better way to find your wonderful business: A stock search engine.

A stock search engine is a tool that filters stocks based on specific parameters. There are about 200 industries, 6,500 sizable U.S. public companies, and about 700 different facts for each company. A good stock search engine stores and indexes all those facts. It's a revolutionary time-saving device for finding a great business to buy in an industry you really like and understand.

To get an idea of how amazing this technology is, think about how you'd have gotten this information only ten years ago. We could still search through all 6,500 actively traded companies in America. Heck yes we could. It just took a little longer. First, you'd write to all 6,500 companies for their annual report and SEC 10-Q filings, which are those quarterly reports required by the Securities and Exchange Commission. Assuming you could do about 30 an hour, it would only take a month to get the request letters out and only cost about $2,000 for envelopes and stamps, not to mention a 12-step recovery program from licking glue off of 300 stamps a day. Within two weeks the first of the 8 x 12 manila envelopes would come in the mail and it'd be time to start reading. Say it takes half an hour to browse an annual report and calculate Return on Capital figures, Earnings Growth, and Debt; within only 3,000 hours you've gone through them all. If you worked hard you could do that job in a year. By which time you'd have to start over because the new annual report was in your mailbox.

Today we do it just a little differently.

Go to the MSN Money home page. On the left menu under Investing, find Stock Research and click on it. On the Stock Research page, look at the left menu for Find Stocks. Below that click on Stock Screener and then Custom Search. On that page it says Supercharge Your Search. Click on that. You'll be directed into the Deluxe Search Tools and they will load automatically. (Note to Mac users: I'm writing this on a MacBook Pro. If I go on MSN Money on my Mac operating system using Safari or Firefox I don't see the Supercharge option. If you can't find it either, crank up Boot Camp or Virtual Machine or Parallels and start up Windows. It will work there. Make sure you've got the latest version of Internet Explorer, which is the browser that works best with MSN Money.) There are lots of stock screeners out there today, but this one works very well and has the added merit of being free.

If I want to restrict my search to my favorite industries, I click on the Industry drop-down menu and select from about 200 industry groups. You remember how we were digging around in Chapter 3 to find an industry we liked? We start our search the same way here — with industries we found by doing the 3 Circles. I put my cursor in the Field Name box, click it, and get the first drop-down menu. I put my cursor on Company Basics, and the second menu appears, where I selected Industry Name. If you're following along, click on Industry Name. Industry Name is now in the Field Name box. Click in the Operator box and select "=."

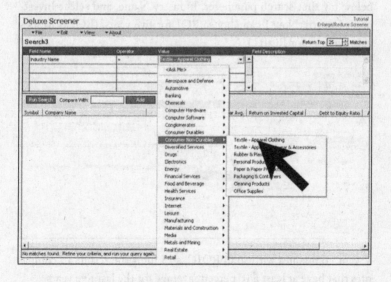

Now click in the Value box and you'll get a list of Sectors. There are thirty-one Sectors at MSN. MSN has decided the nine Sectors we saw over at Yahoo! are too broad for classifying all the stocks, so they have thirty-one instead of nine. I scroll down the list to the first group that looks like it might have businesses in it that I'm good at according to my 3 Circles. My guess is the Consumer Non-Durables Sector has something for me. I slide down to it and see the Industry Group list appear to the right. The first industry is Textile–Apparel Clothing. I want to look in that industry to see if there are any good businesses, so I click on it and it loads into the Value box. You can only do one industry at a time, so this search will be about the stocks in the Textile–Apparel Clothing group.

The beauty of doing it this way is I can swap any industry in for this one and then the rest of my search will be run on that new industry. You'll see what I mean in a minute. First, I have to add some parameters, or facts about a company, that tell the computer what I'm looking for in a business. My first choice is a business with a solid Return on Invested Capital. I put my cursor in the Field Name box below my first search parameter, Industry Name, and select Investment Return. Now I can choose ROI for five years. (ROI is MSN's abbreviation for ROIC.)

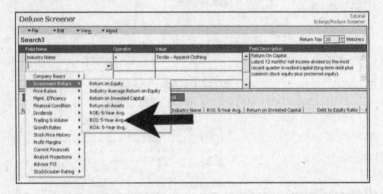

I want companies with solid ROIC, so I limit the results to companies that have at least a 10 percent average for the last five years.

What else should I ask for? How about Earnings growth? Again I'll demand it be at least 10 percent for the last year. I'm not doing a range of years, because if a company got decent earnings in the last year, they're doing really good. I can look at the range later. Add that search parameter by again putting your cursor in the Field Name box below the last search parameter you added and then dig around until you see EPS Growth. Now add Debt as a search parameter. We'll use the debt-equity ratio to find companies with almost no debt.

If you're struggling with this searching stuff, head over to my website, PaybackTimeBook.com. I show you how to navigate these site pages step by step so you can follow along click by click. I've also created prebuilt searches for various industries that you can access. Try searching for a stock just once with this tool and you'll know how to do it forever. It really is that easy.

Now click on the Run Search button and the program rips through the Textile–Apparel Clothing industry looking for companies with these four parameters. It puts the result on the page in less than a second.

Our completed search request looks like this:

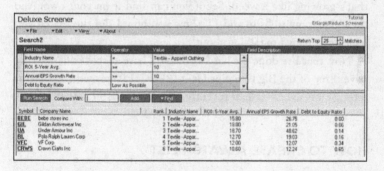

This is a heck of an improvement over the old way of gathering data. So far I've invested zero dollars and licked no glue, and it's taken me less than a minute. I clicked a button and got magic.

And that's not even the cool part yet. Once you've built a search that you like, you can change parameters simply by clicking on the parameter you want to change and putting something else in the same space. The way I like to do this is to work through industries I'm interested in by having the search engine tell me what businesses in a particular industry meet those three Moat parameters we inputted. All I have to do is swap in another industry and run the search again. Try it. Click on the Value box where it says Textile–Apparel Clothing and change it to Specialty Retail — Sporting Goods Stores. Click Run Search and see if any stores come up that meet our minimal Moat numbers.

Okay, what if you do this and find that there are no industries in your sweet spot that meet all our minimums? Then you might want to expand your search area to include industries that show up on 2 of your 3 Circles. You can also look at the Sectors, pick industries you connect with, and look in those for a business.

I was doing that — just messing around — and I clicked on Restaurants, since I eat in restaurants all the time and I worked a bit in my mom's little restaurant in Sausalito, California, years ago. It's an industry I could figure out without too much trouble. And I might be motivated to do exactly that if I found a really interesting business to research.

Try that search now. There's a fantastic company in this Sector that's growing like a weed. See if you can find it on your own. And then check my website and I'll show you how I did the search and which company I'm talking about.

Now that I've done the hard work and I have a few businesses that have three of the Big Five plus Debt (ROIC, EPS growth, and Debt) more or less right — at least recently — I'll put these on a "Watch List."

HOW TO CREATE A WATCH LIST

A Watch List is a list of businesses you're interested in. They've passed some screening but still have a ways to go before you're ready to put them on your Buy List. You can create a Watch List on MSN Money. You don't have to do it on a computer, though. A traditional notebook works just fine, too.

On MSN Money, click on the Investing tab and then in the left column click on Quote Watchlist. The MSN Watchlist page will come up. In the symbol box, enter the symbol of the stock you want to research. Let's put in RL for Polo. Click Add and it's on the list. You can stack up a bunch of stock symbols to work on. I'll put UA (Under Armour) in there, too, since it's a competitor of Polo that came up in my initial industry search. And BWLD — Buffalo Wild Wings — because I like eating their wings, so I did a quick and dirty valuation and now I want a reminder to check out the business sometime.

Symbol(s)	to: My Watchlist				Add			View: Standard				
☑ Quote watchlist								Update quotes | Manage accounts⌄ | Customize view⌄				
	Symbol⌄	News	Chart	Message board	Last	High target	Low target	Change	Shares	Market value	Today's change	StockScouter rating
My Watchlist												
⊞ ⅄	BWLD	📊	📈		30.14	24	15	0.72	0	0.00	0.00	6 delete
⊞	RL		📈		37.27	0	0	-1.02	0	0.00	0.00	7 delete
⊞	UA		📈		15.82	0	0	-0.70	0	0.00	0.00	4 delete
	Total:									$0.00	$0.00	
Total:	$0.00	Today's change: •••										

This is a handy tool. Once you've done your work and have decided you want to buy, you can enter the price you'll pay in the High Target or Low Target boxes the way I did with BWLD.

INDUSTRY RESEARCH

If we haven't done it already, let's go get educated on the industries the companies on our Watch List are part of. Put yahoo.com in your URL box, get to Yahoo! Finance, and enter the symbol of one of the candidates in the symbol box. Now look at the left menu bar, find Companies, and click on Industry. The industry of the business you are researching will come up. Note the competitors in the industry and jot them down for further research. Read about the industry. Check out the websites of the major players. Read, read, read, and keep digging until you decide yes or no to this industry, and then move on to the next business on the Watch List.

By the time you're done digging, it's possible you'll say yes to the industry but no to the stock that started your research. Happens all the time. It's likely in that case you found another business in the industry you like better, and now that one's on your Watch List or Buy List.

Before you start to be concerned about the amount of time you're putting into this without a business to buy, remember that Abraham Lincoln said, "Give me six hours to chop down a tree and I will spend the first four sharpening the axe." The work you do preparing at the beginning will give you the best return in the end. Much of it is reading you only have to do once, because once you've learned the business you don't have to keep reading about it. From that point you're just keeping tabs on it and watching your favorite business for an opportunity to buy in or stockpile more.

STEP TWO: VALUE IT

See Chapter 4. Do the Rule #1 Valuation (find the Sticker Price). Then do the Payback Time evaluation. Be sure you have plenty of Margin of Safety to allow for errors. You want to buy at a price low enough that if you owned the whole thing you'd get your at-risk cash back in a short time (ten years max).

Always remember that price is not the same as value. The reason it's not the same is that we have a partner called Mr. Market who is willing to buy any public stock we own when we want to sell and to sell us any public stock when we want to buy. Our deal with him is that he gets to set the price but we get to say yes or no.

Embrace Our Partner, Mr. Market, and Reject EMT

In October 2008, we witnessed panic and irrationality kick in big-time in the financial world. Highly leveraged derivatives markets melted down as fear tore through credit markets worldwide. The stock market lost 20 percent of its value—about $3.6 trillion—in a matter of days . . . and then continued to deteriorate.

The stock market is a place just loaded with the twin stresses of fear and greed, so much so that we can conjure up a bipolar character whom Ben Graham named "Mr. Market." Mr. Market is usually rational, but then again, he's usually taking his meds. When events in the world happen that Mr. Market didn't expect, he stops taking his medication and gets into a bipolar episode. If the news is unexpectedly good, he'll get manic and be so full of enthusiasm for the future that he'll pay exceptionally high prices for stocks—prices far above their value. On the other hand, if the news is unexpectedly bad, he gets so depressed that he'll sell wonderful businesses at prices far below their value.

The beauty of Mr. Market is that he'll act as our partner no matter what mood he's in. If he's depressed, he'll sell us everything we want at fabulously low prices. If he's manic, he'll buy anything we want to sell him at fabulously high prices. He's a great partner as long as we learn to take advantage of his moods—and not be swayed by them. If he's full of fear, it's time for us to be looking for deals. If he's full of greed, it's time for us to be thinking about selling him businesses we own. We have to remain rational while Mr. Market is acting like an emotional prima donna.

A rational reaction in this market meltdown, one that eliminates emotion, is to see whether the value of what we own is significantly higher than its price. If it is, then a rational reaction would be to buy more even if we expect the price might go even lower in the near term. That's exactly how you take advantage of the system that failed you and guarantee your financial future. If we own something with $10 of value that's selling for $5 now, why not buy more, even if two months from now the price is $4? If it's really worth $10, then we're still buying $10 bills for half off. And if a panicked Mr. Market is selling the $10 bill for $4 in a couple of months, say thank you and buy more of them at that price. Someday we're going to be able to sell the $10s back to Mr. Market for $10 or more. It won't matter a great deal whether we paid $5 or $4. We made a killing either way. This is rational investing. This, as you know by now, is *stockpiling*.

Most big investors talk a lot about "value" but they don't back up their talk with action. If a stock is going down, instead of being excited by the possibility of buying more on sale, the mutual fund manager doesn't really think much about the value of the stock. He thinks, "Why is the price going down? There must be a problem I don't understand. Time to run away." This is Efficient Market Theory (EMT) speaking and, since the theory is BS, when things start to go down, the fund managers panic—often for no good reason.

EFFICIENT MARKET THEORY

The quickie on EMT: Efficient Market Theory basically states that since all the information about stocks is widely known to investors, and since investors act rationally in their own interest, the price of any widely traded stock reflects everything known about it and, therefore, the current price is the current value of the stock. In other words, you get what you pay for—always. Warren Buffett disagrees. So do I, as well as every millionaire who makes a killing in the market when it tanks. EMT is based on a serious error about the real world. It assumes investors act rationally all the time. But they obviously don't. Fear is a powerful emotion that overrides rational thought in the stock market, as it does in many situations in life. For more information about the power of emotions in the market, read Robert Shiller's *Irrational Exuberance*. Dr. Shiller called the top of the market in 2000 and the top of the real estate market in 2005. Anyone who gets it right that often deserves to be read.

When the Big Guys panic, it makes a huge difference, because 85 percent of the money in the market is being managed in large funds—by exactly those same panicking Big Guys. Most fund managers were trained to expect Mr. Market to be rational and price things properly at their real value. Therefore, when Mr. Market isn't rational, his huge emotional waves sweep individual fund managers into their own upwardly spiraling irrational exuberance (driving prices up) or down into irrational fear of utter ruin (pushing prices down) and they begin to act irrationally out of greed or fear. And they take the entire market with them. We don't get caught up in these emotional waves because we don't subscribe to EMT. We *do* love Mr. Market, though, because once you understand him he's such a predictable partner. When he gets very fearful, we buy, because he is, predictably, going to become greedy in the future and everything we bought when he was fearful is going to go straight up. He does it over and over and we love him for it.

It is our job to hit hard when Mr. Market is overly emotional: We will buy when he's fearful and sell when he's greedy. The rest of the time we just lurk in the bushes, waiting for the next great opportunity from Mr. Market. By doing so, we're able to achieve remarkable returns even if the overall market goes nowhere. All the price has to do is to return, post-fear, to its value, and our profits will be excellent.

Once you see a potential opportunity, and you've done your valuation, the next step is to watch it. You wait for Mr. Market to get off his meds and go crazy.

Factoring Dividends into Valuation

Before we move on to the next step, I need to cover a bit about dividends here. A lot of people are interested in buying stocks with dividends these days. It's nice to own equity in a business and get paid as if you owned a T-bill on top of it. Some people even think the dividend is the only reason to own equity in a public business, since it's the only real cash you'll ever see from the business itself. Any other gains you make from owning the business come entirely from selling what you own to someone else. This is quite different from owning a private business. In a private business, the free cash flow is yours to do with what you will. Keep it and invest it in some other business (or trip around the world) or let the business use it and, perhaps, grow.

Dividends are paid by public businesses for two reasons, only one of which is a good reason. The good reason is the business has more cash than it knows what to do with. A good CEO knows that this excess cash belongs to you. The only justification he has for keeping it is if he can use it to grow the business at a rate high enough to justify keeping the money. We call this rate the ROE (Return on Equity), and you already know it's a very important number. A good CEO will judge the performance of his team, in part, by how well the team invests owner capital. In fact, overseeing the allocation of owner capital is arguably the most important job of a CEO. One of the legitimate choices for allocating that owner capital is to give it back to the owners when the CEO can't think of something better to do with it. (Some CEOs think "better" means they can buy a new Gulfstream jet, but when they do that without a business justification, it might be time to look for a new business to own.)

The second reason is a bad reason: Some businesses set a percentage of their earnings aside as a dividend to provide the *illusion* of being a solid business. This common practice is driven by Mr. Market, who prefers the illusion of stability to the real thing. If the earnings fluctuate, so does the amount that can be paid as a dividend, and that makes Mr. Market nervous. Mr. Market does not want a fluctuating dividend. He wants a steady dividend that produces cash flow like a bond. If he gets that he will put a high price on it. Some CEOs, being human, respond to Mr. Market's desire by delivering a rock-solid dividend quarter after quarter. This steadiness attracts investors, particularly retired investors who think, wrongly, that a steady dividend indicates a steady business and therefore low risk.

GM has had a steady dividend for many years. They were paying a steady dividend of $0.25 per share in 2008. This is quite the magic act, considering they were completely out of cash and in the process of going bankrupt. They got the money by borrowing it, because they didn't have any profits or cash flow to get it from. But in the illusion business the show must go on, so they continued to pay it. And ignorant investors continued to hold the stock because of the dividend. An eighty-four-year-old friend of mine in Jackson Hole got hit by this. Before her husband died, he told her to hold on to GM stock because of the dividend. He didn't see the last ten years coming, and she didn't know any better than to do what he said. She held it from the time it was in the $80s per share down to today, when it's at $0. That loss of $80 took eight years and was offset by $13 of dividends. That's not really that good a trade-off. Why did she hold it? Because GM had always been such a steady producer of dividends that she couldn't believe the business was in trouble. In 2002 I took her to a friend's birthday party and we got to talking about her investments. I told her I thought GM was in trouble and she should sell it. She didn't believe me. She said, "But it keeps paying the dividend, so it must be doing okay." She believed the illusion, and she lost most of the money she had invested in GM. Good people like her are being faked out by a close-to-fraudulent practice.

Again, dividends are fine if the business has no better use for your money. If you're retired and need the cash flow from dividends to live on, then investing in a great business with steady dividends is a good idea *as long as the dividends come from real free cash flow.* Here's how you know if the dividends are being paid from something other than cash flow. Look at the Cash Flow Statement for the business on MSN Money or Yahoo! Finance.

▶ Financing Cash Flow Items	-5.0	2,490.0	6,029.0	4,723.0	2,237.0
Total Cash Dividends Paid	-567.0	-563.0	-1,134.0	-1,129.0	-1,121.0
Issuance (Retirement) of Stock, Net	0.0	0.0	0.0	0.0	60.0
Issuance (Retirement) of Debt, Net	-5,021.0	-5,694.0	-1,415.0	17,881.0	58,664.0
Cash from Financing Activities	-5,593.0	-3,767.0	3,480.0	21,475.0	59,840.0

Look at the line that says Total Cash Dividends Paid. See the last three years, where GM paid out $567 million, $563 million, and $1,134 million? Now look two lines below and you'll see where they got the money. In 2003 and 2004, GM borrowed a total of $58 billion and $17 billion. In the next three years it paid back $12 billion of it and used some of it to pay dividends. Clever, no? They put the owners, that would be *you,* on the hook for a loan and then pay you dividends with it and you thank them for the money by keeping their stock even while it loses 100 percent of its value.

Dividends, particularly large, steady dividends, are to be viewed as if you are the business owner, not as if you are an ignorant coupon clipper. If you're going to own a business in part for its steady dividend, be sure you understand the business well and, in particular, that you understand where the dividend money is coming from.

Every word here applies equally to DRPs (pronounced "drips"), Dividend Reinvestment Programs. DRPs are usually run by the business itself to save you the cost of a commission on buying more of their stock. Once you've signed up for their program, they will automatically reinvest the dividend payment by purchasing stock at the price Mr. Market has set that day. If this sounds smart to you, I want you to reread the part about Mr. Market above, along with all of Chapter 3. Don't be tempted by convenience to buy stock at a price over its value. DRP programs contribute to overpricing because they're on autopilot and they have an idiot flying the plane who has no clue about value. Your DRP is going to buy at whatever price Mr. Market offers up, no matter how stupid it is. The *only* advantages to doing this are (1) it's on autopilot so it's going to get done, and (2) there is no commission so you can afford to buy small pieces. But you'll pay a price for that by buying when you shouldn't.

Okay, you've found a wonderful business and you know its value and MOS Price. You did your Payback Time evaluation and you selected a price you're willing to pay. This is your Stockpile Price. Now you wait. Patiently.

Stockpile Price equals what you're willing to pay.
This can be the MOS price or Payback Time price. And,
again, your Payback Time price is the price at which
you can theoretically get your money back in
ten years or less. (See Chapter 4 again.)

STEP THREE: WATCH IT

When a candidate on your Candidate Watch List makes the grade and becomes a business you want to buy at a certain price, it goes to your Watch List. Your Watch List is a list of the businesses you want to own. These are no longer just candidates. They are all businesses you will buy if you get a chance. Your Watch List won't be long. It may have one name on it. If you're willing to do a little more work, you can put a second or third name on it. Ideally, there will be a place on your Watch List where you can list the price you're willing to pay. Again, this is your Stockpile Price. It might be the MOS Price. It might be the Payback Time Price. It will not be higher than your MOS Price, however. In any case, essentially from this point you're just watching the price of the stock.

Your Watch List can be kept anywhere you can keep a list. It doesn't have to be on a computer. Just write down the names of the businesses you want to buy and the prices you want to pay. That's all a Watch List is — a list to watch. Stick it on your refrigerator and check on it occasionally. The fact is, if you're paying attention to the industry you want to invest in, you'll probably notice when the price of the stock you want to buy is dropping.

You can put your list on a smart phone and check it daily if you have nothing better to do. The free stock research websites, Yahoo! and MSN, have places where you can set up Watch Lists. Go to the

MSN Money home page and click on Investing on the upper tabs and then click below that on Portfolio. At Yahoo! Finance, click on the tab My Portfolios to create Watch Lists.

Now comes the part that might take a while. You have to be patient. I sit on cash for months. I did that recently, from August 2007 until January 2009, waiting for the right price on a business I wanted to own. Mr. Buffett sat on $45 billion for years until just recently. During the time you're waiting, it's important to keep up with the business and the industry. Keep reading. Be sure you listen to the CEO's quarterly Q&A with analysts. Those are fun if you've never done one. Go to your Watch List businesses' websites and get the dates of the next call from the Investor Relations page.

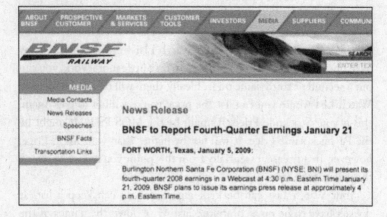

This press release is a typical invitation to hear the quarterly presentation. Good CEOs will tell you and the rest of the analysts listening what they think their growth will be for the next few months or years. They'll talk about the business as if you know as much about it as they do (and you should, since you're trying to buy it). If you have a pressing question you can e-mail it to the Investor Relations Department and the answer might be included in the presentation.

Adjust the value as necessary as you're waiting. Each quarter of the year, your target businesses will release the latest financial information. The information goes to the SEC in a format called a 10-Q. Every fourth quarter the business does its annual report to the SEC in the 10-K format. The company provides the dates for these quarterly and annual releases on its website. Keep those dates on a calendar and be there for the releases and the CEO's press conference as if you owned the entire business.

The only adjustment to the value comes from major changes in the fundamentals of the business or the economy. For example, by late 2006, Whole Foods had been growing its business for a decade at 19 percent to 20 percent a year.* Then the CEO, John Mackey, announced the company would grow at about 12 percent per year because of major competition from the big chains. That's a 40 percent drop in earnings and a corresponding big drop in the multiple of earnings—from 40 down to 24. This represented a sea change in the entire valuation analysis. That one announcement dropped WFMI's value by two-thirds overnight. The stock dropped from the mid-$60s to the mid-$40s and continued falling to $8 before rebounding back to its recalculated Sticker Price. For a full analysis of Whole Foods, go to PaybackTimeBook.com.

GET UP CLOSE AND PERSONAL

Tip: For extra credit, and only if you have the time, you can really boost your understanding of an industry by going to one of its big annual conventions. These usually take place in a convention center and are attended by every business remotely connected with its industry. Many of these businesses will set up booths ranging in sophistication from a simple table with

(continued on next page)

---

*If you read my first book, then you know that I extolled the virtues of Whole Foods in it and used it as a prime example of a wonderful company. What happened to Whole Foods in the years since that publication is a clear lesson on keeping your pulse on what's going on and reevaluating the business and its industry routinely.

brochures to a mock building full of sophisticated technology. Wear your running shoes. You'll walk miles. Bring a big empty suitcase. You'll be taking home pounds of materials. And bring your questions. You'll have a chance to interview every single serious competitor of your business at its booth. There is no better place to get the competition's view of a business than direct from the company at its booth. Bring a business card that identifies you as a potential customer. Again, this is extra credit. Mr. Buffett does not do this. Neither do I.

If you can't take the time to keep up with the business on at least a quarterly basis, then you need to reexamine your reasons for buying stock in that business. Managing your own money means taking responsibility away from someone else and embracing that responsibility yourself. This is a rubber-meets-the-road issue. You can't expect great returns without checking in with your businesses on a regular basis. A little homework is all that separates the successful investors from the wannabes.

WAITING FOR MICROSOFT

I've watched Microsoft for many years, waiting patiently for it to get to a MOS price. Every time it gets to what I'd consider a retail value, Microsoft starts buying and the price stabilizes. This makes a lot of sense for Microsoft. It can't find a place to put all its cash. It's declaring dividends and giving the excess cash to the owners. But if it can buy the stock at a price that represents a 15 percent compounded return, that's like investing the same money in something that produces a 15 percent ROIC without all the trouble of doing the business. Microsoft's CFO is very good at this, and as a result, it has been impossible to buy Microsoft on sale. In March 2009, I had MSFT valued at $21. The price was $15, just below the 80 percent MOS. The Payback Time was six years. It had a Payback Time with zero growth of nine years. This was the first time in forever that MSFT had been close to buyable. Yes, it's a tech stock, but nine years? I was so tempted. Except I use Apple, so I didn't pull the trigger and buy it. By October, it was at $26. And I said these words: "I knew it!" These are words every investor must get used to saying. Go practice in front of the mirror. For more about tech stocks, see my website.

Okay. You've been patient, you've done your homework, you've adjusted the price for any major changes in the fundamentals. Now your business is *finally* on sale. Now whatchagonnado?

STEP FOUR: BUY IT

When the price is where you want it, you buy it.

Decide how much of your available capital you want in this one business. While the mega-rich usually make their money by focusing on one business, they're usually insiders who have a great deal to do with the long-term success of that business. We want to have some diversification but not much. As you'll see in Step Five, there's a lot to keep up with when you own a business. The more businesses you own, the more you have to do to stay informed. If you have too many, you'll start to make mistakes and lose money because you aren't on top of things.

The right number of businesses for you depends on how much time you have to keep up with the business and how much money you have to invest. With a small amount of capital, you can own more than one business, but I don't encourage you to do so. If you're stockpiling several businesses with a small amount of capital, the commissions on your purchases are going to be a significant expense. You need at least

$10,000 to begin to diversify, and I'd recommend you wait until you have $20,000 before you actually buy the second business.

To put this into perspective, the investor who runs GEICO's $2 billion fund owns eight stocks. Warren Buffett and Charlie Munger said that in the early days, when they were only working with a few hundred million, they would buy five stocks, with their biggest position being about 25 percent in one. The author of *The Little Book That Beats the Market,* Joel Greenblatt, boasts a ten-year 50 percent compounded rate of return on several billion dollars and, last time I checked his portfolio, owns two stocks. Eddie Lampert, with a multibillion-dollar portfolio at ESL Investments, has a 29 percent twenty-year compounded return and owns eight stocks. Great investors focus. You should, too.

Capital	Number of businesses	% of capital allocated to each initial buy
$1,000 – $20,000	1	25%
$20,000 – $40,000	2	25%
$40,000 – $70,000	3	25%
$70,000 – $100,000	4	25%
$100,000 – $100,000,000	5	25%

This chart shows the amount of capital you should have before you move to the next business. The third column is the percentage of your total capital you expect to invest in your *initial* buy of that business. For example, if you have $10,000 you want to invest in a business, your initial buy will be with about $2,500. If you have $10,000 right now and expect to add from an outside source of capital $1,000 a month to your capital for the next year, I'd up the initial Buy-In to $4,000 and then be ready to stockpile with the balance plus the new capital coming in. More on that in Step Six.

STEP FIVE: OWN IT

Owning your business is just like watching your targets, except more so. You now have skin in the game. Now you're going to have to deal with the *emotions* of ownership. In *Rule #1* I talked about something called ERI — the Emotional Rule of Investing.

ERI: If you buy this business, immediately after you buy it, the price will go down, down, down. But if you don't buy it, the price will go up, up, up until you do buy it, at which time the price will then go down, down, down.

But now we know another way to deal with the emotions of a stock price dropping after we buy: We stockpile it. As stockpilers we want the price to go down, right? The further the better, as long as the fundamentals haven't changed.

In *Rule #1* I also wrote this:

You bought a business and the price started going down the day after you bought it. And it is still going down with no sign of relenting. In case you've never experienced this, investors who have tell me this is not fun. (Okay, I admit I've goofed and experienced it, too.) One way to deal with this is to say to yourself that even though the stock has gone down in price, as long as you don't sell it you haven't really lost any money. In other words, we'll just pretend we're not losing money and, therefore, not violating Rule #1. Right? Wrong. Big-time wrong. Escaping-from-reality wrong.

And in fact, if you're trading, you're losing money as the trade goes against you. Traders want the stock to go in the direction they expect it to go in, and if it doesn't it's an emotional trauma. But again, if

At a minimum, do the following six things to keep up with your business:

1. Attend quarterly teleconferences with the CEO and analysts.
2. Read quarterly SEC filings (10-Q and 10-K).
3. Read the annual report, including the chairman's letter.
4. Read the news about your company.
5. Keep up on the top competition.
6. Read the industry trades.

Go to my website at PaybackTimeBook.com for more information about these six homework assignments.

you're stockpiling, you're making money hand over fist as the stock price goes down, down, down, and you're having a blast.

Still, the thought can lurk, "What if I got it wrong?" It will occur to you that a lot of very smart Harvard and Cornell types think you're wrong, because they're selling and driving down the price. And what if they're right and you aren't? You might think, "And I'm buying? I must be nuts."

If you have that thought, you're having it because you're not sure of the value of the business you bought. If you know the business's value is $50 and the price is going down like a brick, this is the same as knowing someone's selling you a $10 bill for $5, then $4, then $3 . . . If I'm selling you that $10 bill, you won't give a damn where I got my degree or how smart I think I am. If you know the value of the $10, you're going to buy up all the bills you can at $3.

And there is another reason to not be too concerned about what the Harvard boys are doing: They follow the crowd. They have to. They cannot hold something that's going down in price. It's going to make them look bad to their investors and then they will lose their investors and then they will lose their jobs. These guys are very bright, but they have a different drummer to dance to. They're in the business of keeping their clients and gathering more assets to manage. You're in the business of making a lot of money. These two businesses can dictate very different responses to a market situation.

Today's market affords us a great time to find wonderful businesses on sale. But they aren't *all* on sale by any means. Lots of fund managers, though, do talk as if everything is on sale. They're shouting that this is a great time to buy their fund so they can buy up a whole bunch of Coca-Cola and J&J and Wal-Mart (i.e., the "recession"-type stocks). But guess what? Those stocks have already been bought up by other fund managers, so they aren't on sale at all. In fact, if the analysts are right about the next five years, there is no way you'll make a 15 percent return in any of them. By Rule #1 standards they are all at or above their retail value. And this is what the "smart" boys are buying. Because the other "smart" boys are buying, too. It's a game we don't play.

Do not be afraid of going against the guys from Harvard. They're playing a very different game than you. They know their game well. You learn yours. Rule #1 and stockpiling are made for the small investor who has no one to answer to but himself and his family. And the more you do this, the more confidence you'll have that you are every bit as qualified to invest your own money as any Harvard guy. And don't forget who lost half the money in your 401(k). That's right. The Harvard guy. Or someone darn near like him.

You own it. You watch it. And you just wait for it to drop so you can add more.

STEP SIX: STOCKPILE IT

Now you own your business and you watch it and you look for the opportunity to snap up more of it at a great price. You're adjusting price for major fundamental changes in the business and the industry. And you are patient. You've only put in about 25 percent of the total capital you want to invest in this business. You want to buy more. You're ready to stockpile it. You just need the price to go down.

Our partner, Mr. Market, gets to set the price. He doesn't care if we buy or sell. He'll take the other side of the trade. The thing we have to remember about Mr. Market is that he operates on fear and greed. The more the news is bad, the more fear he feels, the more he's afraid he'll get stuck with a bunch of bad businesses, so he drops the price. You *must* know your business well enough so that when Mr. Market becomes very fearful and begins dropping the price, you *know he is wrong* to be afraid. And so you buy.

You entered the business with a Buy-In of 25 percent of the capital allocated to this business. Your next purchase will be for the same amount as the first investment. Your third purchase will be for another 25 percent. The last 25 percent allocation is yours to split up however you want. You can go the whole 25 percent and be done; or if the stock seems to want to keep sliding, you can split up the last allocation and buy in pieces. Just keep the pieces big enough that the commission isn't an issue — $2,500 or larger.

Beware: If you buy $500 worth of a business and
pay a $10 brokerage commission, the commission
represents 2 percent of your investment. That's a lot.
Avoid purchases where the commission is a significant
chunk (i.e., 1 percent or better) of the purchase.

Whatever your initial Stockpile Price was — from 20 percent off the value for experienced stockpilers to 50 percent or more off the value for novices — it's going to have to stay at or below your MOS to stockpile and it's going to have to stay below a ten-year Payback Time.

Although you want to get all of the capital you allocated to this business into the business, if you bought in at a 20 percent discount off the value, try to wait for an opportunity to buy the next allocation at 30 percent off value, the next at 40 percent off value, and the last at 50 percent off value. If the price continues down with no changes to fundamentals, then scrape together more capital and stockpile as much of this business as you can.

If you made the Buy-In at 50 percent off value, you can continue to stockpile at or below that price.

Buy-In % below value	2nd allocation	3rd allocation	4th allocation
20%	30%	40%	50%
30%	40%	50%	50%
40%	50%	50%	50%
50%	50%	50%	50%

Of course, this isn't a science. You can get your allocation of capital invested any way you want, as long as you follow the rules of price and value. What this sort of discipline does for you is increase your compounded rate of return in that investment. On one hand, we don't expect to get many opportunities to buy wonderful businesses when they are on sale. On the other hand, we want to try to maximize our return when we do get the opportunity. As you saw in Chapter 1, the compounded rate of return skyrockets when you get to stockpile at every dropping price. Once again, an example with a $10 bill says it all:

If I sell you $10 of value (in the form of a $10 bill in this case) for $8 and you buy one, you have a nice 25 percent return with no risk and you made $2. If I sell you a second bill for $7, your return goes up to 33 percent and you made $5. Buy a third bill for $6 and your return goes up to 43 percent and you've made a profit of $9. Buy a fourth bill for $5 and your return goes up to 54 percent and your profit is $14. Buying these bills at every dropping price changed your rate of return from 25 percent to 54 percent and your dollar return from $2 to $14, a 700 percent increase. And that is what we're after.

It takes discipline to buy like this. You're going to miss getting allocations into your business if you wait for the price to drop and it doesn't, but when it does, you reap the rewards big-time. In the next chapter I'll show you a very cool way to know when to do your buying, called FACs.

And don't forget that you own a business that can change. If the fundamentals change, so does the value — and it can change a lot with just a small change in growth rates. Keep doing your homework as if you own the whole thing. It's the only way you'll ever make enough money to retire.

If Mr. Market goes crazy in the other direction, gets completely greedy, and prices your business higher and higher because he's afraid you're going to try to buy more and he doesn't want to sell it, then it might be time for you to take the next step.

STEP SEVEN: SELL IT

"The best time to sell a wonderful business is never." When Mr. Buffett said that he said it from the perspective of one who owns the entire business and therefore gets to keep or invest the cash flow. We don't sit in that chair. While the best time to sell may be never, for us little guys selling is inevitable. That being the case, there are three times to sell.

1. *Sell when you need the money.* Someday you'll need money and you'll have to sell some or all of your wonderful businesses. I hope that on that day you have many choices of what to sell and the selling hardly puts a dent in your net worth. Try to plan for that day. It would be a shame to have to sell, as many do today, right when Mr. Market has decided he's terrified and wants to sell everything. It's tough to ride something down 40 percent in six months and then have to sell it. If you do a good job of financial planning, you should be able to forecast when you'll need cash from the businesses you stockpiled. Sell the ones that have the highest prices relative to their value.

2. *Sell when the fundamentals change for the worse.* Sometimes

wonderful businesses become not wonderful. They might have had a Moat for a hundred years and then it's gone because of some kind of technological revolution. Think of how the horse business got whacked by the automobile. It didn't happen overnight but it happened, and people in the horse business who kept stockpiling horse businesses got smoked. The smart investors were selling out, because they were keeping track of trends in their industry and they saw the automobile coming at them from miles away. Be on top of the fundamentals of the business and industry. If you see any of the Big Five slipping, be on guard. Find out why. Particularly if ROIC slips. That's a huge red flag. If equity is getting eaten up by the business, that's a red flag. And Cash Flow is critical. Hey, the Big Five are all critical. That's why I call them the Big Five. Watch them all. They were the canary in the coal mine for me with GM years before the collapse. And watch debt. If the CEO is loading up the debt, that's a big red flag. Find out why. If you don't understand it, then this business is no longer something you understand and that means it violates one or more of the four Ms and it's time to get out. If you wouldn't buy it at any price, don't own it.

3. *Sell when the price vastly exceeds the Sticker Price (retail value).* When we start buying shares of a business, we try to buy at a low price. We're buyers. We want a deal. When we sell, we want a full price so we hold on until the price exceeds the Sticker Price by 20 percent and then sell it. Chances are, Mr. Market's euphoric greed won't last and you'll be able to buy the business back from him at a discount within a year or two.

STEP EIGHT: REPEAT UNTIL RICH

And all you need to do that is mo' money, mo' money. And in Chapter 8, I'm going to show you how to use a specific type of investment account I call a "Berky" to gather capital to invest.

There's a way to use technical analyses to determine what a stock price is likely to do in the near term. Obviously there's nothing scientific about using technical analysis, but people's psychology is remarkably predictable and we can use that fact to help decide if we should make our next Buy-In now or wait awhile. I call this technical concept "getting the FACs."

TAKEAWAYS AND ACTION ITEMS

Stockpiling maximizes your long-term returns when the near-term prices fall, turning down into up. It is prices falling below calculated MOS that create BIG Money opportunities.

To consistently turn down into up, follow the eight baby steps to wealth.

1. Find it: Screen the market for prospects. Are there any red flags?
2. Value it: Is the Payback Time good?
3. Watch it: Create watch lists. Use the tools available on my website at **PaybackTimeBook.com** to monitor your candidates.
4. Buy it: Focus! Don't buy more businesses than you can understand and manage.
5. Own it: Act like an owner. Track performance by—at minimum—attending quarterly company teleconferences and reviewing the company's public reports.
6. Stockpile it: Continue to buy at or below your MOS/Payback Time Price whenever you have the money. Don't buy in amounts so small that commissions affect returns.
7. Sell it: Sell if the Big Five numbers worsen significantly, or when price exceeds 20 percent of the sticker price, or if you need the money.
8. **Repeat until you are rich!**

JUST the FACs, MA'AM

Shallow men believe in luck. Strong men believe in cause and effect.
— RALPH WALDO EMERSON

While it sounds simple enough to say we begin buying our target business whenever we have a Margin of Safety (MOS) price, in practice we run into a practical problem: If we buy every day we have a MOS price, we'll quickly use up the capital we've allocated to stockpiling this business, thus missing out on future price drops and the chance at compounding. But if we don't just buy every day until the money is gone, how do we know when to stockpile more once we've made the initial purchase? We can stockpile over extended time periods using one of the following two methods: Monthly Allocation of Capital (MAC) or Floors and Ceilings (FAC).

MONTHLY ALLOCATION OF CAPITAL (MAC)

Once we've bought in with, say, 25 percent of our allocated capital, we could make the fifth of every month "Stockpiling Day" and buy another 25 percent of our allocation that day each month thereafter *if the price is lower than the Stockpiling Price.* I call this method MAC. But remember: you buy only when you have a Stockpiling Price, not every time you have capital to allocate. If the price isn't right, you wait for the next month.

Let's assume we're adding $1,000 a month to our account to allocate to stockpiling a particular business that has passed all four M tests. After six months, we'll have all of our initial $10,000 invested (assuming Mr. Market cooperates and keeps the price low), as well as $5,000 of new capital. As new capital comes into our account from any source, we'll save it and invest it in similar-size increments using the MAC Stockpiling method. Here's how that looks in a chart:

MONTHLY ALLOCATION OF CAPITAL METHOD (MAC)					
Stockpile Date	Old Capital	New Capital	Beginning of Month Total Capital	Stockpile $	End of Month Total Capital
5-Jan	$9,000	$1,000	$10,000	$2,500	$7,500
5-Feb	$7,500	$1,000	$8,500	$2,500	$6,000
5-Mar	$6,000	$1,000	$7,000	$2,500	$4,500
5-Apr	$4,500	$1,000	$5,500	$2,500	$3,000
5-May	$3,000	$1,000	$4,000	$2,500	$1,500
5-Jun	$1,500	$1,000	$2,500	$2,500	$0
5-Jul	$0	$1,000	$1,000		$1,000
5-Aug	$1,000	$1,000	$2,000		$2,000
5-Sep	$2,000	$1,000	$3,000	$2,500	$500
5-Oct	$500	$1,000	$1,500		$1,500
5-Nov	$1,500	$1,000	$2,500	$2,500	$0
5-Dec	$0	$1,000	$1,000		$1,000

The MAC Stockpiling method works best if you have a small amount of capital to start with and are adding to it in regular increments as in the above example. Its main strength is that it requires no particular strategy about when to stockpile. You stockpile when you have a Stockpiling Price and enough cash in the account to match your previous investment amounts (e.g., if you put $2,500 toward a business you're stockpiling last month, then you'll buy $2,500 worth of it again this month if the price is still right).

The MAC method is great for taking the guesswork out of stockpiling. You just stockpile mechanically whenever you have the capital and the price is right. If the Stockpile Price is $50 and the actual price is fluctuating between $25 and $50, you don't have to deal with ERI: If you wait and hope the price goes down, according to the Emotional Rule of Investing, the price will go up. On the other hand, if you guess that it will go up and so you buy, the Emotional Rule of Investing states that during the next two weeks the price will go down and you won't have the funds with which to stockpile it. MAC preserves your fragile emotions. If you're using the MAC method and on the fifth of the month you buy at $50 and by the fifteenth the stock is at $25, you tell yourself that next month you'll get to buy at $25. If by the fifth of the next month, when it's time to buy, the stock is at $60, well, you just tell yourself it will all even out in the long run.

EMOTIONAL RULE OF INVESTING

Remember, ERI stands for my Emotional Rule of Investing: If you buy a piece of a business, the price will go down immediately after you buy it. But if you don't buy it, the price will go up, up, up until you do buy it ... at which time the price will then go down, down, down.

Here's the obvious problem with the MAC method of stockpiling: It's the fifth of the month and the price is below the MOS price but it's dropping like a brick with no let-up in sight. You buy on the MAC schedule and then watch the price drop by 30 percent. You realize if you'd waited you could have stockpiled at a much better price. But how would you have known the price was going to continue to go down? There's a method of timing your purchases based on the overall movement of the stock's price that I call FACs, short for Floors and Ceilings.

FLOORS AND CEILINGS (FACs)

The Floors and Ceilings (FACs) Stockpiling method uses repetitive patterns in the price of a stock to predict the future direction of price.

While it isn't quite as subjective as seeing lions in the stars or bunnies in the clouds, not everyone will agree that a certain Floor or Ceiling exists. In other words, FACs aren't an objective method as a MAC is. On the other hand, FACs are a lot more useful. FACs are a big help in getting the timing right to stockpile at big discounts to the MOS Price.

FACs are based on the experience that the Big Guys — the fund managers controlling billions in the market — get certain price targets stuck in their heads. FACs are purely psychological. But even so, they are very real. If a Big Guy has it in his head that he's going to buy at $75 the very next time the stock hits that price because the price bounced off that price and went up two times before, then, to that trader, $75 is as real a floor on the price as if it were made out of granite.

Look at any chart that tracks prices of a particular stock. You'll notice stock prices never go up for long before changing direction and heading back down at least a bit. Even in "straight-up" bull markets in a stock, there are regular times when the stock goes down for a short time before resuming its upward path. The authentic Wall Street gibberish for these times includes "pullbacks," "retrenchments," and "corrections."

The reason for these regular pullbacks is built into the psyche and emotions of the investors who control the price of any stock— the infamous Big Guys. They get, in a word, scared (or greedy). If a stock's price is headed up, the Big Guys who own it eventually begin to worry it's maybe peaked. They know how far it traveled in both price and time the last time it ran up, and that information plays into their trading psychology. Since it takes Big Guys weeks to get all the way out, they have to anticipate a mass exit. To do so, they start to sell. Selling also lets them take profits. There is a saying among mutual fund managers that nobody ever went broke taking a profit. Taking a profit protects the fund manager from criticism for staying in too long, and the profit helps their portfolio's rate of return.

But if, after they start selling, the price stops going down, they get their mojo back and buy back in. This starts another run-up.

The FACs Stockpiling method calls a recurring price level a "Floor," as in, if you're falling you'll stop falling when you get to the floor. When the price repeatedly bounces up off that price and doesn't break down through it, we know we're at a Floor. The more often it bounces off, the stronger the Floor.

There's also a name for the price point where the stock price stops rising and either heads down or stays put for a while. The FAC method calls that recurring price level a "Ceiling," as in "you can't get past the ceiling."

When the price finally breaks through the Ceiling and moves up, the Ceiling often becomes the Floor. Just as in a high-rise apartment, your ceiling is your upstairs neighbor's floor and your floor is your downstairs neighbor's ceiling.

And just like that, a stock price seems to move in somewhat consistent steps from Floor to Ceiling. Then it breaks through and moves on, or it can eventually return and drop down to test the old Ceiling to see if it's really become a Floor.

On a chart that shows a business's changing stock price over time, Floors and Ceilings are represented by (imaginary) horizontal lines where the price stops and reverses direction. They are formed by recurring reversals at a specific price. We'll be taking a look at these shortly so you see exactly what I mean.

There is one more thing to look at: the Trend. The Trend is the general direction of the price over a relatively long period of time. Trend lines are drawn at the top and the bottom of the jagged lines created by price swings within the Trend. The top prices of the diagonal trend form an imaginary Resistance on the price-timeline chart, and the bottom prices of the diagonal trend form an imaginary Support on the same chart. These lines are different from Floors and Ceilings because they're diagonal, not horizontal, but they're used the same way as Floors and Ceilings: to predict where the price will reverse itself. We could call these price levels Floors and Ceilings, too. But it helps me to think of them differently. Trend lines are imaginary diagonal lines that form over a long time. Floor and Ceiling lines are imaginary horizontal lines that form over a short time.

Floors and Ceilings and Trends can help us determine a better time to stockpile our business than the robot-like purchases of the MAC method. They help us pick our Stockpile Price and maximize our returns.

Let's take a look at Burlington Northern (BNI), for example (see graph below).

BNI's Trend, Floor, and Ceilings

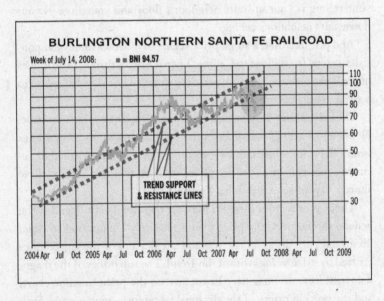

The bottom dashed upward line is the Support Line of this Trend. The top dashed line is called the Resistance Line. These lines do not appear on Yahoo! or MSN charts. I drew them. I just looked at the graph and saw there was a consistent Trend produced by Support and Resistance and drew the black diagonal dashed lines. You can see there is a long Support Line. The more often the price touches it and bounces off, the more solid the Support Line grows. From early 2004 until July 2007, the Trend was consistently upward on that Support Line. That Trend would have been well established by July 2005 because of the many times the price bumped against the Support Line from March 2004 until September 2004. I'm sure, given how clear this Support Line was, that traders were making trades using this Support Line from July 2004 onward. Each time the stock price came down from a previous high point, it "bounced off" the Support Line. It took a nice bounce in July 2004, and then moved on to a new high. Then a series of bounces off the Support Line happened in August and September 2006, and again in January 2007, and one last time in July 2007. That was a heck of a Support Line on an upward-trending stock. Traders can make a lot of money on a Support Line like this one, betting the price will bounce up off it over and over again.

I circled the point (see graph on page 170) where the three-year Support Line was broken for the first time — July 2007 at $90. That was the end of the Support for the Trend, and so the end of the Trend. From that point onward, anything could happen. It could have gone up or down from there. But often the end of a long Trend signals the beginning of a new Trend in the other direction . . . or the beginning of a Ceiling.

In the graph on page 172, the top dotted horizontal line (#3) is a Ceiling Line. The Ceiling for BNI here was created by traders recognizing that a long Trend was broken at the $90 price point. The Ceiling begins in July after the $90 Support Line (#1) is broken (#2). Price points like this can become a kind of psychological barrier. Whenever the price gets near the $90 Ceiling, traders can get nervous and start to sell off. It has nothing to do with rationality. It's just a sophisticated form of guessing, but if enough Big Guys are guessing the same way, the guesses turn out right over and over. After a few

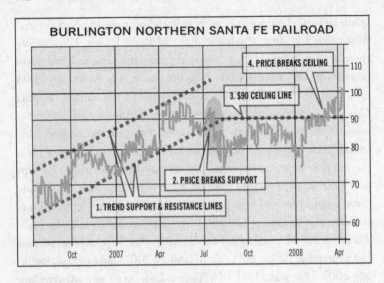

tests, the Big Guys get it in their heads that $90 is like the third rail. If you buy at $90 you get fried, so don't touch it. When that happens, $90 becomes a Ceiling. By October, when the price reached the Ceiling, there were no buyers. Just sellers. In this case, the BNI stock price was swinging between $75 and $90 a share from July 2007 to March 2008.

A big event can break a price through a Ceiling. In this case, the big event in late March, early April 2008 was the news of Warren Buffett's yearlong purchases of BNI. Mr. Buffett used this psychological barrier, this Ceiling, as an opportunity to buy without sending the market into a buying frenzy.

Mr. Buffett began buying at $79 and kept buying right through $84, and the whole time he was buying 10 percent of the business, the price stayed under the Ceiling. Finally the news in March 2008 that Mr. Buffett was in BNI big-time overcame the third-rail psychology and the stock price broke through the $90 Ceiling and started to run up (#4).

As the price broke through the Ceiling, we naturally wanted to know how far it was going to go before it stopped going up. Notice that from September 2006, when the price was at $66, to October 2006, when it hit $80 and dropped back, the price moved the distance from bottom to top in about two months, and the price increased about $14. The next run-up started in January 2007 at $74. Back then, if we were to calculate the distance it might run up before it stalled, we would have estimated that it would run about two months, like the previous time, and, according to our Support and Resistance Lines, the new high would peak around $90 two months later in March. What actually happened was that the price peaked at $86 in March and then headed back down. That was pretty close to our educated guess. The next run-up started at the Support Price of $78 in April 2007, and again, we'd estimated about a two-month run-up to Resistance at $95. And that's what happened. This repeated pattern told us that BNI traders were psychologically tuned to about two months of upward price moves and a price change of $12 to $17. So we

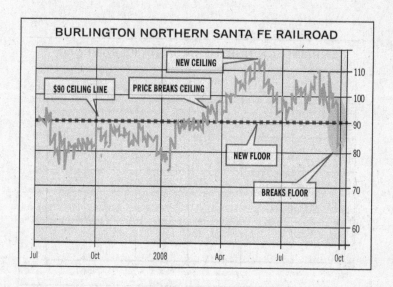

expected something like that for the next breakout. That's why, as the price went through the $90 Ceiling, the Big Guy traders began to think about $102 to $107 as a top. As you can see in the graph on page 173, it made it to $112, which then became the new Ceiling. Then the price came down fast, hit $90, and bounced. The old $90 Ceiling had become the new $90 Floor.

The $90 Floor held, as did a $112 Ceiling, for a total of six months. Then in October, the price broke through the $90 Floor and headed down.

In this final picture, we can see the FACs that BNI made on its price journey from 2004 to 2009, including the big price drop through the $75 Floor. As the stock market crashed in late 2008, the price of BNI also crashed down through our MOS Price of $72. As it went through $72, the FACs kicked in and, given previous distances between Support and Resistance, we could see the price was likely to fall to about $60. As it bounced off $60, it was time to buy. Then (and again I know this sounds cruel) we waited and hoped for another big drop.

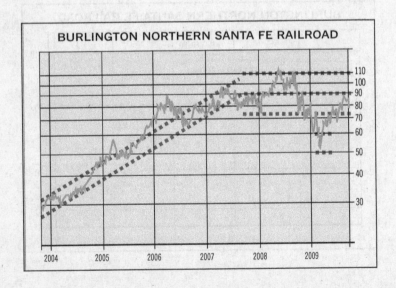

The price bounced off $60 in January 2009, climbed up from $14 to $74 in a bit less than two months, and then plummeted through the $60 Floor. Where was it going? Probably down the next step to $50, right? In fact, it went down to $51, started up, and that triggered another buy.

This is the power of having the FACs. Without the FACs, we have only value and price to determine when to buy. We would buy as soon as the price hit our MOS of $72 and, using the MAC method, buy more in a month. But with FACs, we can pick a Stockpile Price and not be worried we're going to miss buying at a good price by trying to wait to buy at a great price. We can see the great price coming and wait for it with a good deal of confidence.

As FACs form up, we'll sit tight and let the price test the Ceiling. If it bounces off the Ceiling, we can hope it will break down hard enough to blow through the Floor. And if it does, then we look back at previous price ranges and times and we'll have an educated guess about how long and at what price to expect that Floor to stop the price drop. If it cracks our expected Floor, then we just set a new Stockpile Price at the new expected Floor. Obviously, a general market meltdown is a big help, and a general market meltdown isn't at all impossible in these times. Hey, we can only hope.

I know that sounds cruel. I don't mean that in a mean-spirited way. I feel a lot of empathy for all of the mutual fund folks who are getting hurt in this market. I'm writing this book to help them. It's never too late to learn and to change. You can learn to buy businesses, and when you do, won't you also want to buy them as cheaply as you can? Don't feel bad about it. Consider what would happen if no one was willing to buy. The panic would become general. Stockpilers perform a valuable service for all the rest of the fund managers and ignorant investors who are panicking out of great companies. We give them someone to sell to. For them, a down price means their returns go down. For us, a down price means our compounded returns go up. Down is up for stockpilers. Anyone who is willing to learn can join us.

HOW TO DETERMINE FLOORS AND CEILINGS

The bad news is that you are not going to learn to determine FACs and Trends from this book or from any other book any more than you can learn to fly a plane by reading about flying in a book. You have to actually go fly the plane and get the feel of it for real. And it might be a good idea to have a qualified instructor on board when you give it a shot. You'll learn faster and without any pain.

The good news is now that you've read about the FACs, they are available for you to play with on your own. But won't you get burned on your own? Well, no. If you've done your four M homework and know your stuff, you'll stockpile only when you have a nice Margin of Safety. Using FACs to determine the time to stockpile can't hurt you. Even if you don't get the FACs right, it's not a problem, because you're not *trading* on the FACs—you're *stockpiling* on the FACs. As long as you're buying at or below your Stockpiling Price, you're going to be fine. Using the FACs correctly is icing on the cake, not the cake itself. You can't mess up stockpiling your target business if you have the four Ms right. Just know that it's a wonderful business and it's on sale. Everything after that, especially the FACs, is just there to help maximize and accelerate your overall rate of return.

That said, here are a few tips about how to read a chart and spot the FACs and Trends:

1. **The more often the stock price bounces off of the Floor or Ceiling, the stronger the Floor or Ceiling becomes.** You can use the FACs for any time period, from one minute to decades. Psychology is psychology. It doesn't change whether you are day-trading FACs that last eighteen minutes or you are a long-term investor on an eighteen-year hold. The psychology is the same.

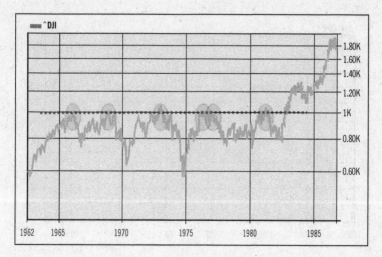

Here's the Dow Jones Industrial Average index for eighteen years from the mid-1960s to the early 1980s (see graph above). Notice that the Ceiling price of 1,000 got into the Big Guys' heads and became a third rail. Nobody wanted to touch it. Whenever the price got up there, the Big Guys unloaded. The price hit 1,000 at least once in twenty-two different months and bounced off every time. That sets a price in stone in the Big Guys' heads and makes for a self-fulfilling prophecy.

At the top of page 178 is a graph of the Dow Jones Industrial Average since 1996. You can see a very solid Floor at about 7,300. The market price punched through that line on February 23, 2009, and technical traders, who would have expected a significant drop in the Dow, sold it off all the way down to below 6,600.

Now let's look at Cognizant Technology (CTSH, a software company that trades on the Nasdaq). As you can see from the graph on the bottom of page 178, CTSH has a very strong Trend Support line from October 2005 to May 2007.

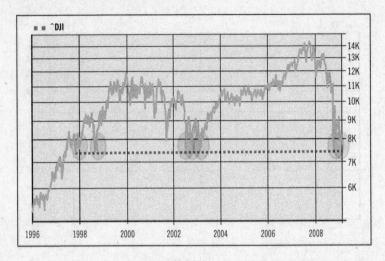

You can bet the Big Guys were watching that diagonal line and trading on it. The price bounced off that diagonal Support Line many times, dozens of times, and all those bounces created a very strong psychological price Trend. But when the price broke through Support, it broke down hard from $45 to $38 in a few weeks, down 16 percent.

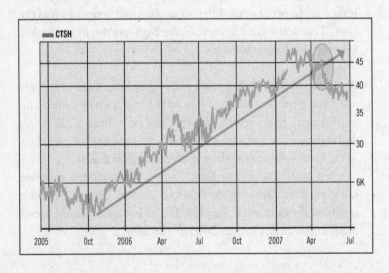

2. **To determine how far the price will climb from the new Floor to reach the next Ceiling, look at the distance between the last Floor and the last Ceiling.** Another look at CTSH (see graph below) shows the distance between Support and Resistance in this Trend was very consistent. It averaged about $5 from bottom to top. That would be a useful number if we were stockpiling this on the way up. We'd be able to get a lower average stockpiling price and therefore increase our compounded rate of return.

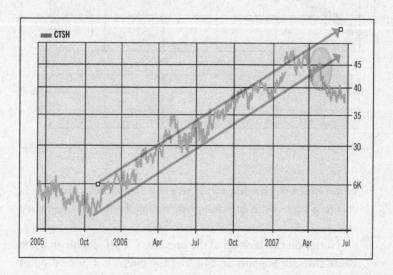

3. **A price move of over 3 percent above the Ceiling or below the Floor, accompanied by 150 percent of the average daily volume, is a significant sign of a breakout that will last.** The "average daily volume" refers to the average number of shares that trade over the last three months; it's represented by the mountains and valleys at the bottom of this chart (see graph on page 180). Since the volume of shares being traded is significant information for many traders, volume is automatically shown on most charts. The higher (taller) the mountain, the greater the vol-

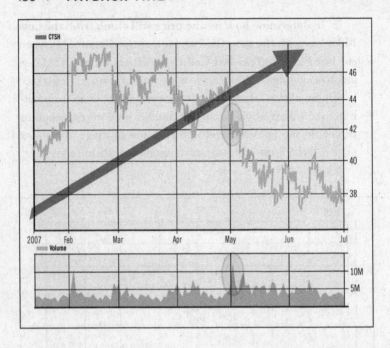

ume. One of the hardest things to know is whether a breakout is real or a fake-out. A big change in volume helps us to know it's real.

Notice on this blowup of the previous CTSH graphic that the break through Support at $44 (the top circle) is a price drop of over 3 percent and is accompanied by a big volume increase (the bottom circle) of double the daily average—from an average of about 5 million shares to over 10 million shares. This is a classic breakout and it was followed by a long price drop.

These three suggestions will give you a starting point for learning how to use FACs. They aren't magic but they do help you with finding an answer to the question "When should I buy more?" The more you use FACs, the more comfortable you'll be with them. Eventually you'll get to where you can look at a chart and the FACs just appear. Keep playing with the FACs and you'll get to where you can maximize your stockpiling returns by buying at the right time or near to it.

That said, having a good instructor will speed up the learning curve for you. For information about finding a qualified instructor, go to PaybackTimeBook.com.

Now let's put this all together and see how our old friends from *Rule #1,* the Connellys, are handling stockpiling.

TAKEAWAYS AND ACTION ITEMS

The Floors and Ceilings (FACs) are predictable patterns in the price charts that show you the appropriate time to buy and sell. You can stockpile any time the price is below the MOS/Payback Time price, but buying on the FACs will help you buy at the best possible price. Being patient and stockpiling near the floor price will maximize your long-term investment returns.

- Be patient. You can invest monthly allocations of capital (MAC) when price is below MOS, but using the FACs is better.
- To increase your rate of return, use the FACs and stockpile during short-term floors.
- Review my must-read posts at **PaybackTimeBook.com** to find out more about the technical tools that can help you apply the FACs method.

A TALE of ONE FAMILY

It was the best of times, it was the worst of times.
      — CHARLES DICKENS, *A TALE OF TWO CITIES*

A t this point in the book you probably have a pretty good idea that you must invest your own money or risk financial failure and economic distress. You've learned how to find a wonderful business (or perhaps a few) you would like to own—one that has Meaning to you, a big and durable Moat, and Management you trust. And you know how to find a Margin of Safety price by doing a Rule #1 valuation. You also know when, if you owned the whole thing, you would have your money back in your pocket from earnings—the Payback Time.

You've learned that if you want to be rich, you do what the richest people in America have always done—buy into the business and stockpile it whenever the price goes *down*. You've learned from the best investors and most successful people that investing is completely the opposite of what it is for everyone else. For the rich (and I hope, now, for you) a volatile market presents an opportunity to see your returns skyrocket.

Will you have the courage to swim against the mainstream? Will you be able to buy when Mr. Market is fearful and sell when Mr. Market is greedy?

Twice in the last few years the stock market has proven it can collapse. And now you and millions of other mutual fund investors and stock market novices are at a financial crossroads. Whatever way you go now will completely determine your financial future. If this market continues in this way for the next ten years, will you continue down the accepted but fruitless path, or will you change direction and try a new road? This is a very big question and a very important decision. To quote Robert Frost in his famous *The Road Not Taken*:

> *Two roads diverged in a wood, and I—*
> *I took the one less traveled by . . .*
> *And that has made all the difference.*

Let me walk you down both roads in the hope of helping you decide.

MEET SUSAN AND DOUG (AGAIN)

In my first book, I introduced you to a couple who represent many people looking for financial independence, Susan and Doug Connelly. Their goal was to retire well by 2023—about fifteen years from now. They are middle-aged and have a combined income of about $80,000 a year. They're looking for at least $4,000 a month in 2009 dollars from investments by the time they reach retirement age. They recognize it will take about $2.6 million to get that from passive investments by the year 2023. In other words, they need to come up with $2.6 million by the time they are ready to retire if they want to live well in their retirement years.

They started investing on their own with $20,000 in 2003, because they were afraid to leave their money with fund managers in a market that might produce a 0 percent rate of return for the next twenty years or even crash. One alternative to letting fund managers lose their money was to play it safe and put their savings in a Treasury

bond, but they believed inflation would make this fixed-income scenario a nightmare. A second alternative was to speculate on real estate, oil, or gold, but neither was comfortable with the gamble. With
those two extremes staring them in the face, it wasn't a difficult decision to take the middle road, learn Rule #1, and start investing wisely
on their own.

They did the 3-Circles exercise and determined that they should
learn the restaurant business. Soon they went through the four M
analysis on a number of restaurant companies and settled on buying
into The Cheesecake Factory (CAKE). CAKE's Big Five Numbers
were excellent and consistent, pointing to a Brand Moat. Debt was
zero. They loved David Overton, the founder and CEO. And they felt
they understood the restaurant industry. And in 2003, CAKE was selling at $18 a share — just below their calculated MOS price of $19. The
technical tools (these are explained in *Rule #1*, but don't worry about
them if you don't want to) all said "Buy," so they opened a brokerage
account and bought 1,000 shares at $18.90. They traded (i.e., bought
and sold following the Big Guys in and out of the market as the technical tools indicated) CAKE eleven times in two years and added about
$500 a month to their stake, and by July 2005 their nest egg had
grown to $78,000.

Then CAKE started having glitches.

In 2006, Sales growth was okay but Earnings growth suddenly
slowed. Equity growth slowed down, and Cash Flow growth went
negative. The Big Five were starting to raise red flags. The Connellys
came to the reluctant conclusion that their wonderful business was
struggling and not something they would buy in 2006. It was losing
its "wonderful" qualities. So they sold their shares and moved on.

Determined to be rich, they were part of an early wave of Rule #1
students to adopt the stockpiling strategy. Rule #1 trading had
worked well and they planned to continue, but the strategy of stockpiling was compelling. They wanted to turn that $78,000 into $2.6
million as soon as possible, as easily as possible, and with the least risk
possible. They liked the concept of accelerating the compounded re-

turn by buying as the price went down. It made sense, it was easy to do, investment risk decreased as the price went down, their compounded return would grow automatically, and the time to reach their goal would decrease dramatically.

Searching for a Business to Stockpile

In August 2006, they began looking for the right business to buy and stockpile. They chose to stick with the restaurant industry, since they felt they understood it well. The Cheesecake Factory was out, of course. Too many red flags. And Doug thought the red flags were going to affect all sit-down restaurants, because the entire retail industry was showing signs of slowing down. In looking at competitors, however, they noticed that several fast-food restaurants looked quite good; fast food, unlike sit-down, could do okay in a big economic downturn. In particular, they liked their Meaning, Moat, and Management results for Chipotle Mexican Grill, McDonald's, and Buffalo Wild Wings, each for different reasons. Chipotle had growth and they liked the Chipotle story — natural fast food and quality farming methods. Everyone they asked who'd been there liked it *a lot*. And a lot of people had never tried it yet.

Susan, in particular, thought they had a lot of room to grow. She also happened to read an article that said this new category of dining, called "fast-casual," was the fastest-growing segment of the restaurant industry. McDonald's was on their short list because it was going to expand all over China and was a good business to own in a recession. And Buffalo Wild Wings also had a great growth story in the sports bar/fast-food segment. By combining bar revenue with cheap food and entertainment, it also could do very well in a recession. All of them had Brand Moats and were best of breed in their respective segments, and all three businesses were very well managed with a strong and proven owner orientation. The CEOs showed passion for their businesses.

Susan did a Rule #1 Valuation analysis on each of them. (Remember: it's August 2006 when she's looking this data up.)

Check Rule #1 Valuation. The basic approach to value is a simple Rule #1 Valuation. Susan started the process by going to MSN Money, typing in CMG (the symbol for Chipotle Mexican Grill), and then clicking on Company Report. Under Fundamentals she found Earnings/Share of $1.51, which was the TTM EPS for CMG as of July 2006.

Chipotle Mexican Grill Inc: Company Report	
Fundamental Data	
Earnings/Share	1.51

A look at Finance Results: Key Ratios: Price Ratios got her the historical high and low PE ratio — a range of 18.5 to 119.

Chipotle Mexican Grill Inc: Key Ratios

Growth Rates
▶Price Ratios
Profit Margins
Financial Condition
Investment Returns
Management Efficiency
Ten Year Summary

Price Ratios	Company
Current P/E Ratio	10.2
P/E Ratio 5-Year High	119.0
P/E Ratio 5-Year Low	18.5

She knew she'd refer back to this PE range after she did the growth-rate calculations on the four Growth Rates (Sales, Earnings, Equity, and Cash). But first she looked at ROIC, Return on Investment Capital. On the same page, she clicked Investment Returns and saw Return on Capital was 12 percent.

Return On Capital	12.0

That worked, she thought (it's above 10 percent). On that same page she clicked on Ten Year Summary to look at Debt and Book Value per Share (see chart below).

Chipotle Mexican Grill Inc: Key Ratios

Growth Rates
Price Ratios
Profit Margins
Financial Condition
Investment Returns
Management Efficiency
►Ten Year Summary

	Book Value/ Share	Debt/ Equity
12/05	$11.77	0.00
12/04	$9.99	0.02
12/03	$7.29	0.07
12/02	NA	0.00
12/01	NA	0.00
12/00	NA	0.00

The Debt/Equity Ratio was zero (see chart above), which means Chipotle had no debt. That's good. BVPS was growing nicely (although she didn't have as much info as she liked; no data was available for 2000 to 2002 — it was not a publicly traded company then, so they probably didn't report it). Between 2003 and 2005, though, BVPS climbed from $7.29 to $11.77 (see chart above). Using the free rate calculator from my website PaybackTimeBook.com, she got a 27 percent growth rate for BVPS. Back on MSN, she clicked on the left menu below Financial Results on Statements.

To do a Rate calculation in Excel, go to my website for step-by-step instructions. Or just use the calculators on my site at PaybackTimeBook.com. No math required; just plug in numbers and click Calculate.

Total Sales went from $67 million to $625 million in five years (see chart on page 189). That's 56 percent growth (again, you can figure that rate in seconds with a downloadable calculator from my site). Net Earnings grew from -$0.77 to $1.37 (see chart on page 189). (Most rate calculators can't calculate a Growth Rate that starts with a negative

Chipotle Mexican Grill Inc: Financial Statement

| Income Statement | Balance Sheet | Cash Flow | 10 Year Summary |

Income Statement - 10 Year Summary (in Millions)

	Sales	EBIT	Depreciation	Total Net Income	EPS
12/05	625.08	30.24	28.03	37.7	1.43
12/04	468.58	6.13	21.8	6.13	0.24
12/03	314.03	-7.71	15.09	-7.71	-0.34
12/02	203.89	-17.29	11.26	-17.29	-0.68
12/01	131.33	-24.0	8.73	-24.0	-0.94
12/00	67.76	-19.54	4.99	-19.54	-0.77

number, so I built the Rule #1 Calculator for you to use, which can accommodate negatives.) Susan plugged in the net Earning numbers and time and got 30 percent Growth Rate for Earnings. And finally, the Cash Flow Statement showed Operating Cash Flow growth from $22 to $77 in two years (see chart below). That's 87 percent compounded Growth Rate.

Net cash provided by operating activities	77,431	39,672	22,069

She then looked at the four Growth Rates: 27 (BVPS or Equity growth), 56 (Sales growth), 30 (Earnings growth), and 87 (Cash Flow growth). This was obviously a very fast-growing company, but she knew she couldn't expect the business to keep these Growth Rates up for long. The 27 was from Equity, which she knew was the best figure to use if she had to choose one of the four. She decided to take it down a notch and use 24 percent for an even more conservative rate. No real pressing reason. It's high but not impossible for sustained growth over the next five to ten years. It means the company will double in size every three years. And it's lower than all the historical Big Five numbers. Doug said, "If Chipotle can handle growing from 500 to 4,000 restaurants in the next ten years, the growth number isn't insane. Micky D's has 36,000, so 4,000 is high but not insane."

Then she peeked at what the pros were saying. She clicked on

Earnings Estimates in the left menu and learned that the analysts were projecting 24 percent per year. It's nice when it all works out like that; she settled on a Growth Rate of 24 percent.

Susan then referred back to historical PE and noted that there was almost no data on the MSN "Ten-Year Summary-Avg PE: just one year and it averaged over 42. She knew the Rule #1 PE was 2 x the Growth Rate, which in this case 48 (2 x 24). She went with 42, the lower of the two numbers.

And her minimum acceptable rate of return (the MARR) for buying a business was 15 percent per year. That number never changed.

Here were her numbers for her Rule #1 Valuation calculation:

1. TTM EPS: $1.51
2. Growth Rate: 24 percent
3. PE: 42
4. MARR: 15 percent

She ran the calculation using my website and got the following:

1. Sticker price: $136
2. MOS price: $68 per share
3. Current price: $48
4. Was there a Margin of Safety? Yes (MOS $68. Price $48)

She ran through the same process with McDonald's. ROIC was just below 10 percent. Sales and Cash were growing below 10 percent, while Earnings and Book Value growth were at 12 percent. Debt could be paid in exactly three years from earnings. Then she ran the Rule #1 Valuation using 12 percent Growth Rate and a 24 PE — well above average for MCD but doable — and she got a Sticker Price of $42 with an MOS Price of $21. But the stock was selling for $32.

Here's the MCD summary:

1. Sticker price: $42
2. MOS price: $21
3. Current price: $32

4. Was there a Margin of Safety? For a novice, no. But for an expert, yes (80 percent MOS $34. Price $32)

And then she did it again for Buffalo Wild Wings. Return on Capital was low but coming up fast. Almost no Debt. Book Value was growing, at 15 percent, Earnings growth was off the charts over the previous three years, at 49 percent, Sales were going strong, at 32 percent for the last six years, and Cash was growing, at 28 percent. Analysts were giddy about the future. She dialed it down a bit because of the 15 percent BVPS and put the Growth Rate at 20 percent with a 30 PE — well within the range for BWLD. Her calculations arrived at these numbers:

1. Sticker price: $37
2. MOS price: $19
3. Current price: $15
4. Was there a Margin of Safety? Yes (MOS $19. Price $15)

NOTE: For the complete step-by-step four M analysis of McDonald's and Buffalo Wild Wings, go to PaybackTimeBook.com.

Check Payback Time. To check Payback Time, Susan needed to know how long it would take the growing earnings to pay off the MOS Market Cap, the price she was willing to pay for the whole company. To get the MOS Market Cap, she multiplied Chipotle's MOS Price of $68 per share by the total number of shares in the company, 29 million. She found the shares number on the Company Report page on MSN Money. The Chipotle MOS Market Cap was $1,972 million. Now she grew the earnings at 24 percent per year and accumulated the total earnings year over year until the total equaled or went just over the MOS Market Cap. She found it would take almost eleven years of accumulating earnings to pay off the business at the MOS Market Cap—a little more than the ideal ten-year maximum Payback Time.

The spreadsheet on the right shows the number of years and the cumulative earnings for CMG as it grows 24 percent per year. The graph below shows the accumulating earnings over ten years. The solid line on the top of the graph represents the MOS Market Cap. When the bar crosses the line, it's Payback Time. In the case of CMG, Payback Time is not quite reached by year ten. It takes a little more than ten years.

CMG YEARS	EARNINGS CUMULATIVE
1	$54.3
2	$121.6
3	$205.1
4	$308.7
5	$437.0
6	$596.2
7	$793.6
8	$1,038.4
9	$1,341.9
10	$1,718.2
11	$2,184.9

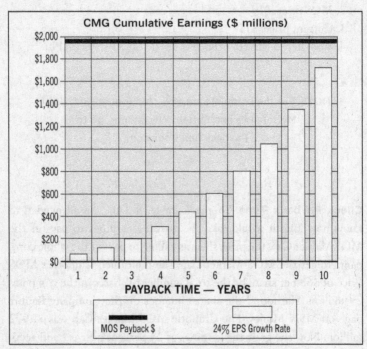

It takes slightly more than ten years to reach the Payback Time.

RECAP ON HOW TO CALCULATE CUMULATIVE EARNINGS

In the first year, the Earnings for CMG grows from $43.79 million to $54.3 million. Again, here's how that works: Earnings per Share at year zero is $1.51. Multiply that by the number of outstanding shares (29) and you get $43.79 million. Now grow that 24 percent for the first year and you get 54.3 million for earnings in year one. (.24 x 43.79 million = 10.5 million; add $10.5 million to $43.79 million and you get $54.3 million). Add the new Earnings ($54.3 million) to the Earnings that you started with ($43.79 million) and you get $98.09 million to grow in year two at 24 percent (.24 x $98.09 million = $23.54 million). Add $23.54 million to $98.09 million and you get a cumulative Earnings number of $121.6 million for year two. Keep going all the way until you reach or surpass the Market Cap of $1,972 million.

MARKET CAP

Remember, Market Cap refers to the total dollar value of all outstanding (sold and held by investors) shares. A business's Market Cap is calculated by multiplying its number of outstanding shares by a price, usually the current market price. For example, a company with 1 million shares priced at $50 per share has a Market Cap of $50 million. An **MOS** Market Cap is calculated using the MOS price per share instead of the current market price. An MOS Market Cap is useful because it lets us see the price we'd be willing to pay for the whole business. A quick comparison of MOS Market Cap and total Earnings will tell you if the MOS price is also a good Payback Time price.

If you do a Rule #1 Valuation on the above company and get a Sticker Price of $40 per share, then the MOS Price would be $20 per share and the MOS Market Cap would be $20 million.

Susan then figured out the Payback Time for McDonald's: Its MOS Market Cap was $23,100 million ($21 MOS Price x 1,100 million shares). Its net income was $2,530 million and growing at 12 percent. Susan did a Payback Time chart that showed MCD had a six-year Payback Time at the MOS Price of $21 per share.

MCD YEARS	EARNINGS CUMULATIVE
1	$2,834
2	$6,007
3	$9,562
4	$13,543
5	$18,001
6	$22,995
7	$28,588
8	$34,852
9	$41,868
10	$49,726

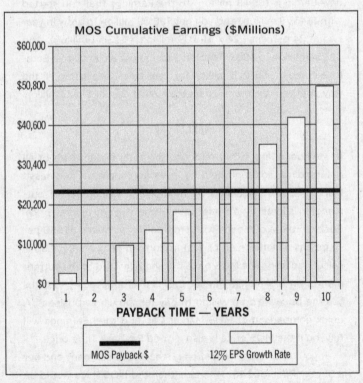

It takes only six years to reach the Payback Time.

Buffalo Wild Wings had an MOS Market Cap of $320 million. Doug ran the numbers and got a Payback Time on the MOS Market Cap of eight and a half years at the MOS Price of $19.

BWLD YEARS	EARNINGS CUMULATIVE
1	$17
2	$38
3	$62
4	$92
5	$127
6	$170
7	$221
8	$282
9	$356
10	$444

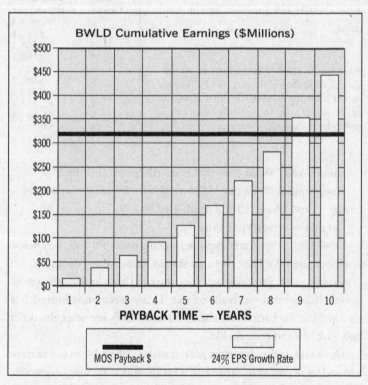

Payback Time is reached in the eighth year with Buffalo Wild Wings.

NARROWING IT DOWN

Susan looked at the Chipotle Payback Time chart and said, "Okay, with Chipotle at MOS price of $68 we've got a Payback Time that's over the limit of ten years. Too long."

Doug said, "So let's drop the price we'll pay until we get a Payback Time under the ten-year limit." Doug looked at Chipotle's Payback Time spreadsheet and said, "If we want to get our money back in ten years, according to the chart, we can't pay more than $1,718.2 million for the whole thing."

CMG YEARS	EARNINGS CUMULATIVE
1	$54.3
2	$121.6
3	$205.1
4	$308.7
5	$437.0
6	$596.2
7	$793.6
8	$1,038.4
9	$1,341.9
10	$1,718.2
11	$2,184.9

Revisiting Chipotle's Payback Time Spreadsheet, look at the line for year 10: $1,718.2 million. This is the Market Cap for Chipotle if Susan and Doug theoretically want their money back (Payback) in ten years.

Susan asked, "What does that make the Stockpile Price?"

Doug replied, "If we pay $1,718 million for 29 million shares, we're paying $59 per share (1,718.2 divided by 29 = 59)."

"So that's our Stockpile Price?"

Doug said, "Yup. And Chipotle is selling today for $48, *way* below the Stockpile Price. Not that that should influence our decision."

Susan smiled. She knew how long they had been looking for a wonderful business that was really on sale. This was tempting indeed. She checked the Payback Time chart and said, "Let's see what the other two look like and then decide."

Doug said, "Okay, but if we get our cash off the table in ten years or less and we're paying less than half what the future Earnings are worth, we should buy it. We don't have to steal it. Remember: 'Better a wonderful business at a fair price than a fair business at a wonderful price.'"

Susan missed the Charlie Munger–wisdom moment. She was too busy looking at McDonald's. "Wow. McDonald's has a Payback Time of six years at the MOS price of $21 per share."

Doug said, "But right now it's selling for $32. What's the Market Cap at $32 per share?"

Susan multiplied the 1,100 million shares by $32. She said, "$35,200 million." She checked the Payback Time graph. "The Payback Time on $35,200 million is eight years."

"Okay, the McDonald's current price gets us an eight-year Payback Time. How does Wings look?"

"Wings looks good. We've got an eight-and-a-half-year Payback Time on our MOS Price. And we can buy it today for less than that."

"Okay, so which one do we buy?"

"The growth rate we baked into the CMG numbers is up there," Susan pointed out, "24 percent a year. A slowdown will hurt us. What's the Payback Time at the current price?"

"Chipotle is at $48 with 29 million shares. That's a Market Cap of $1,392 million. And that has a Payback Time of about nine years," Doug said.

"Okay, and we already know the current Market Cap on McDonald's has an eight-year Payback Time. How about answering the same question for Buffalo Wild Wings?"

Doug checked. "It's at $15 with a Market Cap of $257 million. That puts the Payback Time at just under eight years." Doug smiled and said, "We have a problem. We have about $80,000 to play with. How many businesses should we own with 80 grand?"

Susan said, "Two or three max. Any more and we'd be stockpiling in such small amounts that the commissions would start to affect us."

Doug said, "Let's keep it to two. And I'm not that great a fan of McDonald's." Susan started to object but Doug continued, "I know it's a great business. But it's so unhealthy, that stuff."

"So you're saying we should make McDonald's number three. Go for Be Wild and Chipotle."

"I guess that's what I'm saying. We want to be proud of the businesses we own, and as good a business as Mickey D's is, I'm thinking I'd be happier owning Chipotle and Be Wild."

Susan laughed. "Beer and wings. Now there's some health food for you."

Doug said, "You got that right. Let's see if we can buy 'em today. Go down and drink some of our own healthy beer tonight."

Susan said, "Let's check the FACs and see if we think the price might be headed down some more for either of them. Start with Chipotle. Burritos are better for you than wings."

"Okay. Chipotle it is. We've got a Stockpile Price of $59 per share and a current price of $48. Let's see about Floors and Ceilings."

At this point, their decision to buy Buffalo Wild Wings and Chipotle instead of McDonald's is based as much on what they feel good owning as the numbers. This is how it should be. If you make it personal, you'll own businesses you're excited about, and that's the trick to keeping on top of your homework. If you love the business, keeping up on it is fun.

CHECKING THE FACs

Doug typed "Yahoo.com" in the URL box on his Internet page, and when the Yahoo! main page came up, he clicked Finance and typed in "CMG," the symbol for Chipotle, in the symbol box. The Chipotle main page came up. On the left menu bar under Charts he clicked Interactive to get the Interactive chart. The price was at $48 and had been dropping down from $56 per share. Doug and Susan looked at the price pattern to see if there were obvious price points off which the price bounced. Doug put a dotted line across the chart where they both saw 4 FAC points at $49 per share, right where it was hovering that day (see graph on page 199). Doug asked, "Do we buy or do we wait and see if this is a breakout? Maybe it's going to drop another $5 or so."

Susan asked, "How do you figure that?"

Doug said, "Well, $49 is clearly a Floor and the price is $48, so it's already broken the Floor. It's breaking on more than a 3 percent price move. From $50 down to $48 is $2 and that's 4 percent of $50. Also look at the daily volume. It's been averaging under half a million shares a day and the volume today is almost 1 million, well above the 150 percent volume requirement for a big breakout. It could go to $42, where there's another pretty good Floor. Actually, when I look at the distance between prices on the other FACs, I see a pretty consistent $5-to-$7 range. So if it breaks down we could definitely see it drop to $40 or $43."

Susan said, "We'll know more tomorrow for sure, but if it bounces off this Floor, it's going to move up toward our Stockpile Price of $59 pretty quick and we won't get in at such a great price. And $49 is a big Floor. I think we should buy some now and then . . ."

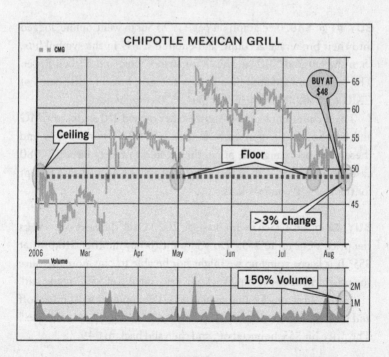

Doug said, "And then hope it drops like a brick?"

Susan replied, "Exactly, my dear. But I don't want Mr. Market to raise the price on us. We're just able to buy in now. I don't want to miss it. I think we should buy $10,000 worth of it now and see what happens. If it really breaks the $49 Floor, we'll stockpile some more at $42 and be happier than if it pops up and we miss this good price."

Doug smiled. "Okay, let's go shopping."

THEN THEY STARTED STOCKPILING

Susan and Doug had $78,000 in cash in their brokerage account from the CAKE sale, plus another $8,000 from saving $1,000 a month to invest. They wanted $40,000 in each business. They decided to start with 25 percent of their goal, or $10,000, in each.

BUY #1 @ $48. (See graph on page 199.) Susan went online, logged into their brokerage account, and entered CMG in the symbol box, then she entered "210" in the "# of shares" box, and clicked Enter. The broker immediately, like in two seconds, bought 210 shares of CMG for $10,080 of their cash plus a $10 commission.

The account immediately showed they owned 210 shares of CMG and had $67,910 left in cash. If they sold CMG immediately and there were no changes in price, they would instantly have $77,980 cash and no shares — all of the $78,000 would be back in cash except for the two $10 commissions.

BUY #2 @ $49. (See graph on page 202.) Over the next two weeks the price went up to $55. "Do you want to buy another $10,000 at $55? If it keeps going up we might not be able to buy more, because the price will be above our Stockpile Price ceiling of $59," Doug said.

"There's a strong Ceiling right at $55. I'm hoping it will bounce off and give us another shot at $42," Susan replied. "Let's wait and see." The price hit $55, bounced off, and then slid back to $49.

"There wasn't much volume and $49 looks like such a solid Floor. It's not going through to $42 anytime soon," said Susan.

"Let's hit it now, then," said Doug. So they bought another 210 shares at $49 per share. They then had a total of 415 shares with about $20,000 invested.

The price moved back up to $51. They waited because the price wasn't moving as far up each time, so it didn't look as though it was about to run off without them. They were thinking that the next time the price came down to the $49 Floor, it was going to break through and drop. A few days later the price slammed through $49 down to $47 on huge volume.

Doug said, "If the Floor holds, let's buy another $10,000 right now, because I don't think this is going to go lower than $48–$49. Maybe CMG management is buying back shares at $48. I don't know, but somebody big seems to be stepping in and buying at $48. If this doesn't break through after all this volume, it probably isn't going to. This may be as good a deal as we're going to get right now. I'm ready to go all in with the other $20,000."

BUY #3 @ $50. (See graph on page 202.) The next day the price moved up right from the market opening. "Dang it!" Doug shouted.

Susan was in the kitchen. "What, honey?"

"Oh, just Chipotle. It just won't go down. It's on its way up again. Let's grab it while we still can." And they bought another 200 shares at $50 per share. They then had a bit over $30,000 invested in CMG and owned 615 shares. They also had about $10,000 more in cash earmarked for CMG.

The price moved up to $52, and Susan pushed to buy the last $10,000. She thought it just didn't seem likely the price would go back to $49 again after that last big dip. Doug said, "We've got the Ceiling at $55. If it gets there, let's buy. But if it bounces off $55 again, let's use the last of the cash at $49."

The price slid to $50, then went to $53 in September, then dropped to $49 again.

Doug said, "Wow. That's the sixth time it hit this Floor in five months. Somebody Big is buying and that Floor is rock-solid."

Susan said, "Let's do the last $10 grand now."

Buy #4 @ $50. (See graph below.) And as it bounced to $50, they stockpiled the final $10,000 worth—200 shares. They now owned 815 shares. They had about $40,000 invested in CMG.

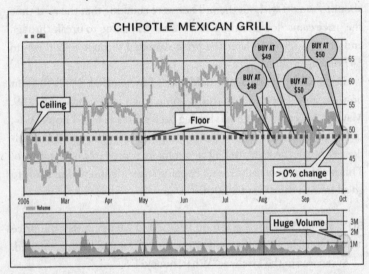

The Connellys valued the 815 shares at $121 per share—about $100,000.

A Note on Diversification

If the Connellys are only buying two businesses, shouldn't they at least be in different industries, especially after their experience with CAKE? It depends on the investor's willingness to get very good at an industry. There is no safety in buying into an industry you don't understand well. Remember, diversification is for the ignorant. If you know you don't know, you must diversify. The best investors stick to their knitting, focusing their capital on the parts of the market they understand well. The Connelleys are becoming experts in the restaurant industry and feel there is less risk buying two wonderful restaurant businesses that will be paid off in under nine years than diversifying into an industry they do not know well.

Be Wild. Stockpiling Buffalo Wild Wings

While they were stockpiling Chipotle, they were also stockpiling Buffalo Wild Wings. To see their FACs charts on BWLD and to see when and at what prices they decided to make their BWLD purchases, go to PaybackTimeBook.com.

PLAYING WITH HOUSE MONEY

As Chipotle sales and earnings grew through the end of 2006 and early 2007, the price continued to go up. Doug and Susan had $40,000 invested in CMG, plus they continued to save $1,000 per month in their Berky (the next chapter will go into full detail about the Berky—the account through which you do your stockpiling). At $55, Doug wanted to buy another $5,000, because CMG numbers were very positive and he thought Mr. Market was starting to love CMG and was going to push the price up; he was afraid that by being too conservative they were missing the boat. Susan said, "Be patient, dear. I think it's going to test that $49 Floor again." So of course it didn't, and over the course of 2007, the price shot straight up to $151.

By the end of 2007, Doug started to think Mr. Market had gotten so manic about Chipotle, its price was getting out of line with its value in the *other* direction. The CMG Growth-Rate numbers were huge for the year, so there was some justification for the high price. Susan did a quick Rule #1 Valuation. Here were her numbers based on Chipotle's September 2007 financial statements:

1. TTM EPS: $2
2. Growth Rate: 24 percent
3. PE: 42
4. MARR: 15 percent

Her December 2007 Rule #1 Valuation on CMG came out at $180, which meant that a 50 percent Margin of Safety price was $90. The stock was trading at $151, making it unbuyable by strict Rule #1 standards. But since Susan and Doug felt very confident about this industry and Chipotle in particular, they could consider buying in as high as 80 percent of value. That meant a price of $144. Susan said, "Hon, if the price drops to $144, should we maybe buy more?"

Doug played with some numbers and said, "Suz, check out the Payback Time." Doug showed her the 80 percent MOS Market Cap of Chipotle at $144: $4,723 million, which he got by multiplying 144 times 32.8 million—the number of outstanding shares. (By December 2007, Chipotle had 32.8 million outstanding shares, not 29 million.) He also showed her the Trailing Twelve Months earnings ($63 million) figures, which he retrieved from the Company Report on MSN Money. Doug did this Cumulative Earnings spreadsheet and said, "At $4,723 million I get a Payback Time of almost thirteen years" (see chart on right).

"Do you want to buy more at a MOS Price of $144, where we won't get a payback back for almost thirteen years?"

"Uh, no," she said.

"Me neither," Doug agreed. "So with all this growth, what do you think our new Stockpile Price ought to be?"

CMG YEARS	EARNINGS CUMULATIVE
1	$78
2	$175
3	$295
4	$444
5	$629
6	$858
7	$1,142
8	$1,494
9	$1,931
10	$2,472
11	$3,143
12	$3,976
13	$5,008

"Let's do a ten-year Payback Time. Check the chart. What's the Market Cap for a Payback Time of ten years?"

Doug looked at the ten-year line on the spreadsheet (see above), which revealed that if Chipotle grew at 24 percent per year, the

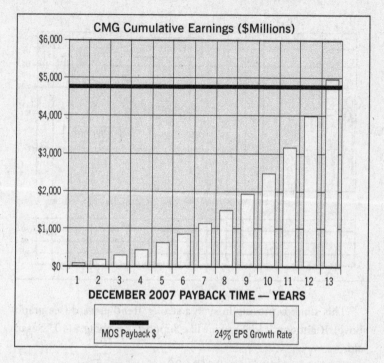

projected cumulative future earnings in year 10 would be $2,472 million. The company had 32.8 million shares outstanding. Doug did the division (2,472 divided by 32.8) and got $75 per share.

"Okay," said Susan, "$75 per share is our new Stockpile Price."

"The market price is double that right now. Let's see if it will run up past the Sticker Price of $180. If it gets above the Sticker by 20 percent, we're selling. Call our Sell Price $220. But even if it doesn't, let's at least get our $40,000 off the table."

"Floors and Ceilings time again," said Susan.

They'd invested $40,000 eighteen months earlier and owned 815 shares. They could sell those shares for $151 per share that day and generate $123,000. Instead, they decided to only take their original investment off the table as soon as the price started to break the long-term Trend Support Line downward.

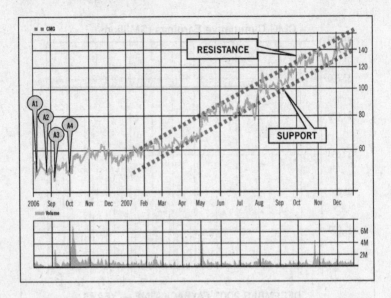

"This stock is moving in such a strong Trend upward (see graph above). Right now it looks to me like Support is at about $140," Susan said.

"If it breaks $140, let's sell $40,000 worth," said Doug.

Sell #1 @ $130. (See graph on page 207.) Within a few days the price crashed through the $140 Support with big volume, and they sold 315 shares at $130 per share.

(NOTE: If the Connellys knew they were going to sell when the price broke through a Trend Support Line or a Floor, they could order their online broker to sell the stock somewhat below that price with what's called a stop-loss order. In this case, they saw a solid Trend Support Line at $140, so they could have put in an order to sell 315 shares of CMG just below $140. Stop-loss orders used properly could have gotten them $40,000 with 290 shares. For information on Stop Losses go to PaybackTimeBook.com.)

Their account showed a $40,940 credit for the sale (their broker charged them a $10 commission on the sale). Since they had this

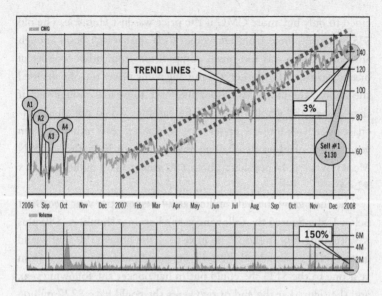

money in a tax-deferred Berky, they had no issues with taxes (more about Berkies coming up in the next chapter). If the price went below their $75 Stockpile Price, they would buy more. Otherwise they planned on letting the money ride. In the meantime, they were looking at other businesses on their Watch List they liked just as much. And they owned 500 shares of Chipotle Mexican Grill free and clear. They were now playing with the house's money.

Reevaluating in 2008. All through 2008, the price of CMG dropped even as earnings continued to increase as projected. As the TTM EPS got larger, the price Susan and Doug were willing to pay changed, too. But not necessarily in the same direction. In October 2008 they sat down to recalculate the price at which they were willing to resume stockpiling.

Susan was concerned about all the economic turbulence. Wall Street banks were going bust. Mortgages weren't getting paid. The market was tumbling down. It was a land of opportunity and there were more and more deals to be had for wonderful businesses. She decided to only buy more CMG if the price was just fantastic. The old $75 Stockpile Price from December 2007 just wasn't good enough anymore. There was too much competition from other wonderful businesses that Mr. Market was putting panic prices on. She decided she wanted the new CMG Stockpile Price to be low enough that if they owned the whole business, the earnings would put their purchase price back into their pockets within seven years rather than ten years. She looked up the Trailing Twelve Months Earnings on MSN Money. It was 2.44 per share, about $80 million (32.8 million shares x $2.44).

She then grew the $80 million at 24 percent per year (see chart below). She figured the following year's Earnings should be $80 plus $19, totaling $99 million. The next year, she hoped, the $99 would grow to $123. She added the $99 she could put in her pocket from year one to the $123 she could put in her pocket the following year, and she figured at the end of two years she could have $222 million back in her pocket. In the third year she figured the earnings should be at $153. She added that to what was already in her pocket— $222—and she had nearly $375 million, and so on until she got to seven years. At right is the spreadsheet she created in calculating the projected cumulative earnings starting with $80 million and growing at 24 percent per year. She then did her Payback Time chart.

CMG YEARS	EARNINGS CUMULATIVE
1	$99
2	$222
3	$375
4	$564
5	$799
6	$1,090
7	$1,450

In seven years the cumulative pile of Earnings would grow to roughly $1,450 million. That was as much as she was willing to pay, because if she paid more and the recession stretched out, she thought the Payback Time might get to be too long to make it worth buying. It would still be a good deal, but in this market "good" wasn't good enough, not when there were fantastic deals to be had for anyone with a few bucks.

Given a seven-year Payback Time, with accumulated earnings of $1,450 million, and with 32.8 million shares out there, their new Stockpile Price was $44 per share (1,450 divided by 32.8 = 44).

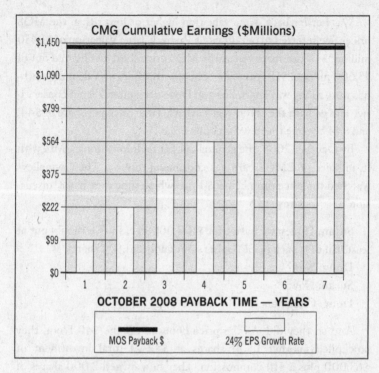

CMG Cumulative Earnings ($Millions)

OCTOBER 2008 PAYBACK TIME — YEARS

MOS Payback $ 24% EPS Growth Rate

Susan redid her Rule #1 Valuation to see how it came out using the 24 percent growth rate and 42 PE. Here were her new numbers for the Rule #1 Valuation:

1. TTM EPS in October 2008: $2.44
2. Growth Rate: 24 percent (from her own analysis)
3. PE: 42
4. MARR: 15 percent

She ran these four numbers through the Rule #1 calculator she downloaded and got a Rule #1 value of $220 per share and a 50 percent MOS of $110. To calculate the Rule #1 value of the entire business, she multiplied $220 per share times 32.8 million shares and got $7,200 million. The MOS Market Cap was half of that number—she rounded to $3,600 million.

Was her Payback Time valuation higher or lower than the MOS price? She referred to her previous Payback Time Valuation of $1,450 million, $44 per share versus the MOS price she'd just figured out of $3,600 million, $110 per share. She saw that her two valuation methods were a long way apart. She and Doug decided to keep it conservative and go with the seven-year Payback Time price per share of $44, and $44 became the new Stockpile Price.

By October 2008, the general market meltdown took CMG with it, in spite of CMG's earnings continuing to grow. The Connelleys watched the price drop below $44, at which time they had a "discussion":

Susan: Honey, we have over $100,000 in cash. We should put at least half of it back in CMG. Let's buy another 1,500 shares.

Doug: Now?

Susan: Now.

Doug: Okay, honey.

And so they did. As the price bounced off the $40 Floor, they stockpiled another 1,500 shares at $42—a total investment of $63,000 plus a $10 commission. They now owned 2,000 shares of Chipotle.

PORTFOLIO RESULTS FROM AUGUST 2006 TO OCTOBER 2009

In October 2009, Doug and Susan had $45,000 in cash in their brokerage account. That included the $38,000 they had contributed from their jobs since 2006, plus the $80,000 they got when they sold enough shares of CMG and BWLD to get their original investment back, less the $10,000 they put back into BWLD in 2008 and the $63,000 they paid for CMG in October 2008. Plus they had 2,000 shares of CMG that they valued at $220 per share (worth $440,000) and 1,961 shares of BWLD they valued at $95 (worth $186,295 total).

The Mark to Market Valuations were determined by multiplying the number of shares of stock by the stock price in the market on the day they created the balance sheet.

By saving, using FACs, and stockpiling a wonderful business when the price was right, Doug and Susan had increased the value of their portfolio to between $275,000 and $633,000, up from $78,000 in 2006. They achieved a compounded annual return of between 48 percent and 92 percent on invested capital. But they were still a long way from their goal of $2.6 million by 2023.

DOUG AND SUSAN BALANCE SHEET AS OF OCTOBER, 2009				
	Current Price	Mark to Market	Current Est. Value	Total Est. Value
ASSETS				
Cash		$45,000		$45,000
CMG (2000)	$95	$190,000	$220	$440,000
BWLD (1961)	$40	$78,440	$95	$186,295
Total Assets		$313,440		$671,295
Total Liabilities		$0		$0
Net Worth		$313,440		$671,295
RETURN ON INVESTMENT				
	CAPITAL	RETURN	TIME	COMPOUNDED ROI
MARK TO MARKET	$78,000	$275,440	3.2 YEARS	48%
ESTIMATED VALUE	$78,000	$633,295	3.2 YEARS	92%

Here's a look at the Connelly's Balance Sheet in October 2009, with two types of analyses of their financial situation: Mark to Market and Estimated Value. Mark to Market uses the current price of the asset in the market to determine the asset value. Estimated Value uses an informed estimate of the value of the asset as the asset value. Return on Investment was calculated with the return consisting of cash and stock value but not including additional cash saved from the Connelly's jobs.

DOUG AND SUSAN LOOK AHEAD

One night in late 2009, Doug and Susan did a little fun calculation. How long, they asked, would it take to grow their $275,000 portfolio (based on current market prices) to $2.6 million if they could keep going at a 48 percent rate and if they kept adding $1,000 per month? The answer was five and a half years. They looked at each other. They could be retired in 2015 with $2,600,000. They might not have to wait until 2023. They realized Mr. Market's fears were directly responsible for their high rate of return, but they had high hopes that his fear would not go away anytime soon. The economy was showing no sign of improving. President Obama signed a $781 billion bailout bill on top of the $700 billion President Bush gave away, but banks still weren't lending. Home prices were still dropping. Congress was in the mood to regulate everything. Labor unions were in line to see pay raises and restrictive tariffs. China was getting worried about lending to the United States.

In other words, from the point of view of Rule #1 Stockpilers like Doug and Susan, 2009 was the opportunity of a lifetime to make a fortune. While they certainly couldn't count on Mr. Market continuing to want to sell wonderful businesses at fire-sale prices forever, they could certainly see that between Rule #1 trading and Rule #1 stockpiling, they were going to easily achieve their goal of retiring comfortably. It was one thing for them to feel pretty good after turning $20,000 into $78,000 while the market was going up. Taking $78,000 to $275,000 in three years while the market went down gave them a whole different level of confidence. They were happy owning small pieces of wonderful businesses and planned on hanging on to them tenaciously. Someday way off in the distant future they might consider selling their piece of Chipotle and Buffalo Wild Wings, but for now they were planning on continuing to stockpile these and other wonderful businesses every chance Mr. Market gave them.

ELIMINATING THE FEAR FACTOR

By every financial measurement—percentage return, compounded return, total dollar return—you are better off stockpiling. And by the most important measurement of investment success, your *fear* factor, you are in another *universe* by stockpiling. You eliminate fear completely.

Let's look at this Chipotle example. Remember when Doug and Susan were hoping the stock price would break through the $49

Floor and go to $42? They owned a bunch of CMG stock but they still were hoping the price would go down. When it did, they weren't worried—they were excited.

Now let's look at this same situation from a different perspective. One investor, someone who didn't know anything about stockpiling, had $100,000 to invest and an additional $100,000 in six months from the sale of a house. In December 2007 he bought $100,000 worth of CMG at $150 per share. He then owned 666 shares. That should tell you something right there. And sure enough, a year later the price of CMG dropped with a precipitous stock market decline to $42. This investor became fearful and depressed.

He assumed the value of CMG was the same as the price, so when it dropped from $150 to $42 he was shocked at the significant loss of value. Down 72 percent was a lot. It had to go up 350 percent in price just so he could break even. If he sold now, he'd lock in the $72,000 loss but he thought, "What if I sell and it comes back?" So part of him was afraid to sell. On the other hand, he was thinking, "If I keep the CMG shares I could lose another $15,000. Who knows in this crazy world? The shares may go to zero and I could lose the entire $100,000!" He was thinking this because he didn't see Chipotle as a restaurant business. He saw it as a stock—a piece of paper that could be worth anything or nothing. Because he had no sense of the business of which he was part owner, he didn't know what to do. Fear kept him up at night.

His wife was angry. She said, "Why didn't you diversify more, like our financial planner said? Wouldn't that have protected us against a loss?"

He replied, "Yeah, honey, except that our 401(k) is invested just as our adviser suggested. We completely diversified it with a variety of mutual funds. We have small-cap, large-cap, growth, value, international. We did every single thing he said and we've lost 50 percent of our retirement anyway. So yay for the safety of diversification."

And on top of all that he needed to invest the $100,000 from the house in something, but it sure wasn't going to be this Chipotle turkey or a mutual fund. He decided to keep the second $100,000 somewhere safe until he could recover the loss somehow. And he thought Phil Town was a jerk for saying that the little guy can invest on his own. He thought he never should have watched this guy on TV. He put the new $100,000 from the house sale into a no-risk short-term Treasury bill that paid 1 percent. He was sickened by the fact that his $200,000 nest egg was now only worth $128,000 and growing at a minuscule $1,280 per year. He had no idea what to do. He was literally frozen, financially, with fear.

Look at the difference knowledge makes. The Connellys were happy when Mr. Market dropped the price of a business they were trying to stockpile. They knew this was how the rich got mega-rich. They knew the fundamentals of the CMG business hadn't changed, so the value of CMG was still at least $75. When the price dropped from $150 to $42, they were excited, not terrified. They saw a 70 percent reduction in price as the opportunity of a lifetime to accelerate the compound return on this investment. They were thankful they had focused their investment on an industry they understood so that when this great opportunity came along, they were emotionally prepared to load up the truck. And they're ready to buy more at the right price.

And they're thinking Phil Town is a jerk for knowing how to stockpile stocks and not telling them about it in the first book.

TAKEAWAYS AND ACTION ITEMS

The Connellys are creating long-term wealth by following the Rule #1 principles and applying the stockpiling tactics.

- Review their analysis and decision-making for Chipotle (CMG), McDonalds Corp. (MCD), and Buffalo Wild Wings, Inc. (BWLD) on **PaybackTimeBook.com**.
- Do a similar historical analysis to evaluate your own business candidates by using my predesigned templates on my website.

FREE MONEY with a BERKY

If you would be wealthy, think of saving as well as getting.

— BENJAMIN FRANKLIN

Stockpiling your way to riches wouldn't be possible if it weren't for Mr. Market. But it also wouldn't be possible without a proper place to stash the excess cash that you'll be using for your investments. And that place is a Berky.

A Berky is an account into which recurring money is deposited that must then be allocated to investments. It's where you'll deposit the money you can put toward investing, so you can begin to stockpile businesses. Simply put, if you regularly take money from your paycheck and put it into an account allocated for long-term investment, you have a Berky. It's the "recurring money" quality of a Berky that drives us to the strategy of stockpiling.

The Berky is named in honor of the original Berky, Berkshire Hathaway. Berkshire Hathaway's core business as a textile manufacturer took a downturn shortly after Warren Buffett bought it in the 1960s. Rather than shut it down and take a loss, he decided to operate Berkshire's textile business with the minimum cash necessary to keep it alive. With the excess cash, he could buy other, better businesses.

He realized if he had to find a new business to buy each time he had to allocate the recurring cash flow, it wouldn't be long before Berkshire owned so many businesses that it, like any mutual fund with hundreds of stocks, would not beat the market. He decided he needed to find investments that were also recurring—that is, wonderful businesses he could buy over and over. As an investor, he also knew he should want the prices of his investments to go up. But soon he discovered he in fact didn't want that. Instead, saddled with the need to make recurring purchases of the same product, Mr. Buffett wanted prices of his investments to go down so he could afford to buy more. In other words, he found that his desire to make recurring purchases at great prices changed his strategy from *investing* into *stockpiling*. In time, Berkshire evolved to become a business that receives—from dozens of subsidiary businesses—recurring cash from earnings. Mr. Buffett then allocates that continual cash, whenever low prices allow, into the businesses he already owns pieces of.

The key words that turn a normal investment account into a Berky are "recurring money." With a normal investment account, you load it up and then invest it. With a Berky, you load it up with cash, invest it, and then keep loading it up with cash again and again to further invest. What makes a Berky special is that the cash flowing into the Berky is persistent, and therefore requires recurring investments—more precisely, recurring investments into the same core group of businesses. If the cash is allocated to too many different businesses, the investor will suffer the consequences of an overly diversified portfolio.

To get around this problem of finding recurring investments, most of you pay someone else to invest your cash flow for you. Most of you already have Berkies, but in the form of retirement accounts invested solely in mutual funds, managed by someone else. Someone who, rather than repeatedly buying a small number of recurring investments, buys a large number of onetime investments. This, as I've explained in Chapter 2, is an error that too often leads to an impoverished retirement.

I'll show you how to fix that, as well as how to set up other Berkies, but first let's take a look at what it takes to be a Berky.

QUALITIES OF A BERKY

The following chart outlines the main features of a Berky, based on the model — Berkshire Hathaway.

Qualities of a Berky	Bershire Hathaway	Your Berky
Berky receives recurring cash flow	Cash flow from subsidiary businesses like Sees Candy and GEICO	Cash flow from your job, your spouse's job, your kid's job, and other investments
Cash moves into Berky without being taxed twice (or, if possible, even once)	Berkshire subsidiaries can pass up the cash flow to headquarters without dividend taxes	You avoid or postpone taxes by using IRAs, Defined Benefit Plans, and a certain type of corporation set up for investing purposes
The Berky allows you to reallocate the cash to investments of your choosing	Mr. Buffett is the decider	Through self-directed retirement plans and self-directed investment accounts, you are the decider
The Berky allows you to reallocate your investments	Mr. Buffett can reallocate cash as necessary from one investment to another	You can reallocate cash as necessary from one investment to another
The Berky allows you to get cash for personal emergencies	Mr. Buffett can sell shares of Berkshire	You can sell shares in your corporate account or borrow from your retirement account

Let's go deeper into these qualities that make a Berky so essential to our ability to stockpile companies.

BERKY RECEIVES RECURRING CASH FLOW

Recurring cash flow is the key to a successful Berky, because it's the secret to stockpiling. Without recurring cash, you cannot stockpile a business, because you don't have the cash available to take advantage of dropping prices. Mr. Buffett's recurring cash comes from the way he runs the Berkshire subsidiaries. His subsidiary CEOs are rewarded for maximizing the amount of cash their business can send up to Berkshire headquarters for Mr. Buffett to then invest.

By keeping a lid on expenses and stopping spending where it gets a poor payback, Mr. Buffett (and his managers) maximize the cash flow into Berkshire for investment. Why don't you do the same thing? Keep a lid on family expenses, do not spend on things that don't have a good return on investment (financial or psychological), and maximize the recurring cash flow into your Berky. This will almost certainly require you to put the family on a budget. There are great books about personal finance out there already, so I'm just going to put in a few thoughts on the subject of controlling your money and leave it to you to read more about it. Remember where I came from as I tell you this stuff—thirteen years in a sleeping bag before I started investing.

The first thing I can tell you is we Americans spend way too much money on crap. Spend your money on functionality. Buy what works. The flashy car you drive, the designer labels on your butt and back, and the name on your shoes are irrelevant. You aren't in high school anymore, so no one cares. And if someone does care, he or she doesn't deserve your attention (and probably won't ever be rich). Wear clean clothes and polished shoes, drive a car that runs, and get a grip on yourself. You don't have the money to squander on frivolous symbols. Stand for honor and dignity, not Coach and True Religion. Entire books have already been written on how to create realistic spending plans and manage debt properly. Go get them if necessary and start cracking. I've listed several of the best on my website, PaybackTimeBook.com.

In all likelihood, you have no idea how much money you spend, and at, say, $50,000 a year, you're pretty much just making a living.

You can do better. There are easy ways to save money. A Health Savings Account (described below) could knock down medical insurance to $200 a month, saving $200. Not eating in restaurants can bring food costs down by $100 or, for some of you, more like $1,000. Sharing housing costs could give you $100 per month. It adds up. Even $400 a month can make a huge difference in your financial future, if you can get that excess cash into a Berky and invest it at stockpiling rates of return.

The graph below shows that over a twenty-year period, $5,000 a year invested at 15 percent gives you more than $500,000 you wouldn't have had without some belt-tightening and a Berky to invest money in.

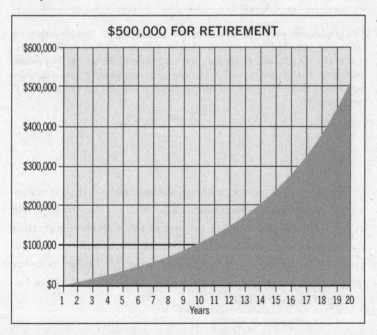

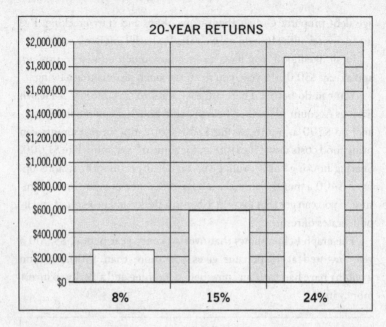

This graph shows the impact of various rates of return in the Berky assuming no tax on your gains. Eight percent is the market's average rate of return. Fifteen percent is the MARR—our Minimum Acceptable Rate of Return. At 24 percent, $400 a month going into your Berky to invest gets your finances shaped up really well. Twenty-four percent, you'll recall from Chapter 1, is what I call a "stockpiling" rate of return.

Whatever your income, it always makes sense to save your money so you can stockpile more businesses. Some of the wealthiest people in the world still pay attention to every penny. A group of executives sharing an elevator with Warren Buffett saw him lean over to pick up a penny off the floor. When he straightened up, Mr. Buffett looked at the penny before putting it in his pocket, smiled, and said, "The beginning of the next billion."

When you're investing money at 2 percent a year, whether or not you save an extra $100 to invest isn't all that important. Save $100, invest it at 2 percent a year, and your $100 will only grow to $200 or so in forty years. At that rate you might as well spend it. But if you can get 24 percent, the $100 you saved will be worth $546,000 in forty years. For an investor of Mr. Buffett's skill, even a few extra pennies are really quite valuable. When he was investing under $100 million in the 1950s, his Return on Investment averaged 36 percent per year. If he picked up a penny on every elevator ride for a year, he might collect $15. At 36 percent compounded rate of return over forty years of investing, those pennies add up to over $12 million.

One of my good friends and fellow motivational speakers likes to tell audiences that it takes twenty doubles to turn $1 into $1 million. It takes ten doubles to go from $1 to $1,000, and then ten more to go from $1,000 to $1 million. The first ten steps are the hardest, because every time you get to $1,000 you spend it on something like a new refrigerator and then have to start the doubling process over again. You begin again with $1 and start doubling it . . . and ten doubles later you finally get to $1,000. Now you've gone through the process of twenty doubles but instead of having $1 million you've got $1,000 and a refrigerator "worth" $999,000.

Probably the single best thing you can do for yourself financially is to become a penny-pinching miser while you're learning to stockpile. The combination of savings and knowledge can make you much richer than you ever dreamed possible.

It almost goes without saying that the first place to pinch pennies is our tax bill. The federal government not only has the largest ownership in the profits of our businesses, it's also the largest expense in our personal budget. Anything we can do to legally reduce our tax burden can have a dramatic impact on our financial future.

That brings us to the second key quality of a Berky—the money comes into the Berky *before* it gets taxed.

CASH MOVES INTO THE BERKY BEFORE BEING TAXED (IDEALLY)

Let's say Mike is a stockpiler with an extra $1,000 per year he wants to invest. First he has to pay taxes at 25 percent on the $1,000, so his actual investment capital is $750 per year posttax. He invests this $750 once a year from the time he's thirty years old. On average Mike holds every business he buys about ten years and makes a 15 percent compounded return and pays long-term capital gains taxes of 28 percent whenever he sells. (Yes, I know long-term capital gains taxes aren't that high now. But just wait.) If Mike keeps this up for forty years, he'll have $460,000 when he turns seventy (see graph below). Not too bad.

Let's say John does everything Mike does but does *not* pay the

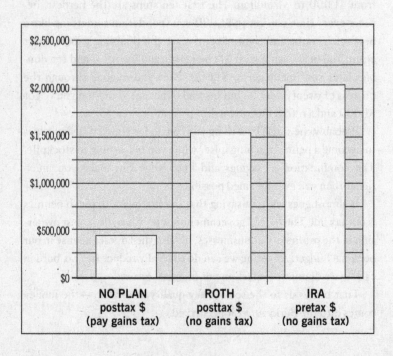

long-term capital gains taxes when he sells because he's got his money in a gains-protected account (more on these below). When John is seventy he'll have $1,535,000. Nice.

And let's say Bill is also a stockpiler with an extra $1,000 that he wants to invest every year, but Bill invests it pretax—that is, before the government gets to take its piece out of it. And when he sells off the portfolio every ten years, like John, he also doesn't pay tax on the gains. When Bill turns seventy, he will have $2,046,000. Very nice.

Taxation will hurt you. How much it hurts you depends on how well you use the tax-deferral opportunities set up by Congress.

John had tax-planning advice. He invested his posttax $750 each month into a Roth Individual Retirement Account (Roth). The gains in a Roth are not taxed. Ever. At age seventy he has $1.5 million that can't be taxed. He's going to have a nice retirement. Assuming he just puts the $1.5 million into a bond that pays 1 percent above inflation, he can spend about $70,000 a year after tax in 2009 money for the whole rest of his life.

Bill also has tax-planning savvy. He invested his $1,000 pretax in an Individual Retirement Account (IRA) and paid no up-front tax. That gave him more money to compound than John, which accounts for the $500,000 extra he's got. However, after he retires, Bill is going to have to pay taxes on it, and the future gains on it as he uses it. Assuming a 20 percent tax bracket, he'll have about $90,000 a year in 2009 dollars to spend the rest of his life.

Mike had no tax planning at all. He invested well, made good money, and retired with, as we learned in Chapter 2, enough to make it seven or eight years in retirement at $50,000 a year in 2009 dollars.

The impact of taxation means your first Berky should be a tax-deferred retirement account, so you're investing without the drag of taxation. You can set up a tax-deferred Berky account through your employer, through your own business, or personally.

SETTING UP THE MOST COMMON BERKY ACCOUNTS

Rules, restrictions, and even types of tax-deferred or tax-free retirement plans seem to change frequently. Let me summarize the most popular ones available today that can be set up by you and/or your employer. I'm sure many of these will sound familiar, and if you have one already, the question is: are you in charge of where your money is invested? If not, it's time to self-direct. And for most of you, that starts with your 401(k).

401(k) Plans

There are several *big* advantages to a 401(k)-type plan. You can pour in a lot of money each year. In 2010 the maximum you can invest in it is $16,500 plus inflation index (in $500 increments). If you're over fifty, you can put in another $5,500 (plus an inflation index in $500 increments) for a total of at least $22 grand. That's pretty good. And your employer can match funds with you up to a maximum between his contribution and yours. And nobody can touch that money, even if you go bankrupt. But there are two really horrible things about 401(k)s: (1) Most plans don't give you much of a choice on what to invest in. Mutual funds. That's it. (2) The average 401(k) fees are over 1.5 percent per year off the top.

As I showed you in Chapter 2, subtract that seemingly innocent little fee from an already anemic mutual fund average return and you're getting clipped for about 60 percent of your retirement money. And even with matching funds, 401(k) plans leave you with so little flexibility that I don't think they're worth it. Many investors are finding that out right now: Last year the stock market crash wiped out about $8 *trillion* of investor capital, the majority of which was retirement fund money.

DID YOU KNOW?

401(k) plans were instituted in 1976 as an add-on to companies' Defined Benefit Plans as a perk for executives. The Defined Benefit Plan, which is virtually extinct in corporations
now, provided a specific amount of income per month for life
and was the responsibility of the corporation. The 401(k) plan
was designed to supplement the limited and fixed income of a
Defined Benefit Plan by allowing executives to invest pretax
salary dollars with matching funds from the company. The
execs could afford to roll the dice on the market with pretax
and matched dollars because they had a Defined Benefit Plan
providing a safe foundation for their retirement. By 1990, however, 401(k) plans were growing so rapidly with the bull market—most were averaging 15 percent per year—that everyone
wanted one. Employees saw the growth in the 401(k) plans as
an opportunity to get rich. And corporations saw shifting to
401(k)s as an opportunity to get rid of costly Defined Benefit
Plans. Of course, with 401(k) plans averaging 0 percent for the
last ten years, giving up a defined benefit for a mutual fund
crap shoot doesn't look so smart.

Some good news about 401(k) plans: You can borrow your own
money. Most employers will allow you to take half or up to $50,000
out of your 401(k) and pay it back plus interest out of your paycheck
over five years. But you're paying yourself back and the interest goes
to you. What can you do with the $50,000? You can invest it however
you want to. (If you leave that job and go to another employer, you will
have to pay back that "loan" quickly or face a large penalty.)

Still, the best choice is to force your company and plan administrators to give you full options. You should have the whole range of
stocks to choose from in your 401(k). There's no reason for your

employer to tell you what you should and shouldn't invest in. You can do that with these magic words, "fiduciary responsibility," as in they have one, and if they don't give you a reasonable range of choices, then they have violated their fiduciary responsibility and are wide open to some other magic words, "class-action lawsuit." Not from you, of course. You would never sue your employers whom you love so much. You're simply letting them know that they're exposing themselves to an unnecessary lawsuit by only providing mutual funds, all of which can (and just did) go down at once. Let them know that a true fiduciary would give freedom to investors who believe they can invest their retirement money more successfully than the people who run the mutual funds. Remember: fiduciary responsibility, class-action lawsuit. Magic words.

Another magic word: "self-directed." When you ask that your account be self-directed, you are requesting that *you*—not a fund manager—can choose whichever investments you want and you are not limited to buying only mutual funds.

Another option that may be available to you: just roll over your 401(k) to an IRA (Individual Retirement Account, see graph on page 227) so you can invest it where you want.

Now, what about this problem: You have a 401(k) and can't roll it over into an IRA. And your company won't give you the option of investing in individual stocks.

What then? Well, borrow $50K first. Then push harder for the option to self-direct. And then, if those two are exhausted, even though your employer is matching funds with you, I'd pull it. Get rid of it. Here's why: The matching funds your company puts into your 401(k) are an expense to your employer and part of your compensation package. Therefore, there should be no difference to your employer whether you take that compensation as part of your salary or as a contribution to your 401(k). They write it off in either case. Seems to me you work for that money, however they pay it. If you don't want your employer to pay you pretax by matching funds in your 401(k), then ask your employer to pay you that money as salary or bonus. Yes, you will pay tax on it. But if you're investing at a solid rate of return, you'll still do better managing that smaller chunk of taxed money than you would letting the fund managers mismanage your untaxed dollars.

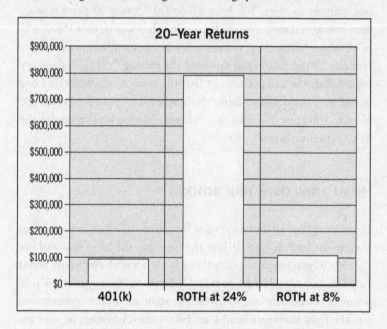

This graph shows the difference between putting matching funds into a 401(k) versus accepting the same money as income, paying tax on it, and then putting it into a Roth IRA. Let's say your company gives you $3,000 matching funds every year in your 401(k). It gets invested for you, pretax, for twenty years at, best case, about 6 percent after fees. When you retire you have $120,000. Then you pay about

20 percent tax, so you have $95,000 after tax. Now let's say that instead, you take the $3,000 as a bonus, pay 30 percent taxes on it, and put the remaining $2,100 into a Roth IRA (more about Roths below). Let's also say you master the art of stockpiling and your money grows in the Roth at 24 percent per year on average; at the end of twenty years you have almost $800,000 after tax.

The third column on the graph shows what happens if you take the $3,000, pay the taxes on it, and then invest it in a market index in the Roth IRA at 8 percent—the same rate you're getting in the 401(k) but without the fees. You have $106,000—about 10 percent more than you would have in your 401(k). In other words, over the course of a lifetime of investing, you do better without a 401(k) in almost any scenario. If the feds would just level the playing field by making the total dollars you can put into an IRA the same as in a 401(k), no one would ever use a 401(k) again! No one with a brain. And once you learn to stockpile, the idea that you were leaving your money to the 401(k)-meisters is just a joke.

How to Roll Over Your 401(k)

If you leave your job before you are fifty-nine and a half, you have four choices for your 401(k): (1) Take the cash, pay the taxes due, and pay the feds 10 percent as a penalty for early withdrawal. You'll have about half of it left. Okay. Don't do that. (2) Leave the money in the 401(k) where it is, and continue to invest like someone who is ignorant and pay the fund managers exorbitant fees—like 25 percent of your annual gain and at least 60 percent of your retirement. No. Don't do that. (3) Roll it over to your new employer's 401(k) plan, and continue to invest like a moron. No, don't do that either. (4) Roll it over into an IRA, and take charge of your life. Yes, do this! How? Go to my website, PaybackTimeBook.com, and I'll show you the fastest and easiest way to do this with the online broker I think is best. (More on IRAs below.)

The only reasonable justification I can find for employers and 401(k) plan administrators determining what you can invest in is this: Your company has decided that you're not educated enough to make good decisions. There's no other possible reason not to open the 401(k) menu to the full range of choices you'd get in a self-directed 401(k) or a self-directed IRA. None. Zero.

Okay, so that may not be the entire reason. Here's why employers limit you, really: Your CEO doesn't want the hassle of making a decision on his own, so he relies on "experts." As you know by now, these "experts" are in the business of making a pile of money on the fees they charge you. So they present your CEO with a bunch of mutual funds that give the appearance of sobriety and solidly conservative low-risk investing. That those very funds will drop like a house price in Detroit the moment the market starts going down makes liars and con artists out of all of these plan administrators. The whole notion that you can protect yourself with a "risk-adjusted," "rebalanced" mutual fund is a complete fiction—as I hope you now understand. Your mutual fund is going where the market goes, no matter what kind it is. Large-cap value, small-cap growth, medium-cap value growth, whatever . . . it's still going down with the market.

IRAs

There are several types of Individual Retirement Accounts (IRAs). Traditional and Roth IRAs are set up by individuals. Get over to my website and I'll show you the steps and the paperwork. Nothing to it. SIMPLE and SEP IRAs, on the other hand, are set up by employers, which could be you if you're a sole proprietor.

While there are various limits and restrictions on all these accounts, you can invest the money in pretty much whatever you want—stocks, bonds, and yes, even mutual funds.

I'll briefly outline these accounts below based on 2009 rules, but for more information, two sites to check out are: (1) the IRS's Retirement Plans Community site, which you can find by searching for "retirement plans" at irs.gov, and (2) the U.S. Financial Literacy and Education Commission, at mymoney.gov. By the time you read this, the exact rules and contribution numbers likely will have changed for many of these accounts. Many limits in 2010 are indexed to inflation.

Traditional IRA. Money you put into a Traditional IRA is tax-deductible depending on your income, your tax filing status, and any coverage by an employer-sponsored retirement plan. You can contribute up to $5,000 or 100 percent of your compensation, whichever is less. If you're over fifty, you can contribute an additional $1,000 of compensation for a total of $6,000 max. When you start to withdraw this money at fifty-nine and a half or later, it's considered income and it's taxed at normal rates.

ROTH IRA. A Roth IRA is just like a Traditional IRA except the money you deposit has *already* been taxed and is not taxed ever again. *Ever.* A Roth is a fabulous Berky, although eligibility currently varies depending on income level (income limits are likely to be eliminated in the future, however). In 2009, you could contribute a max of $5,000 to this type of account ($6,000 for those fifty and above). In 2010, everyone can convert a traditional IRA to a Roth IRA.

SEP IRA (Simplified Employee Pensions). This is a profit-sharing pension plan (used by small businesses and self-employed people) that lets you put up to 25 percent of your income into the plan each year, up to a max (in 2009) of $49,000, pretax. Other than that, it's just like an IRA. And you can invest this money however you want, too. If you're an unincorporated self-employed individual (e.g., you're a freelance journalist or you run a small business from home), you can contribute a maximum of 20 percent of modified net profit.

Self-Employed 401(K). This Berky is technically called a 401(k), but I'm placing it under IRAs because it actually acts more like an IRA than a 401(k). Also known as a solo 401(k) or Individual 401(k), this Berky lets self-employed business owners sock away as much as $49,000 ($54,500 if you're fifty or older) in 2009 into a personal 401(k) account. And unlike traditional 401(k) plans, the self-employed versions don't come with huge management fees and you can buy anything with them (*not* just mutual funds).

SIMPLE (Savings Incentive Match Plan for Employees). With a SIMPLE IRA, you can put away $11,500 per year ($14,000 if you're age fifty or above) with 3 percent matching funds from your employer, which you then get to invest yourself—all pretax. SIMPLE IRAs are typically set up at companies with fewer than one hundred employees.

Keogh Defined Contribution Plans. Designed for small businesses and the self-employed, this plan lets you put up to 25 percent of your income into it each year, again with a max (in 2009) of $49,000. The level of contribution cannot be changed or altered, however, and remains constant throughout its entire duration. (Note: Keogh Contribution Plans are different from Keogh Defined *Benefit* Plans, which are described below.)

These sound complicated, I know. But seriously, setting them up is a cinch. It's much the same as opening a checking account at a bank. If doing it over the phone and sending money in the mail sounds scary, then find a brokerage in your town with a brick-and-mortar office and go speak with someone in the flesh. They will take you by the hand and show you how everything works and which one's suitable for you, and you can hand them a check with your initial deposit. If you need to roll over your funds in your 401(k) to an IRA, they can help you with that, too.

HEALTH SAVINGS ACCOUNTS

This is not a retirement account but it does make for a very nice Berky. You put $5,950 per family into this account each year, lower your health insurance costs, and use the money to pay your much higher deductible. If you stay healthy, whatever you don't use up each year you keep in the account and invest. An HSA gives you a chance to squirrel away a bunch more pretax dollars and incentivizes you to stay healthy and away from doctors. And you can invest it just like a self-directed IRA.

One caveat: An HSA can only be established in combination with an HSA-eligible high-deductible health plan. If you have your own health insurance apart from your employer, you're probably eligible. They are typically offered through financial institutions, including banks and credit unions. I set mine up with my local bank. If you don't know whether you qualify, just call your bank and speak with someone who can help you make that determination. If you're eligible, your bank's rep can also help you set one up.

BERKIES FOR EDUCATIONAL PURPOSES

There are two of these available today: the 529 Plan and the Coverdell.

The 529 Berky

This is a savings plan for college education, but you can't actually self-direct the money you put into it. These 529s are all sponsored by states, state agencies, or educational institutions, and every single one of them limits you to mutual funds or CDs or guaranteed-return investments. Every single plan. But the 529 does have a use. If you feel you must set aside dollars for educational expenses, then consider a 529 and crank up the rest of your Berky returns by making them self-directed. (By the way, if you haven't looked at what a public college education will cost in about fifteen years, I hope you're sitting down. Figure about $100,000. And if your kids can get there, the Ivy League will be about $100,000 *each year.*)

Some of the benefits of a 529 include:

- You pay no taxes on the account's earnings.
- You — not your kid — has control of or access to the account.
- If your kid doesn't go to college, you can roll the account over to another family member.
- Anyone can contribute to the account.
- There are no income limitations that might make you ineligible for an account.
- Most states have no age limit for when the money has to be used.
- If your kid gets a scholarship, any unused money can be withdrawn without paying any penalty (just the tax).

Because the 529 plan is a state-sponsored investment program, the state sets up the plan with an asset-management company of its choice, and you open the account with that asset-management company according to the state's predetermined plan features. You won't deal directly with the state, but rather with the asset-management/investment company. Bonus: Most states don't require residency in order to participate, so shop around different states for the best deal.

For more about these plans, go to the SEC's site at sec.gov/investor/pubs/intro529.htm. From there, you'll find links to sites that help you shop for different plans and find one right for you.

Coverdell Educational Savings Accounts (ESAs)

This is another educational savings plan, but it works more like an IRA. (They were formally known as Educational IRAs.) Named for their main champion in the U.S. Senate, the late Senator Paul Coverdell, ESAs are not state-run. You can open them up at most brokerages, and you will not be limited to state-run allocation programs. ESAs allow almost any investment—including stocks, bonds, and mutual funds. A very good thing for a true Berky.

Like a 529 Plan, Coverdell ESAs allow money to grow tax-deferred and for proceeds to be withdrawn tax-free for qualified education expenses at a qualified institution. But the definition of qualified expenses in an ESA includes primary and secondary school, not just college and university as is true for 529 Plans. One of the downsides to ESAs, however, is that they are limited to a max of $2,000 a year per child in contributions (529s have no limits). The money must be used on qualified education expenses by the time the child is thirty years old or it can be gifted to another family member under thirty in order to avoid taxes and penalties (there is no age limit for 529 Plans). And last, your income level may affect how much you can contribute—unlike a 529, which has no such restrictions.

So you can see both pros and cons with 529 Plans and Coverdell ESAs. The main advantage to an ESA, of course, is that it allows you to buy anything, versus the limited options and lousy returns of a 529. Once you take control of your investments and start seeing great returns, you probably won't want anyone else but you managing your family's money. So in that regard, an ESA is the way to go. If you and/or your kid is maxing out that ESA every year in contributions, then it's probably time to set up another Berky in your kid's name (see next chapter).

KEOGH DEFINED BENEFIT PLAN: THE HOLY GRAIL OF BERKIES

Retirement benefits received from this Berky are based on a benefit formula, and you can make tax-deductible contributions as needed in order to reach that benefit goal. The maximum tax-deductible contribution to a Keogh Defined Benefit Plan is the amount needed to produce the required benefits under the formula. Get this: The *most* you can put away is 100 percent of a three-year average of your compensation. If you're making $200,000 a year average, you can "only" put away . . . *all of it pretax.* If you're self-employed, *this is the best legal tax shelter in the world.* Of course you have to be making a lot of money to take full advantage of one. And it helps if you're over fifty — because if you haven't saved much for retirement yet, your financial planner will be able to determine that you need to set aside a large portion of your paycheck to fund a decent retirement. The purpose of this plan is to make it possible for someone who's earning a lot of money to put a big pile of cash away fast — enough cash to create a defined benefit upon retirement that's big enough to match current lifestyle expenses. This can be quite a lot to put away, thus the huge pretax write-offs.

Imagine you're fifty-five right now with a net worth of $500,000 — all of it in your house. You want to be rich, so you sell your house, rent, and begin investing that $500,000. You've learned your four Ms and know how to stockpile, so you consistently make 25 percent per year returns with your $500,000. At 25 percent per year, you're making $125,000 a year, taxable at the highest bracket. So you're only keeping $65,000 of it. The rest goes to taxes.

To help shelter money that would otherwise go to taxes, what you can do is set up a business that, among other things, invests the cash flow coming from your successful investing. This will allow you to treat your investing as a professional would. (You'll want the help of a good accountant for this. A savvy accountant will know how to help you set up a corporation that allows you to write off lots of expenses related to your investing, and direct income to a Berky that has the most tax-savings advantages. For more details on this maneuver, go to my website, PaybackTimeBook.com.)

I know it sounds impossible that you can start making more money investing than at your day job, but it actually happens all the time. I've watched it happen with some of my students. If you do, in fact, get to a point where you're raking in six figures a year from stock-piling — not to mention compounding those returns — you'll want to consider establishing a bona fide investing business so you can keep more money on your side and work the tax system to your advantage.

YOUR PERSONAL BERKY

Chances are that not all of your investment capital is going to be pretax dollars. If so, you'll need one more Berky for your posttax excess cash. This Berky will be set up as a plain old investment account in your name at any brokerage. Any savings you have — beyond what you're putting into your pretax Berky, of course — goes in here. This Berky is perfect for cash you get from anything else you're doing to generate money: real estate rents, cash from your business, inheritance, gifts, and tax refunds. All of it goes in here to be allocated to an investment.

OTHER FINE FEATURES OF THE BERKY

A Berky allows you to do whatever you want with the money you put into it, with the exception of those few types of 401(k) plans, which I hope I've convinced you to get out of. The only rules you have to abide by are any restrictions on how much you can deposit annually. When you set up your accounts, the person who assists you will be able to tell you everything you need to know about these restrictions.

If you don't know which brokerage to use, again, just go to my website, PaybackTimeBook.com, and I'll show you the most up-to-date information on brokerages along with my recommendations. Some people like brokerages that have nearby brick-and-mortar stores, while others prefer to do everything online. Different brokerages offer different commissions and provide different tools on their site.

One bonus to having a Berky is that it allows you to reallocate your investments. This means you can move from one investment to another if one isn't working as planned. Few people think about doing that when they're stuck in a mutual fund. They just buy and hold, hoping it all works out. With a Berky, *you* get to decide when it's time to let go of an investment and buy into another.

One of the biggest bonuses of a Berky is that you can tap it for cash for emergency purposes. Of course, you can do that with your personal Berky, but you can also pull your money out of the IRA-type Berkies without penalty if:

- You become permanently disabled.
- You use the money to pay medical bills that exceed 7.5 percent of your adjusted gross income.
- You use the money to pay for medical insurance during an extensive period of unemployment.
- You use up to $10,000 to help pay for or build a first home for yourself, your spouse, your kids, your grandchildren, or even your parents. That $10,000 is a lifetime limit, not an annual one.
- You use the money to pay higher-education expenses for yourself, your spouse, a child, or a grandchild. Allowable expenses include tuition, fees, and room and board for postsecondary education, including graduate work.
- You take the money in equal annual amounts, designed to exhaust the account during the course of your life expectancy (as estimated by the IRS). You can increase this amount by adding

reasonable future IRA investment earnings when figuring the size of the payouts. You can begin this kind of early-withdrawal plan whenever you want, but to avoid the 10 percent penalty, you must stick with it for either five consecutive years or until you turn fifty-nine and a half.

Early withdrawals from Roths are hit with a 10 percent penalty if you cash in before age fifty-nine and a half, and they lose their tax-free status, but there are ways to get money out of a Roth tax- and penalty-free.

First, you can reclaim contributions at any time and at any age without any penalties. Only *earnings* are subject to penalties. But money that is converted to a Roth must generally stay in the account long enough to meet the five-year test. In other words, you have to keep the money in there for four calendar years after the year of the conversion to avoid the 10 percent penalty.

Earnings in a Roth are tax-free if you pass the same five-year test as in a Traditional IRA and also meet the following requirements:

- You are fifty-nine and a half or older at the time of withdrawal.
- The money is used for a first-time home purchase (up to the $10,000 limit).
- The money is cashed out after you've become disabled.
- The money is distributed to your heirs after your death. If you die before meeting the five-year test, heirs would have to wait until the year you would have passed that test to withdraw earnings tax-free.

Many of these rules and restrictions can get complicated, and they can change year to year. Describing all of them in detail is beyond the scope of this book. The bottom line is these accounts offer far more benefits to you than being stuck in a mutual fund. Use them. Stockpile in them. Get rich with them.

FREEDOM IN TWENTY YEARS?

Starting today with nothing but discipline, knowledge, tools, a Berky, and a steady job, you can achieve a decent degree of financial freedom in just twenty years. Let's assume you can find $12,000 a year for the next twenty years to put either into a 401(k) mutual fund or into your Berky pretax. The mutual fund, after fees, gives you a 6 percent return, and you'll have $440,000 in twenty years (see graph below). If you keep investing at that rate after you retire, you're making only $21,000 a year on your $440K nest egg. Good luck living on that in 2029. Instead, let's get crazy and assume you're an excellent investor and you get an awesome 24 percent stockpiling return in your Berky. At the end of twenty years you'll have $3.6 million. If you continue to get those returns after retirement, you'll have $600,000 a year to live on after tax. That's $50,000 a month. You can get by on that, right?

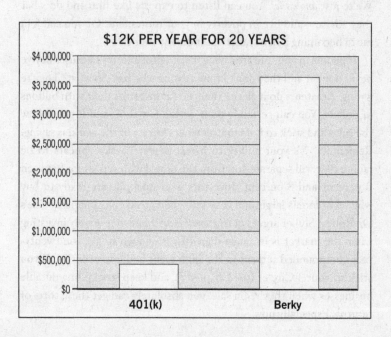

And here's the beauty of going for it: What have you got to lose? You know you can't live on $21,000 a year by 2029. It won't even make a dent.

24 PERCENT RETURNS—AM I SERIOUS?

I'm sure that well-meaning people, people with lots of fancy degrees who use lots of impressive-sounding jargon, are going to scoff at the idea that you can make 24 percent a year. But don't let them convince you. Lots of these folks are blinded to the facts by their worldviews. Burton Malkiel, Professor of Economics at Princeton, adroitly dismisses the problem of those pesky individuals who beat the market by calling them "statistical anomalies." He can prove that professional investors running mutual funds almost never beat the market. Therefore he's sure you can't either. Never mind that there are a few hundred thousand people just like you proving that statement wrong. We're just *anomalies*. You can listen to experts like him and do what they advise—and live in poverty in your retirement. Or you can join me in becoming a rich statistical anomaly. Your call.

If people in your life are saying it's not possible, it's because they've never done it and they don't know anyone who has. So what? They're wrong. Amateurs do it all the time. Great investors do it with billions of dollars. You can certainly do it with a few thousand if you follow the rules and stick to it no matter what the rest of the world is saying. Remember, it's your ability to invest when the sky appears to be falling that will separate you from the crowd who settles for between 0 percent and 8 percent. Investors who stockpile are ready to buy when fear looms large, and they sell when greed runs rampant. Yale's Dr. Robert Shiller argues in *Irrational Exuberance* that merely investing when the market is in single-digit PEs is enough to get you twenty-year compounded returns in the high teens and low twenties. If you stick to your 3 Circles (see Chapter 3), and keep stockpiling durable businesses when they're on sale, you absolutely can get these sorts of returns. Especially now.

Today, in this market, you have the opportunity of a lifetime to make millions of dollars with incredibly low risk. Anyone who says different is either completely uninformed or is selling you something—probably both. Can I guarantee you'll crank out a 24 percent return in your Berky every single year? Of course not. But I *can* guarantee you won't have a chance financially unless you stop listening to these guys and start learning to invest on your own.

GET GOING!

I know you can set up a Berky or two today. All it takes is a few phone calls, the click of a mouse, or the time you need to drive to a local brokerage and bank. Once you have your Berkies set up, it's time to go shopping for a wonderful business you can buy at a Margin of Safety price or less. When you've found what you want to buy and decide on your Stockpiling Price, check the FACs that can show you when to buy. And then stockpile that business every chance you get. This market is an incredible opportunity. A once-in-a-lifetime opportunity. The sooner you start, the better it's going to be financially for you and your family.

This is a well-worn path to riches. It's been walked by great investors for the last hundred years. It will be walked by great investors for the next hundred years. These investors are great because they make money when others are full of fear. For the most part, they're not geniuses but they are intensely rational. They have the discipline to make their minds the ruler of their emotions. Making that happen is simply a matter of learning what I've taught you here in *Payback Time* and in *Rule #1* and then steadily applying the strategy until you wake up one morning and discover you're a great investor, too.

Yeah, I know it's hard to work toward a better future when you're up to your arse in financial alligators. So what you do is take small actions toward your goal. Maybe you start by making your cost of living just one notch below your net income. Or maybe you begin by taking that second job and you put every cent you earn into a Berky. I promise you this: If you just take a few small steps toward becoming financially independent, something unexpected will happen in your life to urge you onward. I don't know what it'll be, but it'll happen. You'll wake up to discover that something you would have never imagined has happened to help you on your way. That small unexpected victory is being sent to you to encourage you to continue doing the right thing for yourself and your family. So take the next step . . . and the next . . . and not too long after those efforts you'll get another gift. And gradually your life will take on a new shape and a new color and a new meaning, and you'll leave behind the struggle you now face. It happened to me. It can happen to you.

TAKEAWAYS AND ACTION ITEMS

Stockpiling requires recurring investments that are best handled in an investment account called a Berky. It is a flexible account that allows you to periodically reallocate cash and investment capital to the business of your choosing. It should be tax-efficient and allow you to get cash for emergencies or personal reasons if necessary.

- Create your first Berky as a tax-deferred retirement account. Subsequent accounts should be tax-efficient because taxation has a huge impact on long-term returns.
- Follow the step-by-step process to set up your Berky account at **PaybackTimeBook.com**.
- Capital earmarked for medium-term financial needs could be contributed to a Berky structured like a Health Savings Account (HSA) or Educational Savings Account (ESA).
- Determine the best Berky structure for you by following my timely alerts and must-read posts on my website.

JOIN the RULE ONE
REVOLUTION

Every generation needs a new revolution.

— THOMAS JEFFERSON

A lot of what you read in this book flies in the face of conventional wisdom and certainly must irritate the institutions that control the stock market. The idea that an individual investor doesn't need to put money in mutual funds and should be finding good investments on his or her own is certainly revolutionary to the existing financial order. In fact, their view is that this is insane. And for good reason. Should you find out you can do this better on your own, Good Lord, who knows what kind of craziness might ensue. Entire institutions might fall. We might lose most of our investment banks. Mutual funds might cease to exist. The financial world as we know it today might end. And, in particular, an unimaginable fortune in fees might be lost forever.

Oh. Wait. A lot of this is already happening. The old financial order is crumbling before our eyes, driven to self-destruction by greed and envy and other people's money. CEOs pay themselves fortunes in annual bonuses while their employees suffer and businesses collapse. Investment banks fail and cause entire countries to go bankrupt. And all the while they, like the old guard of any collapsing antiquated system, keep shouting from the rooftops that everything is fine. Trust me . . . all is not fine!

It's time for you to wake up to the fact that we are in a revolution about money. The old paradigm is dead. A new paradigm has made the scene, and it isn't going to go away. In twenty years, the idea that people once turned over hard-earned money to a fund manager to "actively invest" will be ridiculed. That practice will be as inconceivable as hiring someone to do your reading for you. Financial literacy will prevail; information will be readily available; bad businesses will no longer be able to hide behind smoke and mirrors, false financial information, and fund managers' apathy.

Payback Time is here to sound the alarm, to wake you up and show you how you will need to proceed in revolutionary financial times. Follow what I teach you and you will do well. Ignore me at your own financial risk. There is a revolution on, my friends, and you can either join it or be financially left behind. But there's still time for you to choose.

As more and more people choose to join the Rule One Revolution and begin to take control of their financial lives, more and more chaos will come into the world of mutual funds. But the mutual funds won't go quietly into the night. They have one hundred billion reasons a year to fight to the death. (Yes, that's right. Mutual fund investors are paying them one hundred billion dollars every year in fees.) They are counting on you to remain ignorant and incapable. They will show you false advertising and financial pornography—you know, the images of a blissful retirement because you have the right broker. Frankly, the sooner we stop the madness the better. But it will take some doing because this revolution starts with you, and you want to have the results of the revolution without having to actually change anything. So here is your first revolutionary act: analyze what you already have. It's the fastest way I know to show you that you belong in this revolution.

YOUR "MUST DO" FIRST STEP

You're about to take control or, for some of you, take back control of your own investments, and one of your biggest obstacles is . . . you! Why? Because at this point you don't know how to analyze your current investments. You don't know if what you already own is good or bad or indifferent. You just don't know. It's harder to become a revolutionary if you're not sure if you need to. What if everything is really okay? Well, what if it's not?

If you see the tyranny, you'll join the revolution.

Start by taking a look at what you own. That's called your "portfolio"—just a Wall Street gibberish name for your investments, whatever they are. Maybe you have mutual funds, cash, a chunk of land, a bond or two, a house, a 401(k), and some life insurance. Maybe you have some of these, or all of these and more. Or maybe you're starting like I did—dead broke. Nothing to lose, everything to gain. But if you've already got stuff (and most of you do), then you should know what that stuff is worth and if its value is going to grow or not. Why? Because what you decide to do right now with your investments makes an enormous financial difference in the long run. Getting rich is all about compounding your money over time. The money you invest over the longest period of time will be the money that earns you the most income.

Let's start with your mutual funds. Almost all of you have some, and showing you how to analyze your funds to see if they are any good or not is the fastest way I know to turn you from an ordinary investor into a Rule One Revolutionary. If you could find out quickly that you are investing with mediocre fund managers, wouldn't that go a long way to convincing you that the Wall Street "experts" you are relying on for a decent retirement are not on your side?

You've already read that I think you should sell your mutual funds. But, if you are honest, you must have thought, "What if the fund goes up after I sell it? I will be very angry at Phil Town and think he's an idiot." Okay, you probably will think I'm stupid if that happens! So let me protect myself at least a bit and teach you right here how to determine if you are investing in one of those rare mutual funds being run by a great Rule #1 stockpiling fund manager—someone who will give you a huge, compounded long-term rate of return.

First off, there are virtually no great Rule #1 stockpiling fund managers. How do I know that? Did I personally study every one of the more than 18,000 mutual funds? No. But I know that great Rule #1 investors sometimes stay in cash for years while waiting for a wonderful business to go on sale. And I know that no mutual fund managers can sit in cash for years without having so many of you withdrawing your money that they get fired. Remember, fund managers don't get a piece of the profit they make you. They get a fee. And they are not your friends. They are not going to do what is right. They are going to do what gets them paid the most.

Remember, they get that 1 percent to 2 percent fee whether they make you any money or not. But if they don't do something to make you money quarter by quarter, if they sit in cash and do nothing, then most of you get ticked off and withdraw your money from that fund and invest in one that is performing better in the short run. So fund managers know they have to be active. And that prevents them from becoming the stockpiling money geniuses they long to be.

So let's get this straight right now: virtually none of your fund managers are true stockpilers because the system does not allow them to be. But some of them are at least interested in buying wonderful businesses when they are cheap, even if they can't wait all year for special opportunities.

So if you'll go to your computer, I'll walk you through the steps to see who you're trusting with your hard-earned money.

Step One. Go to MSN Money.

In the little box, type in the stock symbol of a mutual fund in your 401(k). (Don't know the symbol? No problem.) Type in the first name of the fund. "Fidelity," for example. You will get a list of stocks and funds with the word *Fidelity* in them. Now type the second name of the fund: "Magellan."

Now the list shrinks and there it is. You can see the symbol "FMAGX" to the side of the name. (Write it down someplace.) Now, click on the name or symbol, and that mutual fund information will come up in the window. Go. Now. Do it.

Step Two: Click on the left menu called "Top 25 Holdings."

You'll see a page listing the twenty-five stocks that make up the majority of the fund.

Step Three: Click on the top company.

You'll see the window change to the page on that company. Do it.

Step Four: Do a four M analysis on that business.

Just follow the steps in Chapter 3 of this book. Determine if it's a wonderful business on sale, at retail, or overpriced. I just did that to Nokia, the #1 holding for Fidelity Magellan at the time. Without digging into the numbers too carefully, if the analysts are right about the 11 percent growth rate and we start with today's earnings, a fast and dirty Rule #1 analysis says it might be worth $11 billion or so. It's selling for $50 billion. Even if the starting-point earnings are too low because of the recession, we're still way off if we buy this thing for $50 billion, wouldn't you say? We'd like it, maybe, at $6 billion. But the fund manager owns it at $50B. NOT a good sign. He probably can't get out without triggering a huge drop in the stock price. Well, when he does finally dump it and the price crashes, maybe you can be there to pick it up on sale. But only if you join the revolution. Keep doing what you're doing and you are going to keep getting mutual fund results. Which, let's see, have been about a zero return on investment for, oh, the past ten years or so.

Step Five: Follow suit with the top ten stocks.

Chances are good that most of them are overvalued. I did this a couple of years ago on the one hundred stocks in my friend's money manager's portfolio. It took about an hour. Ninety-six were either at retail or overpriced. She got out and then the market crashed, and that portfolio went down 50 percent. Overpriced stocks in a mutual fund are a major clue as to why most fund managers don't give you a good return on your investment. Nokia might be a good business, but it isn't a good investment unless the price is right.

Step Six: Make a decision.

If most of the stocks are overpriced, then get out of this fund now. If some of the stocks are overpriced, but most are at their retail value, then get out of this fund now. There is no need to pay fees when you can do the same job with a no-fee ETF (Exchange Traded Fund). But if most of the stocks are underpriced, you may have found the rare gem fund manager who can actually tell an overpriced business from one that's on sale.

Step Seven: Do more work.

Now dig in and look into the businesses in the well-managed funds. Are the three Ms good? If so, then this is da Man. He must be a Rule One Revolutionary. Let us all know at PaybackTimeBook.com. And, if we agree with you, who knows, maybe we'll all put some money in there! (And we'll be sure to send him a Rule One Revolution T-shirt!)

Step Eight: Sell the funds that are bad or neutral.

You sell the neutrals, too, because there is no sense owning a full retail fund and paying a bunch of fees for it. Don't get nailed by penalties. First check with an adviser who has your real interests at heart.

Step Nine: Buy inexpensive mutual fund alternatives.

If all you want to do is to replace your funds with a cheap alternative to mutual funds that will perform at the market rate of return, buy

Spiders, spelled SPDR (ticker symbol SPY), Diamonds (ticker symbol DIA), and the Qs (ticker symbol QQQ) with the money you pulled out of the funds. Many 401(k) plans do not have these cheap alternatives. Write your congressman. You're being forcefully ripped off.

Step Ten: Fill the Berky.

If you want to get rich, pour cash into your Berky, then learn how to use FACs and stockpile Rule #1 businesses. To learn this stuff firsthand and make sure you're doing it right, get yourself and your friends to a Payback Time Workshop ASAP.

Now . . . what about the real estate, the bonds, the insurance, and the other stuff you own? You have to ask yourself the same questions for each investment: "Is it a wonderful business? Is it on sale now? Is it a good investment if I look at it as a business? Or is it a speculative investment that can only go up if other people are willing to pay more for it than I paid? Bonds, too? Yes. If you're not sure how to put long-term value on your bonds, land, apartment building, or gold, go to PaybackTimeBook.com. I'll show you examples of how to value a variety of assets using Rule #1 analysis. Remember, this is a critical first step, and if you don't do it right, you're starting off wrong. Remember that old saying, "Well begun is half done"? It applies right here.

The money you have right now is going to give you the biggest compounded rate of return. That is just a money law that can't be violated. So what you do with these assets right now will, in large part, determine whether you are going to get rich and stay rich . . . or not. If you aren't sure what you're doing, then get yourself to the Payback Time Workshop and find out what to do next. We're not going to give you financial advice. We're going to teach you how to be your own financial adviser. When you're done with the workshop, you'll go home with a solid basis for making sound financial decisions across all your assets. And for helping others.

HELP OTHERS: SPREAD THE WORD

You can do your part. Spread the word that there is a financial revolution going on, that you don't have to live in fear of a pitiful retirement, and you don't have to depend on the government for your financial future. Tell your friends you're taking steps in the direction of knowledge and experience, and that the sooner they start, the sooner they, too, will be on the path to financial freedom.

Are you concerned at all for others? Do you worry about the less fortunate? Do you think you can help them if you become one of them? The best thing you can do to help others is to help yourself. Stand on your own two feet financially, and then you can support the weight of those who are not yet able to. But get them into this revolution also. You don't want to carry that weight forever.

For your own benefit, and for mine, I want you to make a commitment that, after adopting the Payback Time approach, you will get as many people into this revolution as you can. Give them a chance to think about their financial future in a new way and to see the possibilities of more wealth than they ever dreamed of. Believe me, you don't want to just do this on your own, if only because then everyone you know will want to borrow money. Bring them with you on the journey. It's cheaper.

So how about we work together on this. Commit to getting this book to at least ten people. Start with taking action now. Send an email to ten friends with this link, RuleOneRevolution.com.

We'll take it from there. If you all do that, we could enlighten (and enrich) our nation in a matter of a few years. Can you imagine an entire nation of people who know how to invest, do it well, and are financially independent? Why not imagine it, and then why not take a few easy steps toward exactly that result. It all starts with you.

Get out there and get going, and send me more of your stories. Making big money is definitely the best revenge when it comes to getting payback for your financial future. So tell us how you're winning the battle! Email your stories to me at mystory@payback timebook.com.

Now go play!

TAKEAWAYS AND ACTION ITEMS

Use these steps to analyze your mutual funds and prove to yourself that you must join the Rule One Revolution.

- Analyze your mutual fund's top stocks using the four Ms. Keep the rare "Revolutionary" fund. Dump the rest and buy ETFs or stockpile Rule #1 stocks.
- Analyze your other holdings using the same four M process.
- Pour cash into your Berky.
- Spread the word about the Rule One Revolution by getting this book to ten people.
- Share your Rule One Revolution success story at my website, **PaybackTimeBook.com**.

. . . Before You Go Play

An ounce of action is worth a ton of theory.

—RALPH WALDO EMERSON

I've been blessed. No question about it. You don't go from being a dirt-poor river guide to multimillionaire without a great deal of help. In my first book, *Rule #1,* I talked a bit about the Wolf, the guy I almost drowned in the Grand Canyon. He had a tremendous impact on me. I could never have accomplished what I've done without his help. But there were others. In particular, Dr. Jonas Salk, the scientist who discovered the cure for polio, took the time to teach me that it's in the structure of the universe somehow that the moment you commit yourself, the power of the universe moves, too—that amazing support comes from everywhere to help you. He gave me a quote once that is often attributed to Goethe: "Whatever you can do, or dream you can do, begin it. Boldness has genius, power, and magic in it. Begin it now."

Last year I took that advice and began training people worldwide in the concepts of Rule #1 investing and Payback Time stockpiling. My students paid tuition of $2,995 to attend this workshop, with the understanding that if they were not completely satisfied at the end of the workshop, I'd refund their tuition. Out of all the people I trained to date (November 2009), only one person asked for her money back.

I'm thrilled to see the results my students are experiencing. Of course, we've been in a massively uncertain, volatile market, and that has accelerated the results that can be achieved by my methods. But since there is no reason to think the market is going to get any more certain in the future, I'm excited about your chances of making a great deal of money faster than is normally possible—if you take action.

And you know what? Dr. Salk was right—taking action in the direction of your dream works. Immediately after I started teaching these workshops, I met like-minded people who I would not have met otherwise. I was bold, they are geniuses, and magic is happening. I now am part of an amazing team of brilliant investing revolutionaries who are fully committed to the Rule One Revolution.

Now I want YOU to join my team. I know how hard it is to invest in an education when money is tight and the future is uncertain. But you've taken a huge step by buying this book and reading it to this point. You are one of the people who will succeed, if only you can keep moving forward. Here's how I'm going to help you take the next step: I'm going to give you and a guest a $2,995 scholarship to that same course—the Payback Time Workshop. All you have to do is take action and attend. Go to my website, **PaybackTimeBook.com,** and register now for the Payback Time Workshop or call 1-800-689-6715. You'll each be given a scholarship ID number, which you'll need to bring to the workshop, along with a copy of this book. We'll even give your book an official "welcome to the revolution" stamp.

And yes, I'm giving it to you free. But understand something: *Payback Time* has three meanings to me. It's literally how much time it takes us to get our money out of an investment. It's also about how making money, BIG money, is the best revenge. And it's about paying back those who helped me get on the path to financial freedom.

I learned to invest because people helped me. Now my team is going to help you and your family do the same. Think about your kids:

Will they ever learn to invest and become wealthy if you don't know how? I doubt it. My kids usually do what I do, not what I say to do, and I'm betting yours are the same way. Why not take advantage of our offer to train your children. Bring them. If you've got more than one, go buy another book!

If you're thinking, I'm getting too into the money thing, hey, I know life's not about the money. I'm one of the least "about the money" people you will ever meet. I've been broke living in a sleeping bag, and I did that for years with no problem. I had fun. I laughed. I loved life. But had I not taken action to obtain wealth when the opportunity was staring me in the face, I couldn't have seen the world the way I have. I couldn't have put my kids through elite colleges and into elite professions. I wouldn't have a beautiful home in Jackson Hole, Wyoming. I couldn't have written a bestseller. I wouldn't be writing this book, and I couldn't help you get to this workshop.

I love this workshop! I believe it's the only course in the world that will teach you how to make money the way the richest and most successful investors in the world do it, and also how they generate consistent cash flow while they are getting richer. You're going to go through hands-on training to find wonderful businesses in this market and how to know when they are massively on sale—or massively overpriced. If that's all you learn, you'll never lose money again the rest of your life.

My team will also show you how to buy the business at a discount to the market price—a discount so big that you will hardly believe it until you do it yourself. And they'll show you how to get instant cash flow with Floors and Ceilings, something I didn't have the space to do in this book. By the end of the workshop, you will know why so many smart people have paid nearly $3,000 to attend this workshop, even after they could have gotten their money back. It's just that good. The only way you'll know it's that good is to get yourself there.

It is so critical for you to attend the Payback Time Workshop at this time. I do not want you to be the victim of the very market forces that could have made you rich. So here's my offer to you: For a limited time, I will provide a full-tuition scholarship for you and a guest to each attend my $2,995 Payback Time Workshop for free. Let me spell that out for you. I'm giving you and a friend or family member this incredible workshop worth $2,995 each—free.

There are details about this I'm sure you'll want to fully understand. So in the next pages, I'll explain them as clearly as I can. That way you'll know what you're going to get when you decide to take me up on this offer. It's an extremely valuable course. You just have to get there. Then I believe that, together, we can change your whole life forever. So read on, then come join us!

I look forward to hearing about your success.

Now go play,

Phil

PAYBACK TIME WORKSHOP SCHOLARSHIP

Learning from this book is a great first step, but if you want to put what you've learned into action as soon as possible, then you need to get yourself to a Payback Time Workshop!

So, as a reward for purchasing *Payback Time,* you and a guest are eligible to receive a full-tuition scholarship of $2,995 each and attend a live Payback Time Workshop. (That's right: if you attend this workshop without a scholarship, you will pay the full tuition price of $2,995 each.) All you have to do is take action.

Here's what you need to know about the scholarship.

1. It's available to all purchasers of *Payback Time* by Phil Town. It gives you and a guest a scholarship of $2,995 each to attend the Payback Time Workshop. Two scholarships per book.

2. To activate your scholarship and register, visit **PaybackTime Book.com** or call 1-800-689-6715 to obtain your scholarship ID number.

3. When you attend the Payback Time Workshop, you must each bring your scholarship ID number and a copy of the *Payback Time* book as proof of purchase. Your book will be stamped for validation at the workshop.

4. The scholarship may only be applied to the Payback Time Workshop.

5. Registration for this event is subject to availability and/or changes to the event schedule, and class size is limited. The workshop must be attended by the dates shown on **Payback TimeBook.com**.

At the Payback Time Workshop, you'll receive hands-on training, where you will learn how you can:

- Unload the useless mutual funds while hanging on to those no-load funds run by the rare great fund manager. (This one bit of knowledge can provide immediate payback to your retirement plan.)

- Make up to an additional 2 percent a year or more in your retirement account simply by selecting the right Exchange Traded Funds (ETFs). (Do this and all by itself it has the potential to double the money in your retirement account over your investing life.)

- Open the most advantageous investment account to maximize tax-deferred investments. (Do this right and watch investment capital grow exponentially.)

- Find "wonderful companies" that have the right Meaning, Moat, and Management for a great investment. (Here's the secret to making low-risk, long-term investments.)

- Determine the "below sticker price" of any "wonderful" company, public or private. (You can do everything else wrong, but get this one strategy right and you are certain to make money.)

- Buy in with a huge margin of safety and actually make MORE money if the price goes DOWN after you buy. (This is THE

SECRET to great investing—maximum returns with the lowest risk.)

- Stockpile by using price Floors and Ceilings to maximize your rate of return. (The psychology of traders creates great opportunities every day for long-term investors like us. Do it right and watch your dollars grow.)
- Create a safely balanced but focused group of investments. (Revolutionary returns come from you putting just the right amount of money in just the right number of investments. And it's different depending on who you are and where you are financially.)
- Manage wisely by using Phil's six steps to track the businesses you own. (Keeping up on your investments can take hardly any time if you do it this way.)
- Sell when the time is right to maximize your returns. (Do this one thing at the right time and it can be the difference between a life of financial freedom or financial tyranny.)

You'll leave this workshop a trained Rule One Revolutionary. Never again will you feel the need to let someone else make your investing decisions for you. From here on out, you'll have the knowledge to protect your family's financial future and maximize the return you get on every dollar you have to invest for the rest of your life.

Take advantage of this limited time offer for you and a guest to each receive a full $2,995 scholarship and attend a LIVE Payback Time Workshop now. To enroll, please register immediately at **Payback TimeBook.com** or call 1-800-689-6715. And again, remember registrations are on a first-come, first-served basis, and class size is limited.

Take action now! JOIN THE REVOLUTION!!!!

Here are a few success stories from some of my first students:

"My portfolio has increased nearly 45 percent, give or take, in the last year and a half since applying the *Rule #1* principles."
—*Layne Meyers*

"I finally started using the *Rule #1* system about six months ago. I've worked myself up to 70 percent using your system and 30 percent in mutual funds." —*Ken Popkin*

"As of March 27, 2009, my one-year performance is +21.55 percent (this is in spite of some silly mistakes). Not bad, considering that most fund managers are still deep in the red. I invest only in stocks listed on the Indian Stock Exchange." — *Sunil George Kuruvilla*

"I began trading with real money in April 2007 applying Phil's techniques. Since then my rate of return is an astonishing 37 percent compared to −43 percent had I stayed in my managed mutual fund! Thank you, Phil, for empowering the little guy." —*Chuck Sumpter*

"So when I started taking things into my own hands and utilizing *Rule #1*, it has changed my investing mentality forever. I will never purchase another mutual fund again. I am up overall about 20 percent, buying only three businesses utilizing the "Rule 1" method." —*Christopher DeBary*

"I am an ex–stock broker and thought I understood how the market worked. With your philosophy about 'buying a business,' I am up 60 percent in the market between December 2008 and April 2009. And we all know what MR. MARKET has done in that time!" —*Ralph Sanchez*

"After adding to my positions each month since that time and maintaining my discipline even through one of the largest crashes in history (which created quite a few exciting buying opportunities), I am now up more than 30 percent while the market is currently down 36 percent, since I began. I find the whole process very exciting, and look forward to investing using *Rule #1* principles for the rest of my life." —*Ryan Lee*

Congratulations!

Just for purchasing and reading *Payback Time*, I am rewarding you and a guest with a full-tuition scholarship of $2,995.00 each to attend an upcoming live Payback Time Workshop absolutely free. All you have to do is take action.

To activate your scholarship and register, please visit **PaybackTimeBook.com** or call 1-800-689-6715 to obtain your individual scholarship ID number.

When you attend the Payback Time Workshop, you must each bring your scholarship ID number and a copy of your *Payback Time* book as proof of purchase. Your book will be stamped for validation at the workshop. Let the revolution begin!

Reference #:

RECOMMENDED RESOURCES

We've taken the time to build out a website full of valuable resources—just for you! To access them, go to **PaybackTimeBook.com** and register (it's fast and free). Then dive in!

Phil's FUNdamental Tools

Phil knows how to put the "fun" in fundamental analysis. Access all his predesigned, time-saving tools at the Resource Center. This is just a partial list.

- TOOLS: Run the numbers with these free and ready-to-use tools: EPS Growth Rate, Sales Growth Rate, Cash Flow Growth Rate, Equity Growth Rate, ROIC, Sticker Price, and Margin of Safety.
- MORE STUFF: Jump in and use prebuilt templates, spreadsheets, trading journals, and more to analyze and track your investments.

Take the Online *Payback Time* Investor Profile

Know thyself! It's powerful! Discover your investing personality by taking the *Payback Time* Investor Profile—a very cool evaluation tool we've developed just for you. It's free, fascinating, and, frankly, helpful. Use your newfound self-awareness to develop your investing watch list.

Payback Time Online Video Classes

Sign up for these powerful online video classes, taught by Phil, *Rule #1* coaches, and other revolutionaries. Key *Payback Time* strategies come alive in each online, on-demand class. Ideal for the self-paced investor—learn where and when you want.

The Revolutionary RulesLetter™

Keep up with the Rule One Revolution! Subscribe to Phil's e-newsletter, *The Revolutionary RulesLetter,* and receive timely stockpiling news, industry insights and updates, success stories and profiles, tips, and other investment strategies, plus *Payback Time* news and events—all delivered straight to your email inbox.

The "Big Money" Interview Series

Get a regular dose of stockpiling inspiration, motivation, and information. Each "Big Money" interview features dynamic discussions with Phil and other investors, *Rule #1* coaches, and revolutionaries, plus stockpiling success profiles and more. Check the website for a complete list of guests and topics.

Payback Time Market Commentary

Learn the disciplines and mind-set of an experienced investor. Follow Phil as he shares his thoughts and insights on current market conditions, opportunities, and strategies. Subscribe to Phil's *Payback Time* Market Commentary and eliminate the guesswork.

Q&A

Q&A sections are usually found in books. Not so with *Payback Time*! We want to give you access to a living, breathing Q&A section right on our website. Here you'll find in-depth answers to questions about a variety of investment-related issues, including debt management, real estate, bonds, risk levels, trading, the economy, Berkies, choosing a broker, and more. Delve into relevant questions; analyze the answers.

Feel free to add in your questions and comments as well. This section will build as we grow.

Revolutionary Events

In his past, Phil served as a Green Beret and worked as a river guide. Suffice it to say he *loves* adventure! Join Phil and friends on one of several new journeys designed to combine a cool vacation with exciting investment strategy. Cruise the Caribbean, raft Costa Rica, ride Africa on horseback, or share a private dinner with Phil and friends. Share your stockpiling success with like-minded investors on adventure trips that will energize, motivate, and educate. Check the website for upcoming events.

The Payback Times

Sign up and get our free e-newsletter, *The Payback Times*, delivered to your email box. We'll keep you up-to-date on news and upcoming events. A great way to stay plugged into the Rule One Revolution!

Speaking Engagements

Phil Town is one of America's most sought-after speakers on the subject of investing. He addresses more than 500,000 people annually and has shared the stage with Presidents Bill Clinton, George H. W. Bush, and George W. Bush; First Ladies Laura Bush and Barbara Bush; former secretary of state General Colin Powell; former NYC mayor Rudy Giuliani; master motivator Zig Ziglar; Microsoft president Rick Belluzzo; former world heavyweight champion George Foreman; NFL superstars Terry Bradshaw, Joe Montana, Peyton Manning, and coach Tony Dungy; entertainers Bill Cosby, Jerry Lewis, and Goldie Hawn; gold medal Olympian Mary Lou Retton; Barbara Walters, Larry King, and more. For information on Phil Town's speaking availability, call 1-800-689-6715 or email **bookphil@PaybackTimeBook.com**.

ACKNOWLEDGMENTS

Writing a book is not a solitary enterprise, not for one that is going to get read much, anyway. In my case, it all started with Marci Shimoff, the author of many *Chicken Soup* books, and for some reason my earth angel who continues to mentor me along the author/speaker path that she has been so successful with and influential on. Five years ago, Marci sent me to the best nonfiction agent in the world, Bonnie Solow, who takes care of me on this Alice-in-Wonderland ride through the publishing world. Bonnie proceeded to hook us up with the greatest team in nonfiction publishing — Crown/Random House. We've been together through two books, and I hope we can continue together for many more because they are all so great to work with. Big hugs and thanks to Jenny Frost, Tina Constable, Philip Patrick, Tara Gilbride, Meredith McGinnis, Julian Pavia, and Cindy Berman. A special thanks to my editor, Rick Horgan, who I can say, without any hint of subjectivity, is simply the best nonfiction editor in the world, as well as a man of great patience. Thanks again and again to all of you for another wonderful adventure. A huge hug to my great friend and amazing editor Kristin Loberg, who kept me on track and added so many great ideas to the book. Thanks K, for sticking with me through the entire ordeal of book #2. And thanks to my assistant, Thea, for keeping the train on the tracks, as she always does. And thank you to the amazing Mr. David Hathaway at Barnes & Noble for helping us nail the title over lunch one fine day in New York.

I want to especially thank the team led by Freddie and Mitzi Rick, who absolutely made magic happen with the book, the cover design, and the Payback Time Workshops. Big thanks to Michael Hutchison, John Kilcullen, Judy Hackett, Karen Hutto, Glen Chandler, Shannon Johnson, Jake McCurdy, Bob Stammers, and Sangram Vajre.

But, of course, writing is not all about the professionals; it's also about the team at home. In my case, none of this happens without the love and support of Alaina and Danielle, who are off doing school, and Daniel and Hunter and Melissa, who had to deal with me holed up for months in my backroom cave. They tell me I started writing each morning sitting straight up, and by the time they headed for bed I'd be slumped nearly prone with the computer on my stomach. I don't know. I get in the zone. Personal hygiene suffers. I don't shave. I take irregular showers. I sleep four hours a night. Melissa was complicit in this degeneration. She plies me with Red Bull and puts meals on the side table and even reheats them if I don't notice I'm hungry. No way does this book make the deadline without her and the boys' support. Trust me on this: You don't want to live with a writer unless the book is done. When we're not writing, we're really great people. Really.

INDEX